To my dear,
    It is my honor to share
my story with you. Hope
you enjoyed it.
        Love
        Thongoma

Uproot

A Memoir

Josefina Beatriz Longoria

Uproot/ Josefina Beatriz Longoria.
ISBN 978-0-359-12373-5

Designed by Josefina Beatriz Longoria

For my two sons

CONTENTS

Acknowledgments

When I was a little girl, I watched my mother search for a piece of paper to write a poem. She taught me to love language. I became a journalist with the hope of becoming a writer. After fifteen years of being an editorialist, I lost my column. That is when the idea of writing a book came. It began as a family history, but the more I researched, the more I realized my clan was full of secrets and resentment.

My journey as a writer started in writing workshops at Gemini Ink. Sheila Black and Jan Jarboe Russell made me believe I had a book in me. Then, I had a writing group with Georgia, Josie and Wendy. Georgia gave me *Liars Club* and introduced me to Mary Karr. I celebrated my fiftieth birthday taking a writing workshop with Karr in Patmos. She became my inspiration, together with the other attendees. We called ourselves the Revelators (Revelations was written on Patmos.)

I applied for a writing mentorship and won. My mentor, Amanda Ward, helped me find a structure for my stories. I wrote thirty chapters in thirty weeks. After finishing the writing, I joined a graduate program on creative writing. After a year of editing, I finished my tenth draft.

I want to thank my column readers. Their hate mail and fan mail matured me as a writer. I now face book readers, exposing my private writing. Thank you for holding this book in your hands and letting me share my story. I wrote this book for my own healing but hope my life will inspire you.

When I divorced I created my own support group, and I thank all the women who have been there for me. At the top of the list are my sisters: Alice and Sofia, my sister-in-law Adriana, and my nieces Andrea and Paola. I could not have survived without my friends: Tina, Martha, Dinorah, Ana, Lulu, Lilia, Kay, Gabriella, Ana Elena, Gabriela, Ana Patricia, Gladys, Estela, Alejandra, Aurora, Sheila, Sarah, Annie, Elena, Ninfa, Barbara, Hailey, Lynette, Jan, Rommy, Whitney and Rosa.

I dedicate this book to my two sons. They are my teachers and the source of a strength I did not know I had.

I wake up and it is still dark outside. I do not know where I am. The room is softly lit and my roommate is getting her stuff together. She is an older lady, with short frizzy hair and wears square bifocals. Her zippered bathrobe is violet and she is quiet. Why is my roommate so old? I notice the horizontal scars on her wrists. What happened to her? It is time to wake up, the nurse is here to get a blood sample. She approaches me, while I am still confused about why I am here.

Good morning, sweetie. She asks for my arm and tightly wraps a thick rubber band around it to find my veins. I turn the other way. I am compliant but uncomfortable. Many of my family members faint when they have their blood drawn, starting with my father. She pulls the needle out, and I wince. When she is done, it is time to get up. My roommate, who woke up earlier, is out the door. That gives me the opportunity to get ready in privacy.

I look out the window. It is dawn and silent. The gardens are wide open, like a prairie, surrounding the complex created by red brick units like the one I am in. There are no fences anywhere. This place is familiar. I know because many times my mom took me shopping for a bargain at the Back Room in a discount department store on I-10 in San Antonio Texas. Am I in the Medical Center?

I do not understand this state I am in. My mind is not crisp and clear. It is like a rusty machine that needs oil. I get my things together to take a shower. The bathroom is different, the toilet is made of metal. Why is that? I look at myself in the mirror. My skin is pale. My green eyes stare back at me under puffy lids. My thick brown hair is standing in clumps. The stylish asymmetric bob haircut I got this summer looks askew. I remember how great it looked when they blow dried it at the salon. I try to smooth it down. In the mornings, the longer hair in the front turns into big feathery sideburns. I turned twenty-years-old two months ago and again I have to lose ten damn pounds.

I leave my room and walk to the nurses' station. The lighting in the common area is bright and pierces my eyes. They hand out a tray with tiny paper cups with pills in them. We have to take the meds in front of the nurses. The environment is calm, but feels fragile. I cannot figure out this crowd. There is the old woman, the chubby nerd, the middle-aged handsome man and me. I am probably the youngest. They are absent, their gaze is like a laser pointed at infinity.

Close to the nurse's station, there is a meeting room surrounded by glass, for group gatherings. One of the nurses reminds me that my appointment with my doctor is in the early afternoon. There is some kind of schedule we are supposed to follow. As the day progresses, my mind is oiled and awake. We walk outside, and I can see there is a gym, a small chapel and other units. We pass by a building I recognize. As we sit in the arts and crafts room, I work on a ceramic pad for hot plates. While I gather the small ceramic pieces and glue them together, I mention to one of the nurses: *The unit in the middle, I remember that building.*

She explains that when I first got here that is where I stayed for a couple of days. It is the ICU, Intensive Care Unit. I begin to remember those initials written on big paper bags where others had their clothes delivered. It was a little larger and had more staff. I cannot recall much, but I do remember there were two sections, women on one side and men on the other and a television room in the center.

In the afternoon, we do not do much outside. It is the middle of August. The Texan summer is humid and heavy. Some late afternoons, I sit outside in the terrace with a young nurse, and she listens to me with true intent. She is young like me, and her hair is curly auburn. The nurses are the healers. They are aware that our levels of consciousness are open, and we are floating between this dimension and another. If things go wrong, we could be suspended and never come back. Gently they look into our eyes and hold on to our minds to ground them to this reality, preventing us from drifting into oblivion.

When my doctor comes, he talks softly. He looks like Nixon.
How are you feeling?
Doctor, is this a mental hospital? Why am I here?
Yes, this is a mental hospital. You suffered a nervous breakdown.
But there are no fences, no straitjackets.
Now medications keep people under control.
Is that why they take a blood sample every morning?
Through blood we know if the medications are at the right level.
So, what am I taking?
You are taking lithium. It's a mineral used as a mood stabilizer.
But I am not crazy. Nothing bad happened to me, why am I here?
Then the doctor goes over his notes of previous appointments and helps me go over the recent past. He gives me a journal, knowing that I like to write, and tells me my homework for the day is to write what I remember and try to figure out why I am here.
How long have I been here? When am I leaving?

You've been here for a week. You'll leave when the med levels are stable. If you have noticed your mind is slow, it is because of the sleeping medication. You just need rest and a break from life to get better.

Every moment of the day all I can think of is: I don't understand what I see. Later in the afternoon, when we have group therapy, I do not talk, I just observe. Everybody looks normal. The chubby nerd says he is a veteran. I do not believe him. I cannot see his wounds. My roommate is sweet and speaks softly. The middle-aged handsome man never speaks and wanders pensive alone through the gardens. The pretty and thin housewife is visited by her perfect husband and young children every afternoon. It's hard for me to concentrate.

You seem to have a perfect life.
You do too!
Why are you here?
Why are we all here?

We don't look crazy, we don't act crazy, and yet, we were forced to leave our real lives and take a big pause. Why do we need healing? What is wrong with us? There is no other solution, but to turn to paper and rebuild my recollection of the events that preceded this psychotic break. After the group therapy, we have quiet time, and I sit down to write.

The year 1986 starts in Oaxaca. We are on a family road trip. Coming from a numerous Catholic family, we are large enough to divide into groups. The three oldest siblings traveled with friends, and we, the younger three, tagged along with my parents. The whole trip I eat with no restrictions. It is my fat stage. We drive from Monterrey to the south east of Mexico with two other families. The drive is long and slow, through an old winding highway, but the scenery is unique. Along the way, there are dozens of a special type of candelabra cactus. I have my forehead pressed against the window, alone in my thoughts. The drive is divided by days. We stop in different towns and stay in small hotels. The climax of the journey is our arrival at the ruins of Monte Alban. As we stand on top of the pyramid and gaze at the horizon, I realize how short life is and feel determined to lose the extra weight to enjoy my youth in full. Every year, since I first got my period, I try to recover my pubertal figure and fail miserably. Those hormones kicked me out of the Garden of Eden.

We come back home, and for a whole month, I go on a strict diet and take herbal supplements. A friend in college sells them and convinces me that if I follow the diet I will lose the weight, and I do. Days are numbered. On February twelfth, my brother Anthony is getting married, and I have to fit into a size four dress. Dresses are never bought to fit me, I have to fit into them. The evening gown is made of magenta silk organza.

The torso is draped and tight, the long skirt is layered in ruffles that go down to my ankles, and the straps are made of rhinestones. The wedding is a minor challenge compared to the big event that follows at the end of February: the *Carnaval*. It is my third year participating in a dance choreography and performing in front of the whole club. The costume to be worn is a leopard unitard that hides nothing. We have rehearsals every night, for the whole month of January. I dance my arms and legs off.

Coming home after rehearsal, on a cold winter afternoon, I encounter one of my older brother's friend, a Don Juan type. We talk for a while. We sit around the modern Knoll white circular breakfast table, while I eat a salad. He is not handsome but has a great personality and steel blue eyes. My dancing outfit is damp. It consists of black leotard, tights, shorts, leg warmers, and a bandana to keep my hair off my face. After a month of starvation and hard work, I am slim and getting the attention a thin woman deserves. As I talk about college, my first summer job and a dance program I will attend, Don Juan listens. *You are what my friends and I are looking for.* I am flattered and hold on to that phrase until I meet his friends. He does not talk about himself. He listens, making me feel important. He makes himself attractive by being interested.

A few days later, he calls to ask me out. I am impressed, not just because he is six years older, but because he is socially adept. In restaurants, he knows the waiters by name. When we go dancing, he gets the best table at the discotheque, and when we are on the dance floor the cameras project us on the big screens above. He makes me visible. When I am with him, his friends say nice things about me, like I am a valuable possession. While driving in a golf cart at the Country Club, he tells an older gentleman: *This is my girl.* The man replies. *You're lying.* I don't reflect on his remark and what it means.

We formalize our relationship and agree not to see anybody else. This happens a few days before the *Carnaval*, which takes place at the beginning of lent. Don Juan is the soul of the party. He does not spend much time with me, and I just stand next to him like a prop. I am shy and insecure. When he is performing and telling jokes, I do not know what to do with myself. His friends' girlfriends are older. For a friend's reunion, they bring a guitar player. He grabs the microphone and starts singing "*Somos novios*" as if serenading me. I sit there looking at him.

It does not take long to put the pieces together. He has a thick pink horizontal scar on his neck, where they took out a malignant tumor when he was nineteen. He dropped out of college and started dating Cruella DeVille. For six years, every time he landed in the Houston Airport, where he got his treatment, he would go to the bathroom and throw up. When he became cancer-free, he broke up with his crazy girlfriend, thinking it was time to find a nice girl. That is when we met. But six years is a long time to roam free. He dresses impeccably, has an insider last name and acts like a buffoon with the real heirs. His best attribute is complimenting others. I witness how he repeats his prefabricated flattery to other women with ease. It comes naturally. He cannot help himself, but we all fall for it. Like Don Juan, he praises women of all kinds: blond, brunette, fat, skinny, young or old. I am the most prized in the list, the young beginner.

I am conservative and very Catholic. My entire life I have been in an all-girls school. I am nineteen and have never been kissed. I do not know how to act around men. The only thing that is clear to me is that I have to be pretty and smile. When we start dating, we only hold hands for a week. I am dodging the moment of the first kiss. I am too old. It is too late and for sure I am a bad kisser. I am anxious about managing libido, as I am set on marrying a virgin. When the time comes, it feels natural, but puppy love is not what Don Juan is used to, and that is all he gets. He must feel restrained. There are rumors he had sex with his ex-girlfriend. With me he goes to church, drinks alcohol in moderation and behaves properly. Maybe he wants me to be fun and outgoing, but I am not. We admire each other because he is everything I am not, and I am everything he is not.

The ex-girlfriend Cruella is stunning, a tall skinny fashionista. She models informally. She has short hair with highlights and does her makeup like a movie star, has long lashes and dramatic eyebrows. She is sexy and that makes me jealous. She owns her body, moves and sways, is aware of the effect she has on men and uses her power like a steering wheel. We bump into her often, even in church. How does she know where we are? When we go to a friend's wedding, she arrives in a shiny fully sequined backless dress. It is not a fair game. She is a sensual woman and I am a prudish girl.

It is a Cinderella story, sweet and brief. Like lent, it lasts forty days. Maybe God is trying to tell me something. I am the one who breaks up with him. He gave me no other choice. He was a flirt and ignored me. The breakup affects me more. As expected, he gets back with Cruella. I lose the spotlight and revert to being my nerdy self. No more center stage in the discotheque for me. What makes matters worse is that I have nobody to go out with. Decent Mexican women do not go out unless invited by a man. Dating a man, who was six years older, puts me in a relationship limbo. Guys my age are intimidated and do not consider me for a while. The day I break-up with him, I go into my closet, close the door, lie on the floor in the dark in a fetal position, like a wounded animal. I think I will never leave the closet, but I do. My Catholic brain forces me to expel him out of my life. He is not a wholesome man. The decision feels like a purge. God will help me get through this because I am a good girl, and I turned away from sin.

I get my first job during the summer. I am an aide to the international press covering the matches for the Soccer World Cup. It is a team of young people. We are all working for the first time. We wear tacky uniforms. The turquoise fabric has a print of Mayan hieroglyphics. We stand at information booths at the airport, to distribute brochures to international visitors. When the soccer matches begin, we provide players' lists to professional journalists who narrate the matches for radio and television. Hearing them is a treat. The rhythm they create with their voices, following the ball, is an art form. What happens in this space is being narrated to the outer world by these storytellers. I am excited to become a journalist! The climax is when Mexico plays Germany in the semifinals. It is the tournament that shows the Mexican wave to the whole world. It is electrifying to see a whole stadium filled with thousands of people, stand and sit in waves, roaring like a liquid beast. They go to penalties, and the Mexican team loses.

When my summer job ends, I go to Harvard University for a six-week intensive dance summer program. I board at Elliott House, one of the original seven houses for undergraduates. I have two roommates, one from the Midwest and one from Madrid. We have an audition. With numbers on our chests, we line up on a ballet barre following routines. They observe us and divide us in different levels. I am assigned to the beginner's group. How can that be? I am one of the best back home, front row in all choreographies. The standards are higher here. There are professional dancers in the room. We dance six hours from Monday to Friday. The first ninety minutes, I take ballet with a strict Asian teacher; the second ninety minutes Graham contemporary with a sweet American woman; the third ninety minutes I practice tap with a fun blonde, and the last class is given by a passionate black woman with short hair and long red fingernails. Any one of these dance teachers is better than any teacher I have ever had before. Here, I am not even a star.

I am reading a book titled *A Room of One's Own* by Virginia Woolf. The idea of becoming independent plants itself like a seed in my central cortex. As these thoughts take root in my mind, I meet a Puerto Rican dancer who is living on her own. We talk during lunch breaks, and she makes independence sound easy. I am ashamed to describe my pampered life back home. To me, living by myself sounds like going to space.

What is not clear in my mind, is how I got from Harvard to a mental hospital in San Antonio. I remember I extended my stay in Cambridge and moved-in with a girl from Guadalajara. The last few days remain a blur. I remember starving, skipping meals and still being overweight. My parents were traveling, and it was hard to contact them. At some point, I ran out of money and I booked my flight to go back home. I remember a cab picking me up. At the airport, my mind started playing tricks on me. I felt confused and that is when the conspiracy theories began. I started looking at flags in a hallway and decided the order in which they were placed was a code. It was as if I were the main character in an international thriller. By the time I got home, I decided there was a bomb hidden in my sister's room.

The next morning, my mother called a psychiatrist who went to my house and knocked me out with an injection. Then she called my aunt, who then called influential friends, to borrow a private plane. I could not fly commercial in the state I was in. The priority was to keep this episode a secret. If anybody knew, the information would travel like wildfire, and I would die a crazy old maid. The reason my doctor heard my conspiracy theories was that he looked like Richard Nixon, who in my mind was responsible for faking the moon landing.

Now, I can piece the story together because the med levels are stable, and I am making sense of it all. A good night's sleep and regular meals play a big role. It has been two weeks now. It is my last appointment. I promise my doctor I will take my meds religiously and reach out for help when I need it. The experience scarred me. I do not trust my own judgement. My mind is an independent entity that can betray me, and I am fearful of it. Why did I end up here? My new mantra is sleep well, eat well and exercise in moderation. I am taking lithium, but I am determined to stop taking it once my mind is reliable again.

I am fearful of two things: dancing and falling in love. I don't know which one made me crazy.

Chapter 1.2   1996

Your holiday trip begins in Rio de Janeiro. You see now that it is a unique geographic spot. From the plane, the unexpected marriage of land and sea, flat water and fractured landscape, surprises you. The pictures do not do this place justice. When you settle in the hotel, you take a shower and wait for your tour. Your trip partner is not an experienced traveler. She forgot her detergent and borrows yours. She likes your camera better and wants you to take all her pictures. You have to be diplomatic because you still have three weeks left. You worked together a few years ago. She is now in a better position than you are. Her drive is intense. She wakes up at five to jog and has male employees. With her salary, she could have Mr. Mom sitting at home. She has a hormonal imbalance and constipation issues. Like you, the better she does professionally, the worse she does personally.

You focus on this place. The thing that strikes you most is the complex result of immigration. Brazilian blacks are stunning: slim, athletic, walking half naked on the beach. In America, they sing the blues. Here they dance samba. The weather or latitude makes them blossom. Here they have the *Pardo*, not a half blood or a mulatto, but a mix of European, African and Native. This unique breed exports top models to the world.

Then you go to Argentina. You do the tours, visit *La Casa Rosada*, drive around, take pictures, and buy souvenirs. To ease the traveling friction, you give each other space. You walk around the *Recoleta*, enter a book store and wander. Argentinian publishing companies have a good reputation. You see books you would never find in Mexico. One new book grabs your attention. Esther Vilar is the author of a feminist best seller *El Varon Domado.* (The Tamed Man.) This one is titled *Is Marriage Immoral?* You buy it and start reading, sitting in the Plaza for hours. It gets dark. You have to stop, go back to the hotel and get ready. You celebrate the New Year watching a tango show with a pair of Italian guys from Milan. After the dancing, she falls asleep, and you sit in the bathroom reading. Vilar describes marriage as a contract where a woman grants the exclusive use of her sexuality to a man in exchange for his financial support. The younger the woman, the prettier and more covetable, the older the man, the wealthier and more desirable. The result is a young mother, who soon enough is married to a eunuch and is a widow for thirty years. It dawns on you: you do not want to go out with older men, you need a younger modern man.

When you cross the lakes to Chile, under the snowy mountains, your guide asks you: *Is she your girlfriend?* You get angry. You are odd. Everybody else is traveling with their spouses or family. As you ride your mental roller coaster, the guide flirts with you. He asked to make sure you were available. That makes it worse! It was easier for him to believe you were lesbians, than to believe you were friends? How are single people supposed to travel? Once again, you are modern, but not modern enough. Other women your age travel with their boyfriends, but nice girls do not do that. Are you the only nerds still following the rules?

After Chile, the last stop is Peru, and the whole point of being here is going to Machu Pichu. You suffer altitude sickness in Cuzco. You take the train to the Incan ruins, and once you are there, after a short hike, you face the presence of an older civilization. You bow, asking God for an opportunity to evolve, find a mate and reproduce, give your life a bigger purpose than just yourself, and make a contribution, so you can transcend in time like the Incas.

Back home, you get the traveler hangover: You land fat and poor, with nothing to look forward to. The weather is terrible. It is winter, cold and rainy. Writing editorials twice weekly keeps you grounded. Your television appearances make you feel important, but you are lonely. Your group therapy keeps you on track, you verbalize your needs and wants, trying to heal your communication with your parents and siblings.

On a rainy Saturday night, three days after the gloomy Valentine's Day, a single girl, who is not your friend, calls and begs you to go out. You do not like her. You think she is tacky, but you are twenty-nine-years-old, and you promised to go out with girls to meet men. She wants to go to the new Spanish bar for the older crowd. There is a flamenco show and *tapas*.

I promise we'll be there for thirty minutes and you can even have the car keys and leave if I'm not ready.

You decide to go out and to do it well, you dress up. It is winter and cold. You put on a black leather skirt, black boots, a black cotton turtle neck, and a red suede jacket. When you get there, the bar is over-crowded, there is nowhere to sit. You look around to find a table. Next to an empty seat at the bar, you see an attractive man. He is calling you, rolling his index finger. He is a stranger across a crowded room, and you fly to his side.

Do you remember me?
I don't remember you because I don't know you.
I am a Theriot. We are cousins.
My father is not close to the family, I don't know my cousins.
I didn't know we were cousins either, my friend just told me.
You're drinking Chilean wine. I was in Chile for Christmas.
So was I. Where did you go?"

He is tall and masculine. He is wearing a black polo shirt and jeans. He has hazel eyes, light brown hair, a wide jaw and a beautiful smile. He is seven years younger than you are and your third cousin. He is modern, not a real Mexican man. His mother is American. He probably has a lot of the things on your list, but he is a smoker.

See my mole? Your grandfather also had a mole on his cheek.
I didn't know that.

He knows more about your grandfather than you do. He grew up on the border, in Nuevo Laredo. You enjoy his conversation. Because you are having a good time, you then go to a discotheque. He drives a black convertible Mustang with the top up because of the cold. When you get to the disco, it is crammed and noisy. You walk to the dance floor and he holds your hand, sending electroshocks down your spine. You dance and blend into the massive rocking beast. After that, you go to another bar. He keeps ordering drinks. You drink water to stay under control. You end up eating at four in the morning at *Tacos el Guero*. As he drives you home, you hear him but stop listening, overwhelmed by the combination: magnet chemistry like the Tarzan, business savvy like your boss, well-mannered like Frank and affected by the clan drama like you. He is a man's man: a hunter, scuba diver with a pilot's license. You decide to hang out with him as long as he will let you.

The next day, Sunday, he calls some friends, and you drive out to a nearby town for a long Mexican lunch. His friends are much older than he is, more appropriate for your age, but following Vilar's advice you ignore them. He calls on Monday, and you talk for two hours. He is in college and has classes all day Tuesday and Thursday. On Wednesday, you go to a mall to buy records. After that, he disappears all weekend. You wait for him to call.

Outside your window, there is a Chinese tallow tree, covered in ivy, that blocks the sunlight. The ivy hangs like curtains on the branches. You decide you will clear the ivy from the tree, and cut until there are blisters on your hands. All this time, the wireless phone is in your pocket. You are expecting his call. Using the ladder on one side and then the other, you climb and cut, like a huge haircut, until you can see the tree without the ivy twirling, twisting and suffocating it. Now you see the mountain from your bed, the tree is liberated from the entanglement, the view gives you a sense of freedom.

He calls on Monday. He went home for the weekend to be pampered. The whole week he barely slept. You were talking every night for hours and he still had to go to college the next morning. You continue talking every day about travel, family, Mexico, your editorials, his classes, his friends, and society. The third weekend you go out again with a group of friends. You bump into somebody your age and while you talk to him, he starts talking to a blonde his age. You are jealous and must admit you like him. He drops you off and calls. After being on the phone for two hours you say:

I think we should stop seeing each other. There is too much electricity in the environment.

You make yourself vulnerable, but you can recover from two weeks of infatuation. If you go any further, it will hurt. The next day, he disappears. You think you are too old. Maybe he just liked to talk to you because he is mature, and he is impressed with your job. In the afternoon, he calls. He was having lunch with his buddies, drinking and talking. He invites you to go watch a movie in his apartment.

His condominium has a nice view, located up the mountain. It is spacious and nicely decorated, a long open room with a living room on one side and the dining room on the other. You are going to watch an old movie called *The Russian House*. The music is romantic, drowsy violins and a soft pounding piano. You cannot pay attention to the movie. He is sitting next to you. When you relax with the trumpet, suddenly like a sweet puppy his head is on your lap. For a second, you do not know what to do. You caress his hair softly, as if he were a child before bedtime. The violins are pulling the veins in your heart like strings. He turns, looks at you and pulls your head to his, and kisses you. You know he is younger. It makes you feel safe. The kissing is kind, paused like the rhythm of the music you hear. You like the tenderness, the trust and respect. You stop and continue watching the movie. You need to think about this.

As your relationship progresses, you figure out who Elliott Theriot is. There were eight siblings in the clan, five brothers and three sisters. His grandfather and your grandfather were the two older brothers, the two generals. The three younger brothers were the three soldiers. In the big fight of 1978, the masterminds who put your father in jail were Elliott's father and uncle. That is why you did not know who he was. Your father does not like to talk about his family. When your grandfather had his 80th birthday weekend celebration in Nuevo Laredo, Elliot's parents hosted a party in their beautiful home. You thought his mother was the most beautiful of them all. She was tall, blonde, blue-eyed, and dressed simply and classic, beige skirt and a white shirt. Of the whole tribe, his mother was the only woman who accepted the Wicked Witch of the West, your step-grandmother.

As you continue talking on the phone and seeing each other, hiding the nature of your relationship, you find the courage to ask your father:

Dad, what do you think about Elliott?
You can adopt him. He doesn't like him being younger.
Dad, Elliott says you don't like him.
He's a smart young man.

On his side, the situation is similar. One evening you are driving and bump into his brother and parents. From car to car his mother asks:

Who's the girl?
She is just a friend.

Even after all the tension around you, you still move forward. You do not want anybody to take this away from you. You have been hurt in similar ways and can recognize each other's patterns. You finish each other's sentences, because you share a family history. Your first fight is figuring out if the Wicked Witch of the West will go to your wedding.

Your father comes into your room and sees you on the phone, laughing. *You are talking to Elliott.* He cannot deny that you are happy. He uses a metaphor to explain his perspective. *You are Romeo and Juliet, but you are both Capulets.*

A few weeks later, his family drives to Monterrey, and you have lunch. His sister says to him: *She is old.* It makes sense, you are sixteen years older than her.

You do not stop doing what you were doing because of this puppy love. After four years of working on your short stories, your book is ready. You pick a date and commit to finish the editing. You plan the reception in a big science museum and print the invitations. While this project is coming to an end, you decide to inform your families that this relationship is real. The next step is getting to know them. You get invited to their Easter vacation.

You go to Acapulco, to what was your grandfather's house in *Las Brisas*, the place you went to as a child. The whole scenario is awkward. You get to go because they are close to your grandfather's widow. The house now belongs to your grandfather's daughter, who is almost ten years younger than you. As you arrive, it all comes back. The tropical vegetation, the smell of an ant insecticide, the parking spaces, the steps, the stone floor. You are assigned bedrooms. The master bedroom is for his parents and the adjacent room, where you and your sister stayed as young girls, is for his sister and guest. The four bedrooms above are for him, his brother, his brother's girlfriend and you. It has been fifteen years since you last came here. In the open living-room, you recognize the white tables, with three camel bases, that were in your grandfather's house in Mexico City. You feel like a traitor. You crossed to the other side. You should not be here. These people are friends with your enemies.

You go to your room. This room was for your brothers and their friends. You never stayed here. You take a quick shower and change for dinner. You gather for drinks before going out. Elliott's brother is here with his American girlfriend. Elliott's parents ask about your book coming out next month. The girlfriend asks for your age:
I am twenty-nine-years-old.

My God you are ancient compared to me!

She is only seventeen-years-old. You feel uncomfortable and stop talking. It is time to go. You drive to a restaurant up in the mountain. The food is not good, but you are paying for the evening view of the Acapulco bay.

After the girlfriend's comment, you feel that this is not your place. You are wasting your time. She is a beautiful rich blonde, an only child, and has been part of this family for three years. Her parents are friends with Elliott's parents. What were you thinking when you accepted the invitation? You are twelve years older. It makes sense that to her you are as ancient as the pyramids. As you lie in bed, you feel the blood betrayal.

As the vacation progresses, it becomes obvious to you, there is a gap between his family and yours. Your three older brothers are married, the threshing of the family corn started a long time ago. Here, the corn is still whole. Elliott is the eldest while you are the youngest (of the first batch), and his mother could barely be your mother. You dumb yourself down, lower the level of conversation to disguise the age differences. You like being with them, not because they make you feel special but because they appear special, and they include you. The person who portrays refinement and grace is Elliott's mother. Her face is beauty pageant material. She dresses well, has luscious hair, the perfect manicure and pedicure. The values in this family are different from yours. When they share their family stories, the contrast is obvious. Elliott tells the story of how his mother was asked to leave the classroom in college because she was so pretty she distracted male students. Your mother is not as beautiful, but she is passionate about knowledge. Your professional success is a worthless coin in their currency.

When you get back to Monterrey, you refocus your energy on your book. When there are threats in your personal life, all you need to do is succeed professionally. Your book is a medal you can pin to your lapel for a lifetime. You cannot take much longer. The success of your column is fresh in the reader's memory. The chances of selling the book are higher. You are tired of publishing your ideas in cheap paper that has a life cycle of one day. Your ideas should survive printed on heavier, whiter and smoother paper.

From the day you started your column, you knew you wanted to turn it into a book. Every Friday, a different story would come out. You portrayed the characters and anecdotes that distinguish this demographic area from any other in Monterrey. You have been organizing them by age and subject: the first is the story of a birth, then a baptism, then a small girl, dance classes, and the last one is a widow missing her husband. You got the idea for the cover from a Cindy Sherman exhibit. You hire a make-up artist to transform you into four different characters. You want to translate what you did with words into visuals, becoming somebody else.

The day is near. You call three different kinds of intellectuals to be the presenters: the society lady who plays smart, the literature professor and the sociologist. Each will give the book a different angle. You send out the invitations and buy a red dress for the occasion. You buy flowers, hire a guitar player and the books are ready for sale. The day arrives, and you worry that there will only be ten people there. You have chairs for a hundred guests. The presenters arrive. The podium is ready and the microphone is on. The society lady gives her retro speech on Hollywood reminiscence. The sociologist speaks of an aimless society, and the literature professor gives all the subtle details you cautiously chose. He points out that the name of the book is *Portraits of a Bourgeoisie,* not "the bourgeois" because you only know this one. Then the publisher thanks them and calls you a writer. You have never been called a writer before. Some people have asked you: *Are you the one who writes?* but nobody has said: *You are the writer.* It is your turn to stand up to thank everybody. As you rise from your seat, you see almost all the chairs are taken with different pieces of your past. This room now gathers all the people you care about. As professional as you want to be, your throat betrays you and the liquid emotion drowns your eyes. If you do not ever get a wedding, today your family and friends have gathered here to witness your contribution of handwritten portraits of Monterrey. Your Inca prayer was answered, you did find a bigger purpose than yourself and have transcended into posterity.

Chapter 1.3   2006

Beatrice has accepted her son's diagnosis. Someone gives her a letter titled *Welcome to Holland* written by Emily Kingsley. This letter compares having a child with a disability, to planning a trip to Italy and landing in Holland. The author insists it is not a horrible place, just different. Instead of talking about the Vatican and fountains, people talk about windmills and tulips. The land of disability is exile. It compares more to Siberia, a cold country of hopeless shame. These conditions are not contagious but people keep their distance and stare. Beatrice does not talk about it, if people do not know, it does not exist.

Beatrice is forced to admit her son David has to go to a public school. There they have the proper training and resources to help him. The first week of special education is difficult. When she picks David up from school, his eyes are puffy. He has been crying. They are teaching him to be compliant and follow instructions. He needs to acquire skills in order to be taught. This decision is an emergency landing. How could such a beautiful creature not have the ability to communicate, socialize or engage? This cherub is trapped in another dimension, captured in his own world. Beatrice follows the diet, the therapies, the supplements. She cannot dispel this fog. He does not look at her. He just lines up his toys.

Beatrice lives in denial. She tries hard to prove the teachers, therapists and doctors wrong. She wants to show them how it is done. She will heal her son. He will snap out of this haze and come back to her from his far away land. She does not even say he is autistic, she says he has autism, because one day he will not have it. There is nobody to ask, nobody to blame. All these children are being diagnosed, nobody knows what causes autism. The more she reads, the more depressed she becomes. Research organizations promulgate the image of children having tantrums, screaming and rocking. These stereotypes help them get more funds by appealing to human mercy. David is not like the boys who scream and rock.

Beatrice tries to understand his brain by observing him. He cannot learn abstract ideas. He does not point, because it is an act of abstraction. She cannot teach him to suck from a straw or use the toilet. He figures how to pee by looking at his brother, but it is impossible to figure out when he will have a bowel movement. She reads stories of autistic kids who wore diapers until they were twelve. That idea keeps her up at night.

They had the custom-made house, beautiful and healthy children. Her domestic treadmill was headed nowhere. She was walking in the same place, getting the dream life dictated by marketing. The shiny objects had her hypnotized like a monkey. God snapped his fingers, and she is wide awake. The pillows, the paintings, the rugs cannot give her what she wants. Her personal feelings of failure are daunting. She produced a flawed baby, her human oven is broken.

To overcome the disappointment, she turns to her garden. There was snow last winter in Laredo and many plants froze. As spring starts, she goes out and prunes the bushes to help them grow. She studies her neighbor's gardens. The plants in Laredo, Texas are similar to the plants in Nuevo Laredo. They will not repave the old cracked tennis court. To hide it, she plants six oleanders that will grow quickly. She will see greenery from her windows. She replaces old dry and pale bushes with heat resistant plants. For medicinal purposes, she plants Aloe Vera. It is handy to have for rashes or sunburns. Next to the patio, there are elephant ear plants that drag and take up patio space, she takes them out. She hires a gardening service to prune the oaks. They cut off the branches that touch the roof before the heat comes, to prevent them from getting infested. The previous owner shared stories about how on weekends teenagers would drive over the corner of the lot. To create a sense of privacy, she plants an island of bougainvillea. No walls or construction. Tall trees cannot be unrooted, young plants can re-root.

This year she turns forty. Age is an issue because her husband is eight years younger. She makes an appointment with the plastic surgeon and decides to get breast implants. Her chest and self-esteem are deflated. She calls her friend Blondie, to ask about plastic surgeons. She contacts her doctor and makes an appointment. Many people from Laredo, Texas cross to have surgery done on the Mexican side because it is cheaper. When she goes, she hides in the corner and buries her head in a magazine like an ostrich, hoping not to bump into anybody. When she sees the handsome doctor, she gets nervous. They just talk about options, it is the first appointment. He advises her to think about it and look at a Victoria Secret catalog to choose what she wants to look like. She does not want to look like anybody else. She brings a picture from her own photo album and they set up a date. She hires her housekeeper to spend the night at the hospital.

After the operation, when she goes for a check-up, the doctor cleans her wounds and takes off tubes used for drainage. He tells her about the disturbance in the hospital. One of the leaders of the cartels got shot and had surgery. There were big trucks with armed men guarding the surrounding streets of the hospital. He had to cancel some of his appointments.

What she did not take into account was the effect her operation would have on her children. David was not aware of what happened, but Tomas got apprehensive. He suffered constipation, almost to the level of hemorrhoids. She tried to explain, but all he could see was that she was weak. Three weeks after the operation, she takes him to Disney World for a long weekend. They get a room with Disney cartoons on the walls, and he gets a bunk bed. They walk around the park, wait in line and go on rides. It is winter, Florida's humidity is bearable. She cannot keep up with their friends and decides to go to the hotel and rest for a while. She has become a little autistic. Standing in line, surrounded by people, hearing all that noise is sensory overload. Her tolerance for crowds has diminished. After living on a strict gluten-free-dairy-free-soy-free diet, she has turned into a picky eater, and amusement parks offer only junk food.

They continue with more organized fun. While she sits on a ride, she gets a call. David had a minor accident on the playground. Their nanny picked him up and took him to the hospital. It was a small cut, too small for a stitch, they glued it together. Because there was blood, they cannot release them until both parents give authorization. They call Elliott, who is also out of town, to confirm the woman is their employee. There is a policeman outside the emergency room. They contact the teacher who testifies the boy fell in the playground.

The world of motherhood orbits inside the galaxy of guilt. Beatrice had surgery for herself. Then she did something for Tomas, by taking him to Disney with a friend. While being gone her other son had an accident. She is absentminded at Disney World and feels bad for not being there for David. The next layer of guilt comes from being a bad wife and neglecting her husband. When she comes home, the first thing she does is look at David's forehead. The cut is a fourth of an inch. It is so close to the hairline it is not even visible.

A few weeks after that incident, to quiet the wife guilt, she accompanies her husband on a trip to Napa with a group of couples from San Antonio. There is too much wine involved and they get sick. While recovering in the hotel, she gets another call. Her mother-in-law had the kids in her house, but her daughter was not feeling well. The nanny picked up the children and took them home to Laredo, Texas. When she crossed the international bridge, David was asleep. She was asked to step out of the car. They waited until he woke up to let her go. This incident happened because of child trafficking. Some kids are drugged, kidnapped and sold. When Beatrice shares this anecdote with a friend, she is sent a disturbing video. In the video, there is a beautiful pink baby being set up in an operating room. A doctor opens him up and pulls out of his empty insides a kilo of cocaine.

The border is surrounded by dark forces. Beatrice tries to make her house an island of peace. Her home is a shrine of intimacy, except for the screaming before bath time. Tomas hates to take showers and runs around the house naked *Catch me. Catch me.* David loves to take baths and sits in the water for half an hour. When Beatrice kneels next to her boys at night, she emphasizes *and deliver us from evil, Amen.*

She understands the American government and how it protects children. When Tomas was an infant, she was running errands and left him asleep in the car for three minutes while she dropped something off. A friend warned her: *you cannot do that not even for two minutes.* An acquaintance went to jail for leaving her twelve-year-old in the car for half an hour. Her daughter did not want to go to the mall. Someone saw her alone and called the police. She had to bring in witnesses to testify she was a good mother.

Beatrice cannot talk about David, because when she does she cries. The lack of sleep and the urge to pretend having a normal family are piling up. When she sees David's doctor they can see David is doing better, but she is not. The doctor suggests a *Wellness program for mothers*. She spends a couple of hours working on herself.

Have you noticed that there are people who have a few problems and are always stressed out? Then there are those who have a lot of problems and are always happy and full of joy. What do you think is the difference?

They sleep well?

That does help, but no. They have fun. You see, we have gas tanks of energy and daily life empties our tanks little by little, but doing things we enjoy with people we like is a way of filling our tanks. What is something that makes you happy?

The ocean, swimming in the ocean is one of my favorite things.

You have a problem, you don't live by the ocean. What you can do is get in the bathtub. At the end of the day, when the kids are taken care of, turn the faucet on, light some candles, turn on spa music and have a bubble bath. You have to do this at least fifteen minutes. Now here is the trick: you need to think happy thoughts. That is the most important thing. If your day is all bad and you have nothing good to think about, think about the past or an ex-boyfriend, but no matter what, don't think about the daily challenges you face.

I can do that.

You need to know that even if you feel entitled to worrying, because you have a special needs child, all mothers worry. The problem is that worrying serves no purpose, it just empties the tank. This is not a sprint race but a marathon, you need to manage your strength.

For her fortieth birthday, her husband lets her take a friend to New York for a long weekend, all expenses paid. She chooses her childhood friend Blondie. They stay at a five-star hotel and have dinner in fancy restaurants. They talk about everything. They are honest because they don't interfere with each other's lives. They go shopping, to museums and the theater. They talk from the moment they open their eyes and don't stop until their heads hit the pillow.

Make new friends but keep the old some are silver but the other gold. Blondie is her golden friend. They have known each other since second grade. They were not close as children, but their families knew each other. When she went to Blondie's house they played with Barbie dolls, Ken and the Barbie house. One time they were outside in her garden, and her cocker spaniel *Dragon* bit Beatrice on the ear. They took dance classes together. They were debutantes together: Beatrice was a Princess and Blondie became the Queen of the ball. They traveled to Europe together at seventeen. A European tour: fifty young ladies, fourteen countries in forty days. The first time Beatrice got drunk was in Blondie's house. They were in the lower living room and drank Kahlua while listening to Pink Floyd. They both dated outlaws at the same time. While Beatrice was seeing Don Juan, Blondie was going out with one of the royals. She got married, and Beatrice became a journalist. While she became a mother and breastfed her babies, Beatrice was kissing a few frogs on her way to finding her prince. Coming out of a bad relationship Blondie said to her: *Put your Reeboks on and run.* When she met her younger husband, she said: *Don't panic. So, what if he's younger? From now on you just buy clothes at The Gap.* At Beatrice's wedding, Blondie had two tables to organize their friends. She traveled to see Beatrice's newborn and new house. Now Beatrice belongs to the Autism Club and needs to abandon the life they once shared.

Spring comes and goes. Domestic life is uneventful and the highlight of the summer is yet another trip. Beatrice accompanies her husband on a hunting trip with a couple from South Carolina. While everybody else is hunting, she sleeps late and goes on walks. The first week, she tries to read *Rayuela* by Julio Cortazar. The second week, she reads *La Tia Julia y el Escribidor,* from Mario Vargas Llosa. Every evening, they sit by the fire and talk. One night, an elephant comes to drink from a waterhole close to the camp. They hear him break the branches of the trees as he approaches. When they see him, they are bewildered by his size, his mammoth ears.

The trip is one week too long. Beatrice feels the withdrawal from civilization. To escape the cool fresh air, she chews up a frivolous best seller called *The Devil Wears Prada* that transports her to metropolitan madness. One morning, while taking a break from her reading, she sees a little monkey on a tree. He is agile, smart and alert. They make eye contact. This animal gaze makes her think about her autistic son. How can this monkey make eye contact and her son cannot? On the way back home, Elliott and Beatrice have a big fight at the airport.

You need to know, if you invite me to the moon for three weeks, I will not go. It's not the time, our children are young.

Both their parents left on long trips and left their kids with the help, but Elliott and Beatrice don't have a normal family. Tomas needs company and David demands more attention than they are used to giving.

When they come back, the housekeeper is upset and tired. She demands a raise and starts complaining about the job. They pay for her plane ticket to go see her son in Minnesota. She takes a few days off and comes back in a better mood. After a couple of weeks, one Monday morning she arrives wearing sunglasses. *Is there something wrong?* Beatrice suspects somebody beat her up. She pulls the glasses up and shows her stitches. She had plastic surgery. One of the reasons she is not happy anymore is she met someone. Things get tense and she leaves. Beatrice is devastated. She was raised by maids and every time somebody leaves, she is reminded they are not family and the neglect from her mother and mother-in-law flares-up.

Elliott and Beatrice enter a new phase in their marriage, their seven-year anniversary. Statistics show divorce rates peak during years: one, three, seven and twenty. Year one is the clash of two cultures. For them it was the year they chose his mother's cleaning supplies and her mother's food. Year three is about a new child, house or job. They got them all. Year twenty is the turning point when couples choose to grow old together or go their separate ways. What is year seven about? It is the year pretending stops. When they got married Elliott asked Beatrice to stop drinking coffee. She now decides she likes coffee and starts making herself a cup every morning. They become more honest about their friends too. One of her girlfriends is a divorcé and they have met five of her boyfriends. Elliott says: *I don't want to meet any more of her boyfriends. From now on you see her on your own.* There is also a shift with their relatives. They are a solid family unit and build some boundaries with his and her family.

After a visit, Beatrice has a fight with her mother because she keeps telling her what to do. She suggests moving furniture around, complains about the temperature and makes remarks on her parenting skills. Beatrice suggests next time she should stay at a hotel, where they could be more comfortable. Her mother snaps. *You are not welcome in my house either.* When her parents leave, they drive to the beach and on the way, they stop at an emergency room because her mother thinks she is having a heart attack.

After tests, the nurse asks:
Your heart is fine, what happened?
Her mother narrates the argument and the nurse asks:
And how old is your daughter?
She's forty.
You need to give her some space. She is a grown woman.

At the end of the year, Beatrice decides she needs to talk to someone about her son David. In one of the support meetings for parents, she hears about a workshop called *The Son Rise Program*. She researches it, it is based on *Son Rise: A Miracle of love*, a movie she watched as a teenager. She decides to attend the program for a week in the fall. She flies to the middle of nowhere in Connecticut and learns techniques to engage David. The classes are interesting, but the healing happens after dinner when parents stay in the dining room and talk to each other. They share how their lives have changed, what they hope for and how their other children adapt to the new normal.

Chapter 2.1   1987

While my mother is driving away, I walk towards the office building. My movements are in slow motion because of the meds. The chances of bumping into someone are slim. I do not want to say I am going to the shrink. I get on the elevator. The building smells like mold. I get off and walk alone in the corridor. There is nobody in the waiting room, only a few minutes left to go in. I feel anxious and hold my anxiety pill in my hand. I have never had to take it, but it is nice to have.

Good afternoon. Come in.

I enter his office and sit on the sofa on the left wall. He sits on the sofa by the window. The other wall is covered in books. I get to see a panoramic view of the whole county. This is still the only skyscraper.

The doctor is a middle-aged man with a big mustache like Pancho Villa. I do not say much. He gives me a few minutes. I am coming almost every day. My mother's complaining about the cost is a constant reminder. While I think about what to say, he looks at some papers and is overwhelmed with pending issues.

Last year, I was on top of the world, and now I am at the bottom. My life feels like a steep ascent I must climb. Dr. Villa must think I am a spoiled useless little brat, who does not have real problems and is here just to waste his time. But I feel he has the answer to my riddle.

How are things going?

Bad. I talked to a friend, and she told me that my mother's scheme of keeping the nervous breakdown a secret failed. People came to their own conclusions. Rumors are worse than I imagined. Some are saying I went to Boston to get an abortion. Others think I tried to kill myself. I am humiliated. I would never think of doing either of those things.

How does that make you feel?

Angry. Those stories make sense. What does not make sense is that nothing happened.

We've been over this. Your brain is an organ inside your body. You neglected your body by over exercising, not eating or sleeping and your brain stopped working properly.

You don't think I am crazy?

Of course not. I wonder when did you learn that sleeping a few hours was enough?

Since I was a little girl, maybe because I was number five. I would go to sleep at ten or eleven o'clock in elementary school. My mother would stay awake watching television until midnight. It was the maids who woke us up in the mornings. I didn't put on my own socks until I was twelve. They would do it while I was lying half asleep. The chauffeur would take us to school. My mom woke up much later and had her breakfast brought to her bedroom.

What did you do in the afternoons?

My mom played bridge with her friends and was never home. The maids were in the kitchen. I watched television all afternoon: cartoons from three to four, Old Mexican movies from four to six and then the Pink Panther.

What do you remember about the shows you watched?

I remember the Mexican movies in black and white. They were from a space and time that was difficult to grasp. Men were strong and brave, on horses, with big sombreros, like Pedro Infante. Women were girlish, pure and obedient, or proud and confident half naked cabareteras. The plots were tragic, involved conflict and betrayal. Nobody ever smiled.

What about your friends? Didn't you have any friends?

I was not popular like my sister Alexandra. I rarely had anybody over, when I did, we played store. My friend would pretend she was buying something, and I would charge her Monopoly money and wrap her gift. I guess I played store because my mother owned a gift store called Casa Balam.

Did you participate in any extracurricular activities?

I took all kinds of lessons: piano, drawing, gymnastics and of course dance. My first drawing studio was downtown, a small class where we would make carbon drawings. In my second studio, there were twelve students. The easels were lined up in three lines. In the fall, we painted a still life, and in spring we painted a landscape.

Tell me more about your dancing. It seems to be important to you.

The first studio I remember had a live pianist for the ballet lessons. Even though I was a beginner, I had point shoes, I wore socks over them, to keep them clean for performances. The dance studio was in a small shopping strip. When the classes were finished, before the chauffeur came to get me, I would walk next door to the bakery and buy sweet bread.

What was so special about your dance classes?

The highlight was the end of the school year performance in front of a live audience. We participated in choreographies and wore costumes. There were extra rehearsals, and our measurements were taken by seamstresses. The magic happened at the theater. As a child, I didn't understand that the audience was made up of parents and grandparents, aunts and uncles that were there to see their loved ones. To me it was a faceless public, and it was real. From the outside, the illusion started with the white marquee announcing our show. In front of the theater there was a stone patio. Inside, there was a white marble floor, and down some steps, they sold drinks and snacks. The entrances were on both ends of a round semi-circle. The theater was one when it was empty, and it was another when it was full. The special place was backstage, by the side curtains, where we waited for our exit cue. We would fix our tap shoes, touch up our slick buns, feeling the glamour smeared on our eyelids and lips. Once on stage, everything was blurry. All adrenaline was used up for following our place in the choreography, moving to the diagonal, step right, step left, arms up, chin up and a big smile. I could never see their faces. The light was too bright. I had to do everything right. They were all looking at me.

So that was your happy place. What was your sad place?

School. I went to an all-girls Catholic school. We had consagradas. They were like nuns.

Describe these women.

They were celibate, single and devoted to the Legion of Christ, with no power ladder to climb. They wore dresses below the knee and closed shoes. Many were nice girls from good families. I remember Miss Tania from Ireland. She had fair skin, blue eyes and blonde hair. She spoke Spanish with a heavy accent.

Do you remember what they taught you?

They taught us to be obedient. We had religion class every day. We were taught to pray to our heavenly mother, analyzing the Hail Mary word for word. We were taught that it was the same to have impure thoughts, say impure words or do bad deeds. The plan was to prevent sin at any stage. They also taught us virginity was a virtue. Our body didn't belong to us. It belonged to God, and one day to our future husband. We were part of something exclusive. Father Russell explained that when the boys from the Irish Institute, - which was our brother school - went out to find a wife, they would search among us.

Do you remember when religion became important?

Yes, it was in second grade, when I had my first communion. It was the rite of passage that turned me into an insider. It was like a little wedding. It was the first time I got my hair done at the beauty salon. I had short hair, the Dorothy Hamill haircut. My dress was made of white silk organza and had a big underskirt with a round wire at the bottom. My veil was attached to a little cap covering my head. That day my godmother gave me a medal, carved mother of pearl surrounded by emeralds. The mass was private, only for us. My brother and I walked slowly towards the altar. It was hot under that big dress. I could feel a thread of sweat running down my legs, going all the way down to my laced ankle socks and touching my pretty white patent shoes. When the priest brought the chalice, and pulled out the consecrated host, I was amazed, it was the first time I received the body of Christ. I felt the humid emotion down my cheek.

This made you an insider? What does that mean?

Insiders would follow the system to the letter. We were not allowed to use nail polish, chew gum or whistle. Our green wool plaid jumper dress had to be knee length and our socks pulled up to our knees, even on hot hundred degree days. We would start the day in the patio. Everybody in line, from short to tall. I was always at the front, second or third in line. We had to take our distance, touching the girl in front with an extended arm. The only personal style we had were our shoes, socks, earrings and hair.

Do you have religious parents?

My father is religious but my mother is not. She was raised by nuns and went to a boarding school since she was six years old. She has been going through an agnostic phase, which was a secret, otherwise I would become an outsider.

This system, where does it come from? Who made it up?

The founder of the Legion of Christ was Marcial Maciel. People think he's Irish because he is white and has green eyes, but he is Mexican and grew up in a small town in the middle of nowhere. We called him 'Our father.' The academic program was not the same for boys and girls. For us, the priority was not education, but morals and manners. The teacher would draw a vertical line in the middle of the black board and write down the notes we would copy. When we were finished, she would erase and write on the other side. Our notes had to be impeccable. We also had hands and crafts classes, where we were taught to knit and embroider. In middle school, we learned to type. Not much was expected of us, only to marry the boys from the Irish Institute and lead Mexico into salvation.

Your ex-boyfriend, did he go to that school?

Of course. He is one of us.

Is he religious? Does he want to lead Mexico into salvation?

Not at all. He is a social animal.

What did you like about him?

I have been thinking about that, and I can't figure it out. I guess that what I liked was that he liked me and the attention I got for being his girlfriend.

Did he share your views on God?

Not really. I guess he liked the way I made him look. In the beginning, when he listened to me it was like he was studying me, but once I passed the test, I became part of his curriculum. I am getting upset. I don't want to talk about him.

Who is the most important person in your life?

My older sister Alexandra.

Why is she important to you?

She was the one who explained things to me. One time, when my father was driving us to the airport to pick my mother up from another long trip to Europe, I asked Alexandra who she loved more. She said she loved them the same. I just said I loved my mother more because my dad was never around. When we got home from the airport, she pulled me into our bathroom. I remember it well. She was wearing a knitted striped long vest, over her hippie bell bottom jeans. She was crying because I said I loved my mother more than my father, who was sitting right next to us. She was right, I didn't even think about it. My father was always busy. I didn't think he was listening to our conversation, he never did. I guess that is because she was three years older. It seemed as if she knew everything. She was more aware. I remember another time. We went to Disneyland when I was seven years old. Alexandra had been there before with my two older brothers. It was her second time. I thought she knew her way around. One day, my parents left us in some ride, to go have lunch at the Peter Pan Pirate boat. Suddenly, my brother Gerard was lost. At that moment, I remember holding Alexandra's hand like she was God. She knew what she was doing. She figured out where lost and found was and discovered my brother sitting there. She solved the problem and was only ten years old.

Have you always been close to her?

We were close as children. We had a camaraderie. On Saturday mornings, we stayed in our beds, talking until we got too hungry. There was a special intimacy. Maybe it was because we were still lying down or because we had just come out of the dream world. I remember our white wooden headboards had a pattern of holes, and I would put my fingers inside. We talked about everything. She had her side of the bedroom, where she kept her frog collection, and I had my side, where I kept my

Hello Kitty collection. Our bedspreads matched the curtains in a psychedelic print with huge pink, yellow and orange flowers. We had an orange carpet and two round smiley face lamps hanging from the ceiling.

Did you grow apart?

We grew apart when Alexandra became a teenager. We had the same clothes in different colors. When we went to the theater, she would choose an outfit, and I would put on the exact same one. I loved to dress like her. One day she screamed 'stop copying me!' locked herself in the closet and chose one top from one outfit with the bottom of another. I didn't dare mismatch.

Was there ever a rupture between you two?

Yes. The before and after was the British movie 'Melody.' Alexandra was obsessed with the song by the Bee Gees. She would sing the chorus over and over: 'Melody Fair, remember you're only a woman. Melody Fair, remember you're only a girl.' The break between us happened because she was becoming a woman and I wasn't. She would lock herself in our room with her friends. I would be outside knocking. To get rid of me they went to our neighbor's house.

How did you handle that?

I became closer to my best friend, our other neighbor.

Tell me about her.

We called her 'The Pea,' because she had a small round tummy. We met in second grade but got closer in fifth grade. Her house was in a huge lot of a couple of acres. She was much younger than her siblings, and like me, she didn't have too many friends. She was smart. Her older brothers went to Stanford and MIT. My mom taught me to respect her family. They were the royals. Our house was in their domain. We were surrounded by their big family lots. When she came to my house, she was dropped off by her nanny, the chauffeur and a guard.

Were you intimidated by her lifestyle?

Only in the beginning, but I got used to it. I walked to her house. When I got there, the guards, hiding behind a thin horizontal hole, would ask my name and who I was visiting. After a while, they just greeted me, but my name was always logged in. The extreme security was a consequence of her granduncle being kidnapped and killed. When they opened the gate, I walked to the central patio and waited for the maid to open the door. The house was always extremely cold, the air conditioning at full blast. The hall had dark hardwood floors and a round wood antique table, with freshly cut flowers in the center. Next to the door, there was a brass base with a dozen exquisite parasols and umbrellas. When I had lunch or dinner with her and her parents, we sat at a small table for four, next to the bay window in the dining room. Her mother never ate what we ate, she only had steamed vegetables. All meals were served by a uniformed butler wearing white gloves.

What were her parents like?

Her father had his television room next to the hall, with two down filled dark brown suede sofas and a large screen. I remember he used to watch simple comedy variety shows, which was surprising. He was serious and intimidating. I guess he put up with me, because he wanted his daughter to have friends. He was a wine connoisseur and a food aficionado. I had the most exquisite delicacies in that house, like lychees or dates. One time, we were having dessert, and I dropped a piece of cake on the table, I wanted the earth to open up and swallow me. Her mother picked it up with her long thin white fingers, wearing her ten-carat diamond ring, and put it back on my plate. 'Don't worry about it.' I was grateful.

What can you tell me about her siblings?

They were much older, so most of them lived abroad or were married. She had three beautiful sisters: the oldest had dark eyes and dark hair, the middle one had green eyes and red hair, and the youngest had blue eyes and blonde hair. The Pea was smarter than all of them put together. She also had four brothers: the oldest was serious like her father, there was an engineer, a priest and a painter.

Sounds like a peculiar family. Why were you friends? What did you do together?

In the hot summer afternoons, we walked outside. The property was immense. There was a rose garden, where they got the fresh cut roses for the living areas, a paddle tennis court and a swimming pool. When we were outside I was never completely at ease. They had trained Doberman dogs they would let loose at night. One time, we spent the afternoon at her grandmother's house rowing a boat on the lake and swinging in the big swings. When we went into their kitchen to get something to drink, I kissed the housekeeper on the cheek, thinking it was her grandmother. That is how poised the help was. My friend laughed hysterically.

That does not sound nice. Why did you put up with it?

It made my mother proud to tell people my best friend was a member of the royal family. I felt like she had chosen me.

You were only friends with her to please your mother?

No. I mean of course I was impressed with the butler, the paintings and the Persian rugs, but I was fascinated with the conversations. They had such intellectual domain that they could coexist being close to the Legion of Christ and have books like 'The Third Eye' which was about paranormal powers. Let me explain: the royal family is divided into two branches. Those who have looks and those who have brains. The ones I interacted with are the smart ones.

Were they nice to you?

Not really. I remember when I was thirteen years old, I was invited to go on a trip to Houston, to one of their houses. We were flying private, I dressed up and wore heels. Her siblings literally laughed when they saw me.

How did that make you feel?

Angry and confused. Think about it. To become a man is to be a part of human kind. What the hell does it mean to become a woman? To get your period? The only option I see here is you go from being a little girl straight to being a mother. What about those of us who don't want to do that? What do we do? I want to be smart and confident, but I don't want to be a slut. It is hard to understand what's acceptable. As a little girl I was obsessed with my mother's heels, but as a teenager the minute I put them on they laugh at me?

How is your friend handling this transition into womanhood?

She bailed out! She got married last fall, at nineteen years old, a total traitor. What makes matters worse is I couldn't go to her wedding, because the whole nervous episode was still recent and I didn't want anybody to see me. I was extremely self-conscious, because my hands would shake from the medications. My sweet sister, Alexandra, arranged for me to go give her a hug before the wedding. She was nervous. All she could say was 'What the hell are you doing here?' I know the timing was not the best, but I expected her to be happy to see me.

How does that make you feel?

Betrayed and humiliated. I was her pet, when she needed one.

How long were you friends?

We were close only in fifth and sixth grade. For middle school, she went to France for two years and Germany for one. When she came back, I left for New York for high school. Then she got her older boyfriend, and now she is married.

Are you back to being close to your sister Alexandra?

She just moved to Mexico City last January!

You just lost your best friend to marriage and your sister moved away. How does that make you feel?

Alone, sad and anxious. Things are happening too fast. I tried being thin and pretty, and it didn't work. I am running out of time. I am afraid I am going to be an old maid.

Talking about time, our time is up for today. But I want you to think about two things: first think about what it means to be a woman for you, and then think about how you relate to others. See you next time.

We stand up, he opens the door. I walk out and stand there. It's like I am expelled into the world. When the session is finished I am in a raw state. I feel like this man opens all my drawers, pulls everything out, and then I leave naked because all the clothes are on the floor. As I walk out into the corridor, I feel a mild sense of relief. Maybe not the whole closet is on the floor. Maybe today one drawer is tidy. It is like there is a thread, a line of thought we knit together. When I leave, I hang on to that thread like a rope that swings me to the next challenge. I walk down the corridor holding my anxiety pill on my hand, thinking I only need to wait twenty-four hours to continue the work.

Chapter 2.2   **1997**

Publishing a book did not make you smarter, richer or famous. Your book was a local best seller for a few weeks. It gave you a sense of accomplishment, but you understood the delight was in the writing. You hear anecdotes of people reading it, like a couple living in Mexico City who read the short stories at night and laughed hysterically remembering their life in Monterrey. You are surprised to learn books have a short life span. Books are chewed up like an apple and tossed into a bookshelf.

You are still in a relationship with Elliott, but your friends don't take him seriously. When you ask The Pea *When are we going out with you and your husband?* She says: *When you two have been together for a year.* They do not think it is going to last. Making friends is challenging because of your age difference. Your boyfriend is in college. Your friends' husbands graduated years ago. And still your relationship deepens. You sleep over every other day and wake up early to go back home. Your mother insists you should not be doing that. Now sex is not enough. You want to wake up together. His room has a view, and his King size bed, covered with an emerald plaid comforter, feels like your own. He and your father are getting to know each other.

You do not see your childhood friends often. Most are married and busy with their domestic lives. You call some of them and gather for lunch in a new Chinese restaurant. You all arrive separately, order your food and start the conversation with small talk. By the time your entrees are at the table, somebody says:

There's a small newspaper in Connecticut that just published accusations against Marcial Maciel, (the founder of the Legion of Christ), for sexually molesting nine priests when they were boys...Yeees!... How did you get this information?... I haven't read anything anywhere?... It's public knowledge in the United States.... Those are rumors, pure envy. The Legion has never been stronger... No, honey. These are facts. Who would want to come out to the world to say 'I was raped by a priest.'. These men are old, they have nothing to gain... Our Father has many enemies, they are jealous of his success. He has schools all over the world now. He is a favorite of his holiness John Paul II. We need to stay strong because the devil works in mysterious ways... Correction dear, it's God works in mysterious ways... Girls don't get upset maybe this is not a good subject... it's a great subject! We grew up thinking this guy was enlightened, and he is a fraud. Just think about it, if these men were abused as children in the forties they have been keeping this secret for fifty years! He told them he had permission from the Pope to seek them sexually for relief of physical pain... Please stop! At least half the people here have their children in our alma mater. I will not accept you insulting Our Father. I don't believe anything you are saying.

It is like an earthquake cracked the table into two pieces. Some ask for the check. They cannot take this any longer. Everybody leaves, two of them cry and hug each other in the parking lot. As you drive away, you feel disgusted. You are not invested in this cult anymore, but feel enraged to think that the one authority who has been managing sexuality in the world is not even living by the standards they preach but depravity. You know it was not only your sexuality that was damaged. You have heard friends narrate how on their honeymoons they get to the room anxious and turn the television on, take a long shower, not knowing how to handle the holy permission to enjoy something that was a sin for so long. You are struggling with feeling your bodies and accepting this force inside you as natural. Your libido is damaged, like a wild horse that was bridled harshly to be trained. Those who preached abstinence were not even having intercourse with the opposite sex, not even having sex with adults of the same gender, but abusing young children and stealing their innocence. You wonder about the courage it took for those nine men to tell their story.

You make the decision to write about it. You approach the subject in an analytical manner, but you do something you have never done, you get personal. You start by explaining the concept of the *hidden curriculum*, which is what you learn while you learn. *I studied in one of their schools from second to ninth grade. As part of my hidden curriculum, I was taught that white people are better than dark, rich are better than poor and the people with power always get better opportunities than ordinary people. The priests of the Legion are European, blonde and blue eyed, who perpetuate Colonial catechization. They teach their students to use liquid paper to hand in clean homework. The boys have to get to school early with a good short haircut. Girls have to wear long skirts, no nail polish and no whistling. That is for construction workers. They also teach boys to confess when they have impure thoughts, if they kiss their girlfriends or stare at lingerie ads on billboards. All the while, they guarantee the Legion girls that when the time comes the Legion boys will choose them for marriage.*

This article passes the editor's radar and gets published easily. You know this information is a continental divide for the city's elite. You suspended your television participations and now read your articles for the radio. When you read this piece in the studio, your voice shakes. It does not take long for you to hear the reactions. The editor gets in trouble for publishing your piece and the subject is put aside. Nobody is brave enough to address this issue, not even The Compass. Our Father was smart to focus on educating only the richest in Mexico, arguing that when you form a leader you reach thousands of souls. In real life, he has an army of priests trained to visit old millionaires dying in hospitals and getting generous donations. Anybody who claimed to be somebody was recruited inside the system. It is going to take years for this to come out into the open.

Writing something personal changes you. You have crossed a threshold. All these years, you were only the observer, translator or link between the reader and the subject. This is the first time you are the subject. You used your personal experience as the source of your insight. It makes you feel your voice matters. It is not the applause that builds your self-esteem, but the rejection that bounces your voice back to you.

These thoughts are recurrent. You have been researching the idea of the journalist-writer. Seven years ago, when you finished your college studies, you were required to write a thesis. You did not do it and are finally working on it. After months of work, you present your thesis. One of the readers is the editor of the Daily and the other is a literary intellectual. You deliver the printed copy of the seventy-page proposal beforehand, they read it and your exam is discussing it. To start the conversation, you present the thesis in a nutshell.

The thesis is called the journalist-writer because it explores how journalism and literature are different and the same. Journalism is about content and reality. Literature is about form and fiction. When the journalist gets a fact wrong, the work is destroyed. When the writer gets a fact right, the work comes to life. Journalism was for the masses, literature was for an elite. With time, both have evolved towards each other. The journalist through reportage can be personal in narrative, and the writer can now tell the truth without hiding behind fiction. When the reporter is objective and gives us facts, the news is cold. When the writer makes up a story with no base in reality, he creates fantasy, but fiction has to make sense. When the best journalists get personal, they take us with them to the action. When writers research to create a logical tale, we believe them.

There's the time factor. When sent to a press conference, having just a couple of hours, even Gabriel Garcia Marquez would write a news piece like any other reporter.

I disagree. The writer has a different angle. They process information differently.

The argument continues, your two readers are from different backgrounds. Watching each argue makes you realize the division is real. What matters is you finished the requirement to get your degree.

Elliott is graduating at the end of the year. When you talk about the future, you do not see anything concrete. One day, he calls saying: *Do you have your calendar with you? I need you to write down my family trips.* He is not planning a future with you. He still sees himself as part of his nuclear family. You break up with him.

I know you are younger, but the only way this is going to work is if we both compromise. You might want to marry older but if you want to stay with me, you are going to have to marry sooner than you wanted.

A friend who is studying in Mexico City, is leaving her apartment empty for the summer. You rent it and take a Mexican History summer program, with the renowned author Lorenzo Meyer. You keep your sister company. She is single and pregnant. Even though she is thirty-four-years old, there is drama around this. The baby's father is willing to have a small wedding for the family only. Your mother pushes for invitations and a big party. The deal is off. Now the pressure is on you. You get a few blind dates with older established men. Elliott gets jealous enough to come see you. You get back together with plans to get married.

You continue writing editorials. As part of the elections, you are invited to a house to hear a candidate's proposal. She is Miss Mexico 1981. She is unqualified to run for Mayor of Monterrey. You write about it even though as a little girl you watched Miss Universe every year. These officially pretty women cannot flirt their way into office. Miss Mexico 1981 does not even have a high school diploma. Her fame comes from conducting a television show giving beauty advice. The gossip is she got her big break by being the governor's lover. You write an article about her incompetence.

A few months after that piece, a representative of the television variety show *Sábado Gigante* calls you. *Can we have coffee? I would like to make you an offer.* You meet her in a restaurant. She invites you to the show. There will be a pageant debate, you against and somebody in favor. All your expenses will be paid to go to Miami. You accept and have a month to prepare. You read *Palabra de Reina* (Queen's Word) book written by Lupita Jones, Miss Mexico 1990 and Miss Universe 1991. You research to find out the show is a profitable business owned by Donald Trump. Through Elliott, you get an appointment to interview Miss Mexico 1992.

When you land in Miami, you get a sense of closure returning in a different position than last time. You and other participants get picked up at the airport. You are dropped off at the Embassy Suites. You take a bath, order room service and watch a movie. The next day, you check out and go to the studio. You are taken to hair and make-up. While sitting there, lit like a star with dozens of lightbulbs, the producer runs in to look at you. *Thank God you are pretty. I had to trust our correspondent. You have to look good to have credibility.* She gives the hairdresser a few instructions and leaves. They finish beautifying you and take you to a waiting room. The only person sitting there is Miss Mexico 1981.

I am not from a privileged background like you. My parents were poor. For girls like me, beauty contests were my big break.

I am glad you made something of yourself, but education has not been your priority and in politics you need to be better equipped to serve in office. You could have finished high school.

If you don't believe in this, why are you all dressed up?

This is an appearance on international television.

They take you on stage. There is a large live audience. You are clipped with microphones and wait for Don Francisco. He sits next to her, they fix the lights and you are on.

So why are you against beauty pageants?

Women are treated like objects. They parade themselves to be graded, like pedigree dogs or horses. It's humiliating.

And why are you in favor of them?

Thanks to the opportunity I had of becoming Miss Mexico 1981, I have had wonderful experiences. I have traveled, met interesting people and I get to be here with you Don Francisco. She smiles and flirts with him and the camera. Two months later the show airs. Miss Mexico 1981 gives a press conference to attract more attention.

What does she know about beauty pageants? I participated in one. What can she tell me? She calls you *machista*, you write a reply.

This woman does not even know the definition of the word. A feminist is in favor of women, a "machista" is in favor of men. In Mexico feminists are a minority, "machistas" are the majority. A "machista" woman is seductive and uses her sex appeal to get what she wants. A woman who participates in beauty pageants is "machista" because she uses her beauty to get ahead. When I said to Don Francisco that beauty pageants humiliate women, I was not offending them but defending them. Her participation in no way makes her an expert. She was seventeen-years-old and wearing a bikini. The key aspect was our appearance. We both looked pretty but while I was wearing a light blue suit with pearls and hair pulled back, Miss Mexico 1981 showed up with big hair, in a short red spandex dress with five inch heels. I was there to be heard, she was there to be seen.

You went to Miami to debate against beauty pageants with a sense of duty, but Miss Mexico 1981 had an agenda and established a relationship with Univision. (She became the hostess of a television show on family issues, and supervised family drama with a good haircut and professional makeup.)

Your focus was on journalism. You sent your article to the Miami Nuevo Herald and it was published. Your reward is different. You get an email from a student of *Women Studies* who asks if you can translate the piece to English so she can discuss it in class. Another reader writes: *Thank you for reaching millions of viewers and saying what the majority of women feel and wish we could communicate.* The biggest compliment is a gossip column that asks Miss Mexico 1981: *What were you thinking? You can't pick up a fight with Samson.* You are Samson in this scenario.

Chapter 2.3   2007

Beatrice is now trained to be the parent of a special needs child. She does not pity her son David anymore. She treats him with respect and expects more from him. She uses the new techniques acquired. She plays games to get him to use his words. It takes weeks, but he finally says the word *Tickle* when he wants his mom to tickle him. He does not get what he wants unless he gives her a sound. A sound turns into syllables and syllables turn into words.

David is enrolled in a school close to their neighborhood. His new teacher, Ms. Arlene, is smart and dedicated. Every day she is put together: a modern asymmetrical haircut, sharp outfits and bright red lipstick. The more respect Beatrice shows her son, the more he shows her his capacity. One Friday morning, he insists on wearing a red shirt, but his uniform is khakis with white or navy shirt. He throws a tantrum, she realizes his tone is different, she is missing something. When they get to school, she sees everybody is wearing colored t-shirts with a school slogan on them. He had one of these shirts, it was red, but was given away. She goes back home and calls Ms. Arlene and explains what happened. The teacher calls and gets a yellow one. Beatrice goes back to school and puts the shirt on her son. *I am sorry David. I didn't know you wanted your old red T shirt. I am sorry I gave it away. Here is another shirt.* He knows what day of the week it is and he follows the school's activities.

She is still not sharing with local friends. Through his parents' networking, Elliott gets three telephone numbers. She calls three women who live in San Antonio, who have older children with autism. Even though she does not know them, she calls to talk. They belong to a sisterhood, The Special Mother's Club. They assure her David will mature like other children. *When my son was three-years-old I never thought he was going to be independent. Now that he is twelve, I can see that happening in the future.*

It is time to enroll Tomas in the right school. After a long wait, they get the call. He takes the admissions test and fails on purpose. Beatrice takes him to a psychologist to talk about why he does not want to go to the other school. When they enter her office, Tomas sits quietly on one of the sofas and she gives him paper and crayons.

What is his first language?

Spanish. We left Nuevo Laredo in the middle of the school year.

Was he part of the decision?

No.

He is six-years-old and needs to be involved to collaborate.

The therapist suggests Beatrice come back by herself as her son is too young. Next time she comes, in less than five minutes Beatrice is cursing drug dealers, crying like a baby because she had to leave her house. Her nose starts bleeding, she is drowning in tears and blood.

Had you ever talked about this before?

No.

Do you realize all the pressure your body had built in?

Why didn't she talk about it? Shame? Fear? She did not talk about it for two years, during which her life revolved around autism. She did not mourn the loss of her Mexican life. Nobody talks about it. They all pretend everything is going smoothly. They bump into each other at the supermarket and chat about how well they are doing.

I have other patients who are beginning to mourn. I call you all zombies. You are walking around absent minded and purposeless.

Everyone is confused. The elderly are the worst. I know an old man who had a nervous breakdown and was found running naked on his ranch. Somebody's parents were forced to move. They were fully functional. After the move, they lost their social circle, routines and daily activities. In a couple of years, they developed dementia, ended up in wheel chairs with diapers, and died. Trying to start a new life with grown children and no professional activity is hard.

Beatrice decides to see this therapist once a week for two months. It has been years since she had a therapist. Now she can review, analyze and organize her thoughts about all the changes. They are like a pair of librarians placing books on the right shelves.

Have you asked Tomas what he thinks is wrong with his brother?

She is ashamed to admit but she has not. Beatrice initiates conversations with Tomas about autism. She had been so busy with the occupational therapies and doctor appointments, that she never explained to her eldest son what was going on. He believes that she loves his brother more than she loves him. Tomas wants to sleep with his mom, and she always refuses, but when he wakes up, she is in his brother's room. *Honey that is because David's doesn't sleep well and he wakes up in the middle of the night.* He hears the word special over and over. Why is his brother special? Why does he get special education? There is nothing special about him, he cannot even speak. He gets punished constantly, and David never gets punished. *What can I take away from him? Friends? He doesn't have any. Food? He has a special diet. Toys? He doesn't even play with toys, he lines them up.* She makes an extra effort to do things with Tomas, to give him time. Her two goals are to reestablish his self-esteem and to dissolve his resentment towards his brother.

The other part of the puzzle is becoming part of a community and having a sense of belonging. She addresses this issue with the therapist.

I don't understand why there's no sense of belonging in Laredo. Communities are not tight on the border. There are only family ties. Is that how American society is?

Remember this is called the Gateway City for a reason. People come through, make money and leave, they don't grow roots. These international borders are divided by a river, two different countries on each side, with two different laws. These differences favor illegal activity, drugs are the obvious one, but everyday Mexicans cross to work illegally, and they can't trust their coworkers because they don't want to lose their job. Guns are legal in the United States and illegal in Mexico, and they are smuggled into Mexico. American pharmacies have strict policies about dispensing medication, but Mexican pharmacies are permissive.

You are right. A friend of mine sells used clothes. She knows this is legal in the United States but illegal in Mexico. She knows that those

who buy her merchandise will smuggle it into Mexico. One man's trash is
another man's treasure.

In an atmosphere of fear, it is hard to build a sense of belonging.

As Elliott and Beatrice continue making friends they attend the George Washington's Birthday parade. They sit on a stand and watch the floats drive by with society girls waving, wearing their hand-embroidered Marie Antoinette dresses. The schools march along, and every local organization participates. Beatrice knows that the previous night these girls were presented to society at the Civic Center, because she was a debutante twenty years ago.

The presentation stages a dinner at George Washington's house where his wife Martha receives aristocratic guests. This is a confusing scenario, Washington fought the British crown for independence and did not believe in aristocracy. This eclectic tradition is the product of historical and cultural ignorance. Texas did not become independent from England but from Mexico. The George Washington Celebration tradition began with a group of Americans, who wanted to demonstrate patriotism toward the United States and amity towards Mexico. The morning of the parade, the celebration begins at the International bridge with *El Abrazo*. Two American children from Laredo, Texas hug two Mexican children from Nuevo Laredo.

With time, Beatrice becomes familiarized with American life and witnesses as an insider how this nation is flawed like any other. One Saturday morning, her son David is outside jumping on the trampoline. The nanny, who helps on the weekends, comes inside the house and says she has a headache because of the cloud of smoke coming from the backyard behind. Beatrice goes outside and realizes her whole garden smells like weed. She calls the president of the neighborhood. He calls the police. Beatrice's house borders another neighborhood. She calls a friend who lives on the other side. *Go outside and tell me if you see anything.* Then neighborhood leader calls to say: *The fire department rang the doorbell and asked them to put out whatever they were burning. No further investigation was conducted.*

Outside her garage, on a dead end, Beatrice sees the red and blue lights of a police car. In the middle of the night, the policeman was interrogating a couple of teenagers who were consuming drugs. Behind her house, by the narrow alley, there is a hidden small door. They install an iron gate, preventing this door from opening. They believe through this door they sell drugs on the weekends.

Beatrice shares this with a friend, who has another back-alley story. On family social gatherings, the teenagers hang out in the backyard, while the parents sit inside. There is a service called *Papi Chulo* the kids call. They deliver alcohol through the back. The parents have no clue their children are getting drunk in the backyard.

At the end of spring, Elliott finishes his MBA. After two years of travel, deadlines and meetings, they go to North Carolina to celebrate his graduation. Beatrice buys a formal day dress and a hat. As the graduates receive their diplomas, their teachers congratulate them and their spouses. They are a mature couple. The recognition is not for the parents. After his graduation, Elliott gets gifts for his family member for putting up with him. He takes Tomas and a friend in a Recreational Vehicle to camp by a river. He spends an afternoon driving David around eating French fries, and Beatrice gets a new watch.

As the school year comes to an end, Tomas goes to a summer camp for the first time. Elliott is on a hunting trip. Beatrice takes Tomas to camp. His clothes are packed in a black trunk, a gift from his grandparents. They drive in the middle of a storm and cannot reach the camp because the Guadalupe River is flooded. When Beatrice drops Tomas off and says goodbye, she cannot hold back the tears. *Mom you're giving me a headache.* He does not cry. It is the first time they are apart for so long. The whole month, every morning, Beatrice goes to the camp's website to look at the pictures. She feels at peace when she sees him making arts and crafts, cooking outdoors and playing tennis.

A month later, Elliott and Beatrice pick him up together. Elliott greets the owners and chats about the summers he went there as a child. When they find Tomas's cabin, he is not there. The little boys are waiting for their mothers, and one of them hugs Beatrice. He cannot help himself. He needs a mother's hug, even if it is somebody else's mom. Tomas comes and they hug. He looks tan, but when they get home and he soaks in the bath, the tan turns out to be filth. He has not taken a proper shower in four weeks. He is grateful for the comfort provided at home. Their house is full of life again.

The school year begins, and Tomas starts going to his new school. The academic level is higher. The whole family is introduced to a new social network. Beatrice does not blend in easily. She feels the wall around locals. They do not mean to be rude, but they are. They have their circles and high school stories to share.

Beatrice decides to create her own Book Club. She searches for readers and establishes her own intellectual orphanage. A friend brings other friends and before she knows it there is a painter, a Masters and a PhD in Literature. This group proves the fastest relationships are built by reading the same books. They propose books, select dates and take turns hosting their gatherings.

The woman with the doctorate gives Beatrice an article about her grandfather titled *The Last of the Border Lords* published in a magazine on 1987. Beatrice knew her great-grandfather had committed suicide, but she never knew why or how he killed himself. The article explains he was sleeping in a little room above the family bank. On January 12, 1931, after he shaved, instead of dressing in the suit, coat and vest he had laid out for the day, he found his brother-in-law's gun put it to his forehead and fired. Three pesos and a lottery ticket were in his pocket when he died. His wife Sarah found him lying on the floor. His body was embalmed, making him the first person to be mummified in both Laredo, Texas and Nuevo Laredo. Three days later, his body was taken to a burial ground in an international procession that was twenty blocks and a hundred and seventy vehicles long, this was the largest funeral in Nuevo Laredo's history. This man was Beatrice's great-grandfather as well as Elliott's.

Once Beatrice reads this article, she becomes curious and begins research on her family. She gathers information going back to the original Octavio Theriot I, her great-great-grandfather. He was from Camargo Tamaulipas, married and moved to Mier, a border town. He was a merchant, probably a grocer. When his wife died, he remarried and went back to Camargo. Octavio Theriot II was from Mier. He did not go to Camargo, but went to Laredo, Texas searching for a brighter future. The town was booming because of the new railroads that arrived in 1881. He was an experienced merchant and found a job in a grocery shop. After Octavio proved to be a trustworthy employee, he was given more responsibilities, and with time, he started his own business selling sugar, rice and wheat by the sack in Nuevo Laredo.

Octavio met Sarah, and they married in May 31, 1900. They had eight children, three girls and five boys. The firstborn was a girl, and the second child was a boy, Octavio Theriot III. They called him *muchachito,* and his eldest sister called him *Chito*. Octavio and Sarah had their own grocery store, a new home, and a growing family. The outbreak of the Mexican Revolution in 1910 did not affect Nuevo Laredo in the beginning, but by 1914, the need to recruit men and more supplies reached every corner of the country. Octavio Theriot II tried to sell wheat and hay to the revolutionaries. When he said to the *caudillos*: *Just please tell the General to pay soon.* They laughed and replied. *Pay? This is for the Revolution.* They hunted him down for having tried to collect money from the revolutionaries. He had to cross to Laredo, Texas in the trunk of a car to escape.

During the Mexican Revolution, from 1910 to 1920, the population of Laredo, Texas doubled in size because of the exodus of Mexicans escaping the armed conflict. During the chaos, the grocery store was burned. With few possessions left, Octavio and Sarah took their gold savings and joined a wholesale grocery business.

Even life on the American side was not safe. People would stand on their roofs to see the battles across the river. When an observer was shot by a stray bullet, they decided to send their four older children to San Antonio. In 1924, Octavio sold his grocery business and became a beer distributor. Many Americans who were not in agreement with the Eighteenth Amendment traveled to Mexico to drink; this is how a long tradition began of generations of gringos going to the border to get wasted. The beer was delivered in refrigerated railroad cars and kept cold until it was delivered to the bars. There was no ice house, and the Theriots built their own ice plant with cold storage.

By the 1920s, exchanging dollars for pesos became common. The volume of business turned the Theriots into informal money exchangers of gold coins. Mexico had not recovered from the Revolution. Mexican merchants traveled to the border for supplies. Merchants stored their gold with the Theriots and drew on their accounts when purchasing in Texas. Paper money became acceptable in the 1930s. In 1925, the beer concession was terminated. They formalized their private banking activities and built a two-story building in Nuevo Laredo, to reflect stability. It was built in a Neoclassic style with white limestone, brought from Indiana, and the interior featured white marble and bronze windows.

Ranch lands were acquired as collateral for bad loans. Later, they established a mill to sell cottonseed cake and other cattle feed for ranchers on both sides of the border. They pressed cottonseed to produce refined oils and they had plants for producing cooking lard *Manteca Sara*, laundry soap *Jabon Gloria* and an ice factory *Hielo La Carolina*. They incorporated these businesses into *Industrias Unidas* on November 1930.

Octavio Theriot III, *Chito*, met Alice Penn in High School, the daughter of Justo Penn, owner and editor of the Laredo Morning Times. Chito married Alice Penn on May 18th of 1927. They had four children: Sara Alice born in 1928, Octavio Theriot IV (born in 1929, who died at three months of crib death); Gloria Gilda born in 1931 and Octavio Theriot V born in 1933. The boy was called Chitito, and was by all accounts a most beloved son. Because of his brother's death, he was protected and cared for like no other. That boy was Beatrice's father.

I'm lying on my mother's bed watching television. Her pillows are fluffier, and her sheets are softer than mine. I have cramps and want to stay here. Next to her bedroom she has an office. Now that she is in college, that is where she sits to do her homework every morning. As a child, I was not aware that neither of my parents had a college degree. Maybe they did not think it was necessary. My mother is studying philosophy. She will graduate when she turns fifty-years-old. She walks around energetically, always in a hurry, doing too many things at once.

We're going to have to go pretty soon. I suggest you get ready.

Their German friend from Hamburg, Mr.Wasmuth, is in town and brought his son with him. We are going to dinner and it is my duty to entertain. I do not feel like going, but I have to. It is important to my mother. They met having dinner at the Twenty-One Club in New York. They were sitting next to each other and started up a conversation. His wife died a few years ago. I am going. My mother has been so dedicated to me in the last year, I owe it to her. It has been almost two years since the episode.

I get up and walk to my room, get my clothes ready and turn the shower on. As I get undressed, I see myself in the mirror. For the first time in a long time, that inner monologue against my body is quiet. It is hard to pinpoint the day it dawned on me that this is the only body I have, and I live in it. Last year, I was heavier because of the meds. Now that the dose is lower, it is easy to eat less. I will never look the way I did when I was fifteen-years-old, but having a woman's body is not all bad.

As I wash and enjoy the warm water all over me, I thank God for helping me find journalism as my major in college. Being a good student was not a priority and now it is. My first choice was fashion, my mother insisted I had a talent with colors. While drawing Greek togas in the History of Dress, the girls would talk about soap operas. I dropped out. My second choice was psychology. Many of the students were psychoanalyzing themselves. I dropped out again. I am not the only one. My mother tried different options before she chose philosophy.

Knock, knock! We're going to be late. Hurry up.

My university is the second best in town, the focus is liberal arts. They use a new way of teaching. We read an assignment, go to class and sit in a circle. The first time we were silent, it was uncomfortable, the teacher was waiting for us to say something. The study material was created by us. Inside the classroom I am inquisitive, in social settings I am somebody else. My mother reminds me of a Mexican proverb: "*Mujer que sabe latín no tiene marido ni buen fin."* ("A woman who knows Latin will never find a husband, nor come to a good end.")

Once I am ready, I go downstairs, and the four of us get in the car, - my mother, father, my brother Gerard and I - and drive to the new steakhouse located at the skirt of the mountain. It is still hot and bright outside. Summer is about to begin. When we get to the restaurant, both men stand up to greet us. I know Mr. Wasmuth. He is tall, but his son is even taller. His name is Arne, but his father calls him Musen. He is a true Aryan sample: tall, slim, rosy cheeks, deep blue eyes and dirty blond hair. I sit next to him, and we start talking.

How tall are you?

I am 1.96 meters.

I knew your father was tall, I just didn't expect you to be taller.

I am four centimeters too short to be Hitler's bodyguard.

I am surprised that being German he brings up that name. I thought nobody talked about him out of shame. While we look at the menus and wait for our food to come, we cover our background. Musen just graduated from Columbia University. We talk about New York City like a mutual friend.

I went to a boarding school in New York and would go into the city every other weekend. It was a cultural shock to see such diversity.

How old were you?

When I got there, I was fifteen-years-old.

Where did you go?

The school was north of Manhattan, in a small town called Dobbs Ferry. My sister went there before me, and my mother went to a boarding school in the same area, in White Plains. She chose to send us there.

What a great opportunity! I believe that not leaving your home town before you are an adult is a damage that is irreparable. Your vision is impaired for life.

I never thought of it that way.

New York is a drug you need to have at least once a year.

He was in New York for four years. I was there for two. That gives us a sense of fraternity. He is from somewhere, there are locals in his community, well rooted families that stay in the same place for generations, but he is proud to be a mover. He is well rounded, he speaks German. His English is perfect, and he also speaks some Spanish. He is well mannered. When I excuse myself to use the restroom, he stands up. While walking, I cannot help smiling. I do not think I have ever had a close encounter with a true global citizen. He has no preconceived notions about me and treats me as an equal. When talking with Mexican guys, I listen most of the time and pretend to be interested. With my locals, those two years in New York fell in the Bermuda triangle. With him, I can open my box of memories and talk about a time in my life that manipulated my brain like it was dough.

We are done and get ready to leave. We make plans for the next day. It is uncomfortable to stand next to him, he is a foot taller than I am. As I get in the car I am ecstatic. I can tell my mother is happy. After the year I had, meeting this man is a gift. We get home. My mother and I go to the breakfast room and talk while we drink some tea.

You didn't stop talking all night. You didn't look at us.
I didn't, I was smitten by him.
Gerard grabs something to eat, and before he leaves he says:
I am sorry but I think he's gay.
Why the hell would you say that? You are such a homophobic!
If you two were together, I would have German grandchildren!
Mom it sounds like you are going to make them. She blushes and laughs. My mother also engages in intellectual matches with Mr. Wasmuth. She doesn't have those conversations with my father.

We go upstairs. I try to go to sleep. My sister Alexandra has been gone for more than a year. I still miss her. I wish we could talk about this until midnight. As I lie here, I thank God because Musen exists. All of last year I felt like a sack of potatoes. The meds numbed my mind and body. I felt hopeless and trapped. Even if I never see him again, tonight is important. He exists. He liked me. We liked each other. I feel like the ugly duckling. After growing up feeling awkward, I just spent a lonely winter and now I see this beautiful swan. As I approach him, I can see in his eyes that I have turned into a swan myself.

The next day, I drive to pick him up at his hotel and take him out to lunch at the Club. The conversation continues like it was not interrupted.

How was your flight coming here?
Even though it was long, if you think about it, traveling has become such a common activity it is not an adventure anymore.
What do you mean?
When these colonies were established, it took Europeans two months to get here. Now it all happens in one day.
It's as if just because you are European you have seniority over me. Where do you get this insight about travel?
I am reading a book on travel, and I am journaling.
I have been journaling for years. What role does journaling play in this equation?
To write well you need to be here and now.

That is not at all what I do. At the end of the day, I go over the events in a telegraphic manner, just to remember the sequence. Then I spill my emotions, like vomit. The result is a cleanse of frustrations.

Well, it would be best if you could practice being aware. For example, I am in Mexico, I am a twenty-four-year old German, and you are a twenty-two-year-old woman.

Twenty-one! My birthday is coming up, but I am still twenty-one. Don't make me older. My mother worries I am going to be an old maid.

It's hard for me to understand that. Women in Germany marry older. But why would she say that? Wouldn't it be more constructive to make you believe you'll find somebody?

I guess it's the way things are done here.

You need to get out of here before it's too late. You shouldn't live in fear. Didn't you learn anything in New York?

I did, but there was a disconnect. After coming out of an all-girls Catholic school, at fifteen, I saw the American girls as drunk-skinny-whores, but they were preparing for the SAT. They were not looking for a man who went to Stanford. They wanted to go to Stanford. I knew I was coming back. My options were girl majors like teaching, psychology, design or fashion. A close friend went to college, got a boyfriend and dropped out. She just wanted to meet someone.

He doesn't understand my friends are getting married one after the other. It's the musical chairs game, everybody is grabbing a chair, and soon there will be none. He is a man and he is German, how could he understand? We Mexican women have a small window of opportunity to find the best suitor, and whoever becomes sexually active turns into damaged goods.

As we walk towards the car, I hope to bump into somebody I know. I feel proud and know he would impress anyone. We Mexicans have a deep inferiority complex when it comes to Europeans. It was ingrained in our brains during colonization. As we drive around, I feel like an accidental tourist in my own city. When we drive up to *Chipinque,* we see the majesty of the city in a sunken grey valley underneath us. The mountains guard it like sentinels on every side.

These mountains are regal. Their peculiar forms are unique. They remind me of Rio de Janeiro, except that there is no ocean, of course.

Rio de Janeiro? I think of Brazil as exotic. You could say they are both geographical accidents. But people here are humble because when they look around, they see God's touch in the majesty of these mountains. New Yorkers are proud when they look around. They see man made sky scrapers that boost their ego.

When I drop him off at his hotel, I go back home, and my mother and his father are changing plans. It seems he will be staying with us for a week. My mother's friends will be appalled that she would let him stay in our house, but I assume his father warned him about our conservative ways. He does not even stand too close to me. In the next days, I find out about his mother's death. She was sick and asked to be taken home and died in her husband's arms. He has a half-brother from his mother's previous marriage. She came from nobility.

Explain to me how aristocratic titles work. We don't have them in Mexico, but most Mexicans are obsessed with Royalty and talk about royals on a first name basis.

Titles were given by the Pope for religious or military merit.

Why was it special to be an aristocrat?

Only aristocrats could own land and hunt. They had the blood tax. They had to fight in wars.

That does sound noble. Europeans had a gradual maturation. In America, we started watching the movie after the intermission.

But you have the advantage of native cultures.

For years that was not appreciated, racism persists.

Mexicans are racists?

It's worse. We are caste-conscious. Las Castas classified people into categories: the whiter someone was, the higher their status.

I am not familiar with the caste system.

It was used in the colonies. Las Castas divided people by race and origin, with lower socio-racial categories paying more taxes. Dark skin was associated with poverty and inferiority. I believe that race is a manmade concept.

I am such a hypocrite. Here I am talking about racism, and one of the reasons why I look up to this man is because he is white, blond and blue-eyed. I don't believe in aristocracy, and yet I am impressed with his aristocratic background. After a week of talking and driving around, we go to Mexico City. He stays in Octavio's newlywed house. I stay with my sister Alexandra. He has been telling me for days that he has a special surprise for my birthday. The day arrives. I get dressed up, and he picks me up in a taxi.

Where are we going?

It's a surprise.

We are going to *Palacio de Bellas Artes*. I cannot believe I had never been here! It is a magnificent art nouveau building. As we approach it, we walk and see the murals by famous Mexican artists.

I am happy to be here. This is the best birthday gift ever!

We go inside the theater. We are going to see the *Amalia Hernandez* folkloric dance show. As we take our seats, we wait. On stage, there is a Tiffany glass curtain with the image of the valley of Mexico City. On this window, you can see the *Popocatépetl* and *Iztaccíhuatl*. The lighting is soft. It makes it look like dawn. It is a magical evening. In the end, there is no hugging or kissing. Maybe my brother was right after all.

The next day, I go back to Monterrey and Musen continues his adventure in Mexico City and then on to Guatemala. At the end of the summer, I receive a letter and get to read about all his adventures. It is nice to know our time together was special to him: *I find myself avoiding the places to which you and I have been together, as if they were in some way blessed or sacred by your eyes.*

These lines will fuel me for a lifetime.

Chapter 3.2   1998

After eight years of completing your studies, you finish your thesis. Your graduation day is the exact same day as Elliott's. You go to your ceremony alone and park far away. There are hundreds of students. After all these years the campus is complete, with a green landscape. Here you are, on a cold winter day, sitting among the younger students, waiting to shake the principal's hand. For years, you told yourself that this little piece of paper did not matter, but it does. When you get your diploma, you free your mind from the beast of procrastination.

You are going to a fancy French restaurant to celebrate both graduations. Your mom is getting ready. The two of you stress about how you look. In every family, there is always one woman who is prettier than everybody else. In the Theriot family, it is Elliott's mother. No matter how you fix your hair, or how much make up you put on, she will look better, dress better and smell better.

Elliott arrives with his parents. You arrive with yours. When you get there, his mother looks like a countess. During dinner, you stare at her white silk ruffled blouse, her pearls, her abundant blonde hair, and her perfect complexion. You sit boy-girl-boy-girl. Your father flanked by your mom and you. His mother flanked by them. Elliott and you sit next to each other. You narrate your graduation experiences. Your family is not big on gifts, but his is. You harassed your father to get him a set of Mont Blanc pens as a gift. There is no special reaction from their part, it is expected. You are civilized, well-mannered and polite but the tension is tangible. The past lingers like a dark veil between you and them. You get home and your mother ruins everything with her blunt honesty.

Now that he graduated, they came to take him back home.

You talked about getting married and living here, but Elliott does not make his own decisions. You refocus on your development and start a graduate program. You choose Organizational Development because it is rooted in behavioral sciences.

After the Christmas holiday, you show up on your first day of school. The graduate classrooms are on the top floor. They have carpets and air conditioning. There are only ten students, eight women. Most are older and have professional experience, except for one girl, who just graduated. To look older, she shows up in a suit she never wears, there is a hanger mark at the level of her knees. Most members of the group are employees of large corporations wanting to get a better salary. You meet for a week. The other three weeks are for assignments. Your first morning, you divide into groups to make a collage of your lives. As you sit and cut magazine photos, you glue your past, present and future to a paper board. When you are done, you present your lives to each other. Something strange happens. You explain the images you chose but they are more revealing than intended. The visual icons are raw associations. One of the guys chose an image of suitcases to represent his childhood. His mother was always gone. Your collage is divided in three sections: your past is family and school; your present is studying and writing, and your future is marriage and children.

At the end of January, everything is eclipsed by the birth of your nephew. Your sister Alexandra has a baby boy as a single parent. As much pressure as your mother put on her, Alexandra decided not to marry. You all come to see her. Alexandra is still in bed. You go out to lunch with the proud father, who brags that the baby got all hundreds on different baby scores. There is tension. Your mother is angry at him. She could not bend him. You make sure your mother and his mother do not sit next to each other.

You stay with Alexandra for a couple of days. She has lived in the same house in Mexico City for years. It is an old mansion divided into two. The owner, a spinster, lives on one side. For years, this space was for bachelorettes only, and now it is a nursery. Your father pays for a nurse in the evenings. Alexandra is a new person with her baby. You have seen her struggle her whole life. Once again, she chose an uphill path. You worry about her, but as she holds her tiny baby she becomes invincible. She is not afraid. There is a square of bright white morning sunlight coming through the window, and it hits the bed like a divine beam. She undresses her baby and lays him under the sunlight for a few minutes. He is small and beautiful. Alexandra stares at him with awe and you stare at her with amazement. She has always been brave and now she is even stronger. While your mother suffers because of what people say, Alexandra dives deep into motherhood.

Now that Elliott is living in Nuevo Laredo, you visit often. His parents' house could be pictured in Architectural Digest. It is brand new, built to look like an old hacienda. The entrance has the Theriot family crest at the top. The two big wood doors have shutters. Next to the entrance, there are two tall candelabra, like the ones they have in churches. The house has a horseshoe shape. To the right are the kitchen and garages. In the center are the dining and living room areas, overlooking a pool in a courtyard. To the left are the bedrooms. The ceiling is at least eighteen feet tall. Elliott's parents are always traveling. You stay over many times. There are childhood pictures of him in his bedroom. He has a king size bed covered with a large canopy. In front of it, there is a day bed full of pillows. The doors are tall and solid. The curtains are long and heavy. In the living-room, there is a grand granite table, antique furniture and images of angels and virgins everywhere. At the end of the corridor, there is an altar. His sister says the house looks like a church.

Fifty years ago, your grandfather did the exact same thing. When Nuevo Laredo was even smaller, he built himself a thirty thousand square foot house on the outskirts of town. There were ten thousand square feet for the basement, ten for the first level and ten for the second level. You remember your mother would joke saying: *I didn't know I was poor until I met the Theriots.*

When you are here, Elliott is different, he feels proud and confident. In Monterrey you are the insider, Nuevo Laredo is his oyster. Now that you are talking marriage, his parents have changed their attitude towards you. You are at an impasse. When Elliott's brother was born, their father bought their mom a set of diamond earrings, destined to become their engagement rings. She is not ready to part with them.

Why don't you give me any ring? It doesn't have to be that one.

That earring was bought for my future wife. You are my future wife, it has to be that one.

While that situation is still frozen, you visit the newspaper in Nuevo Laredo to sell your editorials. When you arrive, you are disappointed to see how small the offices are. You meet with the son of the owner, who is surprisingly young.

Did you know your grandfather and my grandfather had a huge fight many years ago? Your grandfather was so angry, he went and founded the other newspaper.

The clan's history is more complex than anticipated. Elliott knows more, he grew up here. His family talks about it. Your father comes up with the idea of you helping him manage one of his properties. Your Nuevo Laredo memories are from your childhood. When you were ten, your cousin taught you to ride a bike outside your grandfather's house.

It is a hot summer afternoon. You are sitting in one of the rooms in Elliott's house, writing. He shows up with both hands behind his back. *Pick one.* You choose the wrong one. He opens the other. It is the earring. That is your marriage proposal. After many conversations, he got his mother to give him the earring. You go to a well-known jeweler and choose the mount. When it is ready, you wear it and look at your hand constantly. When you drive, the sunlight hits your left hand and the prism refracts rainbow-colored sparkles like a tiny chandelier.

As soon as there is an opportunity you show it to your closest friends. They are playing cards at The Pea's modern custom-made house, on her family's private estate. Of all of them, the one you feel closest to is Blondie. You hug her tight to express your joy.

Who was the jeweler? It is a bit yellow.

You tell the earring story. They change the subject faster than expected. Driving home, you reflect on their reaction. You wait for your monthly appointment with your current therapist to go over the issue.

I had to come share this with you, I am engaged.
Congratulations! How does this make you feel?
I thought it was all happiness but it's not black and white.
What do you mean?
My friends saw the ring and made me feel it was cheap or fake.
Would you rephrase. Nobody makes you feel anything.
I expected them to be perfectly happy for me, but they weren't.
Why do you think that is?
All of them have been married for years. One of them has been a wife for twelve years. I was the weirdo singleton for whom they would get blind dates. They felt sorry for me, thought I was never going to marry. Now they are not that happy. I was pleased when they were engaged, had their weddings, built their houses, and had their babies. I am so behind that I was sure this happy ending, after a long journey of solitude and uncertainty, would make them share my joy.
There's a difference. Can you tell me what it is?
All that time I could still hope for a better future?
Correct. You see, single people haven't made choices and can continue fantasizing about their boyfriend, ring, house or babies. Once you make a choice it's real.

Are you saying that they are not happy with their lives?

No. But they might be jealous because you are starting.

I saw them become wives and mothers, it is a different stage.

The word illusion and disillusion are linked. The illusion fades when reality appears. As you progress in this journey, you too will have to accept your new reality and there will be good things and bad things.

One of my biggest wishes was to become one of them, but that will never happen, we will never be in the same stage. I guess I was naive when I thought that just because they were married they were happier.

Your marital state is not static. A widow can be sad when her husband dies, but after grieving she can be happy again.

I thought they felt sorry for me because I was alone.

Did they all marry whom they wanted to marry?

It's seems that way. It's hard to know.

Do you really think you couldn't have married before?

I had a ridiculous marriage proposal once.

Maybe they are jealous for more than your ring?

Well, I was brave to wait. I kept myself busy doing interesting things. I remember another conversation with one of them. We were talking about training and she wanted to convince me she was more fit than I was. I finally said, the difference is that all my energy was mine and she had to share her physical strength with her children and husband, doing things for them.

You will soon learn that being married is harder than you think.

I am still an outsider, they have been through so much. In all those breakfasts, I pay attention and listen. They share but not so much.

Wives like to talk to other wives, mothers like to talk to other mothers. You'll soon be one of them, and the stage won't matter as much.

One of them was making fun of a woman we know, who had professional success, got married and had kids. She said that it didn't matter, we all end up the same. That's not true. When I have children, I will feel different because I did have a career. What do you think?

Yes and no. Yes, it does make a difference in your perception of yourself if you accomplish something or not. No, because it is true that domestic life is just as hard if you have a graduate degree or not, and being well educated can make it harder.

Are you saying it's going to be harder for me to adapt?

Maybe. After being a journalist and coming and going, you might find it harder to sacrifice that part of your life.

I don't think so. I am tired. I want to have a house and make it into a home, take care of Elliott and my babies.

When it comes to being single or married it's all or nothing.
What do you mean?
Don't you think your friends felt that way years ago?
Yes, they were super excited.
So, what changed?

I see. The same thing day in day out. Now I understand, at least with my brain. I know once I am there I will understand what they are going through. To me there's a bigger conclusion to this. There's a saying 'When you are up, your friends know you, when you are down, you know your friends.' I don't agree. I think it's easier to be kind to someone who is doing badly, it's harder to be happy for someone who is doing well. Some of the people who were the nicest to me are not reacting the way I thought.

It depends on their situation. People who have love can be happy if you have love. People who have money can be happy if you have money. If you have something I don't have, how can I be happy for you?

Before I go, I want to thank you for your patience and faith in me. I share this joy with you, and please tell the group, I couldn't have done it without all of them.

You have come a long way. Stay brave. Marriage is both a happy ending and a difficult beginning. On days like these is when I love what I do, I can see how it makes a difference.

As you continue with your life as a fiancée, the adjustments continue. Your future in-laws act distant. They bought an apartment in Paris, and Elliott is there for a couple of months collaborating with the construction workers on the remodel. You miss each other. His father buys you a ticket to go visit and help out. You must miss a family trip, but the Bible says, *a man shall leave his mother and father and be united to his wife.* You have already become one flesh.

You are too excited to sleep and stay up watching movies. When you land in Charles de Gaulle, you get your bag and walk outside. You see him. It is a freezing day in mid-November, and he is only wearing a light jacket and a wool scarf. You hug and smell him.

You are cold. Why aren't you wearing a coat?
This is the Parisian style.

You take the RER to get to Paris and pull your suitcase behind. You come out at *Les Invalides* and walk a couple of blocks. It is a small building, only four levels. After entering the code, you walk inside to a small courtyard. You put your bag inside an old small elevator and walk up the white marble spiral staircase. The apartment is grand. There is a hall, a corridor, three bedrooms, with three bathrooms, and an empty space for a dining room and living room. Two antique chandeliers are on the floor,

Elliott is fixing and installing them. You greet *Chucho*, a Mexican painter working on *trompe l'oeil* decorations. He creates the illusion of a lace edge on the bathroom ceiling. You are exhausted and fall asleep on the bed.

You spend your days with the neighbor, an Asian interior decorator. She takes you antique shopping at the *Marché aux puces*. You hunt for a coffee table, a mirror, a dining room set, and a pair of chairs. You find a pair of yellow silk chairs. You choose a black Italian dining room from Tuscany. Elliott finds a tall golden mirror that goes over the fireplace and a heavy marble top for the coffee table that goes between the silk burgundy sofas. While Elliott continues installing the chandeliers, you buy accessories for kitchen and bathrooms.

To reward your good work, his father pays for lunch at *La Tour D'Argent*. You order duck and get a postcard with your duck's number on it. The jet lag still wakes you up at four in the morning, and you work on your graduate assignments. You are hopeful that his family is beginning to like you.

Chapter 3.3   2008

Researching the past becomes harder for Beatrice with two young children at home. They no longer need to be carried, changed or fed, but are still small enough that she must oversee their physical, intellectual and emotional development. She can still manage the house, the help, the teachers, and attending school functions. It is the traveling that gets out of control.

In her social circle, she is as good as her last trip. For cocktails, she might as well bring her last boarding pass because that is her way into the conversation. The travel industry is a machine fed with lies. When she reaches her destination, she is bombarded with images of other places to go. Airplane magazines are filled with publicity of the next great destination. This vicious circle is nurtured with omissions. The answer to *How was your cruise?* is *It was wonderful, the islands are heavenly.* What really happened?

David wanted to roam around the ship, and the rooms could not be locked for security reasons. The old couple next door was banging on the wall because of the noise. They were four people, Elliott and Beatrice with their two boys, in a tiny little room with limited space. The claustrophobia was like a punishment. David's juices and snacks were set up on their little counter. After a couple of days, when he woke up at five, Beatrice sat with him outside on the balcony. Once the sun came up, she sat him in his stroller and circle the promenade deck.

This cruise is filled with older couples. They give Beatrice a dirty look for bringing a little one. In expensive cruises, wheel chairs trump strollers when getting on the elevators. She gets a babysitter for one night only. After that, the nanny refuses to take care of David. The other nights Elliott and Beatrice take turns. Tomas discovers video games and gets hooked like they were cocaine. He hangs out with other boys in the ship's arcade and forgets to eat. His mother has to go find him.

Beatrice becomes anxious about traveling. For spring break, Elliott organizes a trip to Hawaii. He gets first-class tickets for them, and coach for the boys and nanny, who is coming to help. Beatrice buys David a new toy for the trip. They fly to Houston, as always, and their flight is delayed. Easter is early and for the first time in twenty-two years spring break and Easter vacation coincide. Their plane has a malfunction. Waiting in the airport is torture. It gets hard to entertain David. When they board, Elliott and Beatrice get service first. Tomas complains he is hungry. Beatrice and Tomas switch places. David sees Tomas walking around the plane and wants to do the same. The flight attendants are approaching with their cart. He gets anxious. It is a long flight to Los Angeles. All the passengers are in a bad mood. They wait for hours. It is hard to keep David busy. At the end of the row, a woman lends her computer so David can have something to do. Another woman lends him a DVD to watch. The nanny cannot help much. Nobody can help. When the flight attendant is done with her service, David walks a little in the aisle and one kind young man says *Hi buddy!* Beatrice sees the computer woman walk to the bathroom and follows her. As they stand waiting, she thanks her in tears. *We have someone in the family, my niece is autistic. She is older, and has an itty-bitty life, but it gets better.* Autism is a growing secret club.

Due to the delay, they miss their connection. In the middle of the madness, they grab their bags and walk to the airport hotel. The next morning, Elliott, takes a cab to Best Buy and gets David a tablet and DVD cartoons that he can watch on the plane. The next long flight is at night time, and Beatrice has melatonin. After a day of rest, they grab their bags and head to the airport. They have to wait, like everybody else. Beatrice puts David in his stroller, but he is angry and throws a tantrum. People stare convinced he is a spoiled child. They get on the plane, Tomas in the front with Elliott, Beatrice in the back again with David and the nanny. They arrive in Hawaii in the middle of the night, rent a car and drive to the resort. As they walk to their rooms, they feel the ocean breeze and remember why they came. Elliott and Beatrice stay in one room, the nanny and the boys stay next door.

Elliott leaves everyday with his guide on a hunt, and Beatrice spends it with the nanny and the boys in the ocean and swimming pools. They are both great swimmers and love the water. She drives to Walmart to buy juices and snacks to stock their refrigerators, and after a few days, she walks to the laundry to wash some clothes. One day Elliott takes Tomas with him, and Beatrice takes David and the nanny for a ride. She brings him out of the car to look at the view and take a picture, but he starts crying. He is not enjoying any of it.

When they get back home, Beatrice sees David's doctor. He says: *You are crazy for going so far.* It is the last family trip they take. Beatrice cannot pretend they are a normal family anymore. It is so stressful, she would rather stay home. They start planning trips as a couple or Elliott takes Tomas on hunts. David can only travel short distances. Cars are private spaces, and they can handle him.

Before the school year ends, Beatrice travels with some friends. They are three experienced travelers, one of whom is a travel agent. The conversation revolves around travel anecdotes. As they review hotels, airlines and restaurants, judging the quality of their service, Beatrice feels left out. She does not talk about the limitations she faces. As they brag about their teenagers and their accomplishments, she suffers in silence knowing that David will not have a normal life and neither will she.

As he grows, it sinks in. He is learning and maturing, but not enough. He is not a toddler anymore, and now he just seems spoiled, and it is Beatrice who gets the judgmental looks. As he grows, the development gap becomes larger and can no longer be camouflaged. It is painful for her to keep this quiet, to pretend he is doing well. *How's David? How is he doing?* Beatrice insists he is doing better, but there are standards, and only she knows what her life is like. Mothers and wives hide their problems. They are bound to make their husbands and children look good at all times. Who they are depends on how well their families do. Their accomplishments or failures are a direct reflection of mothers. What did she do to have a child with autism? For her pregnancies, she walked every morning and did not drink a drop of wine in nine months. She breastfed both children and blended their fresh fruit and vegetables for months. She thought she could conquer this challenge, as she had conquered others, but she cannot. Autism is growing and invading her life like a flood.

As soon as the school year is over, Beatrice attends a class reunion in Monterrey with her friends from college. She is excited to inflate a part of herself that is punctured. They gather in a restaurant, in a back small salon at a big table for twelve. They are a small group and sit three on each side. To the left, the three professionally accomplished business owners; in the center, there are those who have a career and family, and to the right are the stay-at-home moms. They look the same, except for a few extra pounds or hair color changes. The pear seed became a pear tree and the orange seed became an orange tree. They go around and give an update in just a couple of minutes. Beatrice is happy to brag about her published book and graduate program, but she does not mention her autistic son. This is not a mother's club but a college reunion. They all want to show their best self and remind each other of who they were. They show how their dreams come true like captured prey.

Beatrice reenters her life, the feeling fades. The achiever dissolves like a ghost. Her consolation is that Tomas is doing better and making friends. He is taking Tae-Kwan-Do twice a week. She taught her son to ride a bike, and did such a great job, she has now taught two of his friends. On weekends, she can find Tomas wherever his bicycle is. He and his friends are like a pack of street dogs. There are advantages of living in a small town with small children.

This is the year Beatrice focuses on Tomas, trying to heal his experience of being the brother of a special child. This summer Elliott takes him on a hunt to Australia. They leave first, and Beatrice joins them later, not to leave David for too long. Elliott and Tomas got their visas through the internet. Hers took weeks to arrive because she is still a Mexican citizen. She packs her beige safari clothes and hops on a plane. It takes her more than thirty hours to get there. She lands in Cairns, grabs her stuff and walks towards immigration. There is a routine interrogation. While she gets pulled aside, Japanese passengers slide by. They consider it suspicious that a Mexican woman is traveling by herself, and want to make sure she is not there to stay. The officer looks decent.

What is the purpose of your trip? Why are you traveling alone?
I am here to join my husband and son. They are hunting.
What are they hunting?
They are getting black buffalo.

They let her go. This reminds her, a Mexican passport is not well regarded in the world. She picks up her things and heads to the hotel. This is the first day she wonders about becoming a US citizen. She needs to stand in the same immigration line with the rest of her family. The next morning, she takes a walk by the ocean. Again, the same idea comes to mind. Australia is clean and safe. Mexico is dirty and unsafe. As a traveler, she can escape to enjoy another country's democracy and safety, but for her everyday life there is fear. Being the mother of an autistic child makes her see things differently. She cannot move freely as usual. She is vulnerable with him.

She spends a night in Sydney. She stays in a nice hotel her husband reserved for her. As soon as she settles down, she goes out for a walk towards the opera house. The city has the feel of London with a touch of Vancouver. Restaurants are full of young people. She has not traveled alone in a long time. She does not have to chase anyone or be an active listener to her husband. She heads back to the hotel to order room service. She is not used to sitting alone in a restaurant. She wakes up before sunrise, and walks to the botanical gardens.

In the afternoon, she heads to Melbourne. When she sees her son Tomas, she hugs him tight. She can see how thrilled he is to be with his father. They all drive to a seafood restaurant to catch up. The next day, they go to their camp in a remote place. While Elliott goes hunting, Tomas goes fishing, and Beatrice becomes friends with the cook. In the evening, they prepare Tomas's catch and have barramundi for dinner. He helps chop the wood to heat up the water for their showers. He is thrilled to be here as an only child. David is not here. It feels good to pretend they are a normal family for a few days.

Beatrice spends the afternoons playing cards with a beautiful eleven-year old half aboriginal girl. They go on walks, and the girl tells her the story of how her mother got lost for three days as a child, and a fairy guided her back home. As they play, the girl sneezes.

Every time you sneeze it means somebody is thinking of you.

When you have a cold people think of you? I'd rather be healthy.

In the evening, her father explains to Beatrice:

She meant to say, when you sneeze in Australia somebody is thinking of you.

As they drive around in an old car, Tomas is hot and cannot open the window because the door has no buttons. The girl makes fun of him. She teaches him to grab the handle and turn it to roll down the window. He is angry that it was a girl who had to explain something so simple to him. When they visit the girl's house, they see their chickens and pick up some eggs for breakfast. They have a small house, but there is a television room with a hundred DVDs of American movies.

The night before they go, Beatrice looks at the night sky and sees the stars are placed differently. That is how far they are from home. In the morning, they leave on a small plane and drop off Elliott in the next camp. Then Tomas and Beatrice fly back to Cairns. In the evening, as they sit in a restaurant by the ocean, Tomas cries. He misses his dad.

Son, try to enjoy this moment. We are by the ocean. I am here.

Being with dad is special, he is not around much.

Beatrice has to respect his feelings, and they have dinner in silence, hearing the crash of the waves. The next morning, they take a boat to the Great Barrier Reef and swim in the cold water with fishes and a small manta ray. Their flight is scheduled for the middle of the night. As they leave Australia, they present their passports. They get the same officer who questioned her before. He looks at Tomas and says:

Did you get your buffalo? He remembers their conversation.

At summer's end, Beatrice's family celebrates her father's seventy fifth birthday in Austin. The eldest brother lost his job, and their father pays for his dinner. Her youngest sister is living in Washington and could not come. Gerard is divorced, jobless, and living with his parents. He did not come either. How much her family has changed. Her mother was the one who made the reservations. She got herself a room with a view to the lake and got everybody else a room with a view to the parking lot. Elliott was furious!

They have dinner together, but the bonds are weaker. As time and daily routines breathe life into their own families, they debilitate the ties between them. Her mother was never good at keeping them together. She never hid who were her favorites, showed preferences and felt in control of them because they were young. Now, they all have in-laws and their own children. Her father's economic situation is not what it used to be. Most of his businesses were on the border. He sold some properties and his remodeled restaurant is turning into a gambling casino. His whole life he felt less than his father, now he begins to live a self-fulfilling prophecy as his economic vitality diminishes.

School begins. David's development is stuck. Beatrice has been doing his occupational therapy for five years and cannot see changes. She feels it is time to try something different. He is turning six. This is a milestone in his brain development. She cannot use the stroller anymore. He does not fit in it.

Beatrice met a nice lady on the winter cruise. They speak on the phone and she tells her about a Mexican neurologist who has an alternative treatment that is curing people's brains. She makes an appointment in Monterrey. Elliott and Beatrice drive to Monterrey with David. At the clinic, they set up electrodes on his head and get an electroencephalography to measure his brain activity. When the doctor looks at the graph he assures he can help them. They set up a three-year program. Beatrice will take him to his clinic in Chihuahua every four months to get the treatment. They receive a stem cell medicine, and after only a couple of days David, starts having regular bowel movements, after years of severe constipation. David's regular doctor is not too excited.

Beatrice decides it is time to stop seeing him. He has done what he could to help.

When the rain begins in Laredo, the heat ends. Elliott and Beatrice reconnect with their friends. She organizes a large group of five couples to go to a concert and hear Luis Miguel, the Mexican Frank Sinatra. When the group leaves, they have dinner at a sushi restaurant and sit outside because there are smokers in the group. As Beatrice opens the door to the terrace, sitting right there is Frank, an old flame. They have not seen each other in ten years. He is as handsome as ever, slim and has abundant curly hair. She only says hi and walks to her table, which is a few feet away. She can see him from her seat. He is uncomfortable. The waiter takes their order, some light up their cigarettes, and Beatrice makes a plan to go to the restroom and greet Frank, but he stands up and leaves. He is with a couple. They go inside. As he holds the door, he turns, looks straight at Beatrice and disappears.

The next day, Beatrice calls the girl who was sitting with Frank to ask why they left so soon. He was upset. Beatrice finds out he is still single and visits Laredo frequently. His life has not changed much in ten years. They used to talk about the future, but Beatrice's future is gone, it is here, all around her. His future is still vague and open. The image of him looking at her stays in her mind. What does she look like to him now? For a mother immersed in her daily life, one day looks similar to the next, and then there is an unexpected encounter with the past, and the present is lit in a different light. It is black and white, then and now, what was and what is. The cloud of what could have been is suspended in the air.

This happens at the exact moment when Beatrice does not have small children anymore, when she has been expelled from the baby section at Target, when her house is done, and there are no more pillows or ashtrays to move around. That sweet smell of the past comes when her stagnant life stinks, when she is hungry for her youth.

Chapter 4.1   1989

After a year of love letters, I am here in London. My sister Alexandra and I just landed. Before we get off the plane, the flight attendant gives me a telegram from Musen. He could not come because there is a public transportation strike. I will have to wait a few more hours. We get our things and take a cab to our cute bed and breakfast. The excitement diminishes the effect of the jet lag. When we get to our room, I get the outfit I selected a month ago, and get in the shower. Alexandra will take a nap.

As soon as I am ready, I go outside and sit on the steps. It is not dark, a late European summer evening. The light here is not as bright and yellow as the Mexican light. It is cloudy and the street is quiet. I enjoy these last few minutes, like a marathon runner who sees the finish line. When I hear steps, I look to see who it is. When a car goes by I look again. Sitting here I caress my memories like a lazy cat. The last time I saw him, I taught him how to take a picture with his mind. I am doing it right now. I look at the street, the white houses in line with different colored doors, and close my eyes to photograph it. I look at the twilight sky with hints of orange and violet, the wet sidewalk and I close my eyes. Then I open them to make sure my mind's photograph looks exactly like the street before me. I hold this triumphant moment and capture it before it fades. There he is at the end of the street walking towards me.

Those days in London did not live up to my expectations. I ignored Alexandra and was all over Musen. He was flattered but defensive. I took German lessons and came prepared to jump into his arms, but he did not want to catch me. The timing was off, and his life plan did not include me. He was not the solution to my problems.

Alexandra and I arrive in Paris. She will be here for a month, and I will stay for six months. I just finished college. She is going back to her real job. Our temporary home is in the sixteenth *arrondissement*, half a block from Avenue Foch, the house of Marquesa de Castejá. She is an old aristocratic lady who rents rooms to young women. Her niece manages the house, smokes all day and drinks only wine in the evenings. She believes water is for frogs. In the mornings, young Indian men set up the breakfast table: fresh bread, butter and marmalade.

Alexandra is a cosmopolitan woman, she has lived in Mexico City for three years now. With her list of contacts, she sets up our lunch dates. Today, we are going to meet two Mexican guys at Brasserie Lipp in Saint Germaine. Alexandra taught me to take the metro and I follow her around, like I always have. We get to the restaurant, go upstairs and find our group.

The two guys have other friends from Mexico City, men and women. They are both lawyers, one working and the other studying at La Sorbonne. This is because Mexico and France share the Napoleonic Code. One of the lawyers, Will, is older and half bald. I sit next to the younger one, Alex. He is so handsome, that I cannot look at him straight in the eye. He has an aristocratic neck, brown curly hair, deep hazel eyes and long lashes. He has an unshaven sexy close-cropped beard. While we order and eat, we make small talk, brief introductions. Alexandra has friends who know them. They compare mutual acquaintances. Alex announces he is going to Belgium.

Who wants to go shopping in Brussels?

Why Brussels?

They broke into my apartment, I have to replace electronics.

We'll go. I kick Alexandra under the table and whisper.

Are you crazy? We are not traveling with strangers.

They are not strangers.

We just met them!

But we all know the same people. Relax!

This is out of my comfort zone. The group is noisy, and they all know each other. We are the extras. With no bags and no plan, we just go. I am amazed at how social and relaxed Alexandra is. I am not. We go straight to buy the electronic equipment, then find a place to stay, and a restaurant to have dinner. Will, who is the only real adult here, takes the train back to Paris. He needs to be ready for work tomorrow morning. He is the first Mexican lawyer to work at the International Chamber of Commerce.

After that get away, for the next weeks Alexandra, Will, Alex and I hang out together. For the bicentennial of the French Revolution, we attend a formal lunch at the Hotel de Crillon and watch the majestic parade from a balcony. At the end of July, Alexandra and the others leave. Will, Alex and I become the three musketeers. We go to the park at *Les Invalides*, with a tape recorder, and do Jane Fonda's workout, which I can do in my sleep. We have dinner with Will's French work colleagues. We gather at Will's apartment and work on making invitations for his birthday party, using photos of Parisian scenes taken by Alex's camera. Then Will's friends are in Paris, and only I get included. Then Alex's grandfather is in town, and only I get invited. We cannot be the three musketeers, because we are not all guys. Our friendship gets awkward.

Will speaks five languages. He is bright and funny. He is nine years older than I am. He listens to opera in his car and pretends not to be as intelligent as he is. He fools people with ease. A French woman said she was seven months into her pregnancy: *Wow! Really? Mexican pregnancies only last six months.* She believed him.

I spend time with Alex, and we talk about our future and love interests. He is only three years older. He talks about his Greek girlfriend, I talk about my German boyfriend. It is a subtle form of flirtation. He is a talented photographer, and we do a photo shoot by the Eiffel Tower. I prefer him because he is handsome. I am not the only one who likes him. He is a chick magnet. I do not want to ruin our friendship. Without telling

Will, I invite Alex to go see the Joffrey Ballet at the Théâtre des Champs Elysées, on Avenue Montaigne.

This is the first time I have dressed up since being here. Most days I just wear comfortable shoes like a tourist. I hang my black silk crepe dress, black tights, and high heels. After having shared a room, - first with an Italian and a British girl, then with a Peruvian -I get to have a bedroom to myself. All rooms face an interior patio. I apply some mascara and wait for him to ring. He is downstairs. When I walk out the door, he is surprised. Men are so predictable! It is still me, but the visual factor changes his reaction. It is fun to manipulate that.

We go to the theater, which is my favorite magic place on earth. The ballet is everything I expected. After that, he has a plan. He drives close to Île de la Cité and parks. He grabs a bottle of wine and two glasses he had in the car. We walk down some steps to the banks of the Seine. We sit on a public bench to talk and drink. I have a low tolerance for alcohol, and we did not have any dinner.

I am getting nervous and excited. I know where this is headed. The chances of ruining the friendship are high. The chances of transitioning into a romantic relationship are low. I do not care and sip more wine.

He is a lawyer by force, but a photographer by choice.

I wish I had my camera to take your picture. I want to remember this view, your green eyes, the street light behind, the reflection of the lights on the river.

We discuss the subject of kissing. It is useless and makes the flirtation more enjoyable, giving us the certainty of what we both want. He approaches me. We kiss and become part of the Parisian scene, *Lovers on Bench*. I enjoy the simmering chemistry, the lasting heat of a flickering flame. In a slow rhythm, our mouths taste each other, our hands touch each other's hair. Our bodies snuggle in different angles. I could stay here forever, but he stops.

We should go. It's getting late.

When we walk up the stairs to the car, there is a policeman next to it. The car was crashed into and while the agent was writing down the first accident, a second crash occurred before his eyes. For Will's party, Alex had bottles of tequila, his grandfather brought him from Mexico. They are broken. He mentions this to the officer, to assure him he is not drunk, but I am. A tow truck is called. We are taken to the police station. The truck driver is a punk with a Mohawk. When we get in the truck, he insists I get in first. He asks too many questions, and Alex gets nervous. I do not like the way he looks at me. Alex decides to call Will. My heart sinks, and I sober up.

Do you really have to call him?

It is hard to know the time, but it is two or three in the morning. Will does not answer. He calls again, and I speak. When Will hears my voice, he picks up the phone.

There was an accident, we are ok but we need your help.

Where are you?

I am with Alex and a weird truck driver.

Put Alex on the phone.

Will picks us up, he asks questions, our stories do not match.

Where were you when the accident happened?

We were walking.

Walking were? Why are you all dressed up?

Well, first we went to the ballet.

Your hair is messy.

We stop talking. I am dropped off, but I cannot sing my way up the stairs like Cinderella, because I betrayed Will. The three of us had worked hard to make the invitations to his upcoming birthday party, but now there is tension. The worst is that I know Will is a better person than Alex, but those full lips were a ripe fruit I had to taste.

I get the silent treatment at Will's party. There is a nice group of Mexicans and some French friends. Will rented a *peniche* boat for the evening. I dance with Alex, but because I saw him flirt with other girls, I keep my distance. Will is watching us. After Alex has a few drinks, he wants us to go to a dark corner. I refuse. He grabs the first girl he finds and after dancing, makes out with her in the corner.

When we have the gathering to review the party. Will points out how Alex was all over her and barely let her breathe. He looks at me while he talks, paying close attention to my expression. My poker face hides my emotions. After the party, things never go back to normal. I do not have anything to look forward to.

I walk around Paris with my walk-man, listening to Carly Simon say: *stay right here because these are the good old days.* What is so good about these days? Most of my life is the future. The uncertainty of finding my way is overwhelming. It is getting cold. The leaves are dancing on the floor. I do not have any more romantic projects. A whole year of daydreaming about a fantasy. When that did not work, I found another one, and now here I am. I stopped attending my French lessons at *La Sorbonne*, the American students were destroying my accent. The touristic portion of my stay is finished. After three months, I now live here. I begin to feel the real city.

I sit at a Cafe and look at people. Dirty tennis shoes with backpack, tight blouses on high heels, big tummies with beard, fast boots puffing cigarette, black fashion on skinny legs, bald head with jacket and sunken eyes. These are the real French, serious and always in a hurry. Where are the mothers and their babies? Not on the Champs Elysées.

When we sit in the *Métro*, we are boxed up pretending not to be. We protect our private space, avoiding each other's eyes, and touch. We are absent, either remembering or planning. That man hides his glance behind a newspaper, the woman covers her ears with headphones. We are isolated waiting for the next stop. The blurry, grey wall goes by. There is publicity to read. Life is somewhere else, a Polynesian beach, not here. A man plays a tune and begs for coins. We are subterranean beings, briefly trapped together each one in our own time.

I visit museums, watch a Woody Allen film festival, then a Hitchcock film festival. These days are suspended in nothingness, a lapse of time inserted in my life as a pause. I know that when I get back home my adult life begins. Besides my summer job at the Soccer World Cup. I have no experience.

These love deceptions force me to face my own contradictions. I want to accomplish things for myself, by myself. At the same time, like thousands of women before me, I learned that my worth as a woman is measured by the success of the man I can reel in. Musen went to Columbia University and I never thought of the possibility of doing it myself. American women can do that, not me. Alex finishes law school, and here I am doing nothing, accomplishing nothing.

I have no role models. My mother married when she was a nineteen-year-old, and by the time she was twenty-five, had five children. I was sent to a boarding school to learn what? It is as if by being relocated I was stripped of a false sense of identity, with no context the meaning of my existence changed, and now I am feeling it all over again. I lost my place and fell behind in the race to get a man. Now, I am really behind. I thought I was too modern for Mexican men, but I guess I am not modern enough for European men. My fantasy was that Musen was going to propose, and we were going to get married. He is trying to figure things out for himself.

In Paris, I am an intruder. In my boarding school, I was part of a community, a custom-made little world for girls like me. What did I think when I saw pictures of the Eiffel Tower? Not this. Only public spaces are open to me, museums, movie theaters, monuments, stores and restaurants.

This city is for display, but its intimacy cannot be penetrated except by the locals, the French people in the metro who live here.

I recently celebrated Mexican Independence Day with a group of Mexican friends. We were drinking hand-made margaritas, and they played *Mexico Lindo y Querido,* a song I have heard many times. Now, I listened. *Pretty and dear Mexico, if I die far from you, may they say I am asleep and have them bring me to you.* I miss Mexico, but I am not ready to go back. I cannot stay here because it is expensive. My mother reminds me of that every time we speak. I came here to do what exactly? I know my parents brag about me being here, but what is the point? I am here to learn French, which I learned in kinder garden in Mexico City. I am here to learn about culture and food, but when I see the franc, I see *Liberté, Egalité, Fraternité.*

We Mexicans are holding on to a system that is non-sustainable, and I belong to the worst kind, the ones who protect the idea of privilege for only a few. A debutante exposed to the right suitors, but spoiled and useless. I do not know how to cook or clean because I have had help my whole life.

My grandfather, the tycoon, died three years ago. There was not as much money left as my father thought. After building an empire of banks, real estate, cotton mills and car dealerships, it is all gone. My father's clan is a pack of juniors, who stood on somebody else's shoulders. All I hear is that we are waiting for the inheritance. I really should not be here. We are becoming *has-beens* by the minute. Good French is what they are sending me into the world with?

Before I go back to Mexico, I visit a German friend I met in New York. The Berlin wall fell officially on November ninth. I thought of keeping the cover of Le Figaro, but lost it. Western Germans are angry because eastern Germans are coming back in their old cars, empty handed. The sacrifice made for years is meaningless. Thirty years of suffering for nothing. Now that communism has failed, what will the new balance be? What system will compensate for capitalism?

I feel like them. My whole life I have been groomed to be a nice girl, a decent member of society. The French lessons, the ballet classes, the all-girls Catholic school, the debuts, were all to train me to be a pretty object to decorate a room gracefully. The mistake they made was to send me to New York. When my mother went there, it was like a finishing-school, but when I went there, American women had changed. I did not become one of them, but the idea of accomplishing something of my own was planted in my brain. Now that I have become a failure at finding a husband, I must reconsider the possibility of making a personal contribution.

Chapter 4.2   1999

The time comes to pick a date for your wedding. You check for Mexican and American holidays, review the weather and choose September the fourth for the legal ceremony, which will be organized by your mother-in-law in Nuevo Laredo. On September eleven, you will celebrate the religious ceremony which will be organized by your mother in Monterrey. You think there is more resistance to come, but Elliott insists you are blending in.

Soon enough, the cat jumps out of the hat with protracted claws. Elliott's parents went to Monterrey to consult a priest about the fact that you are related. The priest said: *As long as they are not siblings, we can't do anything.* Next, they had a lunch meeting with your parents, during which they threatened not to attend the wedding, to which your parents responded: *The wedding will take place, and we'll be there.* The last peaceful lure is a Ferrari. When Elliott resists the temptation, they fire and disinherit him. You go to Monterrey, you get him job interviews, when they see his determination, they back off and give in.

I don't want to be responsible for you losing your family.
You are not the one making this decision.
If it doesn't work, do we stay together to prove a point?
This is what I want, if I make a mistake, it will be my mistake.

The crisis lasts three days, but the thrust is deep enough to leave you wondering: Why are you such a bad option? Why don't they want you? The next time you see your mother-in-law, it is like nothing happened. You set a date for the first bridal shower.

Elliott's parents establish three requirements before the wedding: you have to visit a geneticist; you have to go to a couples' therapy retreat, and you have to sign a prenuptial agreement. You find a geneticist in Monterrey. He puts you at peace by explaining: *It is not the blood relation that is a threat but shared diseases. If you both had diabetes, whatever your last names might be, that would be a red flag.*

Next, you go to a place close to Nashville for a weekend for couples' therapy. There is a total of fifteen couples. You are the only ones who have never been married. Many are saving their third marriage. Some were sent here by a judge, before signing the divorce. You are divided into three groups. The first day, you make a drawing of your lives, talk about the past and who you were before you met. You want to understand what this person was saving you from. The leading couple used to be a nun and a priest, another pair met in Alcoholics Anonymous meetings, another team is a country song writer and his manager. You are the youngest.

The second day, you are supposed to talk about sex. You fear you will talk about penises and vaginas. As it is, sex is a sensitive thermometer, it is the day when it all pours out. A woman married to a diabetic gets unglued, and curses diabetes for taking away her sex life. You are all quiet while she screams and cries. The leader says: *Everybody breathe.* You breathe deeply and start to cry. The last day, you get a warning from one of the ladies: *Honey, set boundaries with your in-laws, I wish I had.*

Your first shower, as tradition mandates, is given to you by your mother-in-law. Her house looks perfect, the candles are lit and the swimming pool fountain jets are on. The table is served with silver trays filled with minute appetizers. Guests come from Laredo, Nuevo Laredo, and your mother's entourage from Monterrey. One of your mother's friends is the mother of the first boy who ever asked you to be his girlfriend. You rejected him because you were leaving for boarding school. He serenaded you on your fifteenth birthday. One of the songs they played under your balcony was *"Aquellos ojos verdes"* (Those Green Eyes) a bolero you have heard your whole life, as both your mother and you have green eyes. It was probably this woman who chose the song for you to hear. You walk towards her, around the elegant buffet table and say: *I want you to know that your son was the first man who made me feel special.* You are making her uncomfortable. She does not know what to say. It is an apology. You have no doubt about who you are marrying, but memories of how you got here surface.

You now understand why in Mexico you call bridal showers *despedidas.* They are farewell parties. A wedding is a parting from the single life and an introduction into married life. Now, your mother's friends start giving you advice. You who are joining a secret society. *Please don't pack for your husband. I still pack for mine thirty years later.* Even funny stories come up. *He wanted me to iron the bed to make it warm, so I just burned it saying I really wasn't good at that.* While you were growing up, these women seemed in control, yet they were having struggles you could not imagine.

The best shower is given to you in Mexico City by your aunt Gloria. She organizes a game. The guests are given tissue paper and divided into four groups. They make you a paper wedding gown: skirt, torso, sleeves, and veil. Like little girls, they play and chat, compete and compare. While the seamstresses work, you look around your aunt's house, your home away from home. You remember when this room was added on to the house. There were garages in this space. You loved staying here. There was always good food, the sweetest maids and everything impeccable, a place for everything and everything in its place. She always had dogs. You can still remember a monstrous Great Dane called Hopi and a fat basset hound called Chencha. There was a pile of newspapers perfectly stacked behind the kitchen door. Tia Gloria said grace before every meal and had a cloth and a paper napkin. Whenever it was your turn to say grace, you did not know what to say. You did not say grace at home. Her garden is perfectly manicured, the lawn surrounded by a long bed of flowers. In the family-room upstairs, there is a built-in bookcase with pictures, she even has your picture. She is always home, not like your mom who is always out doing something. When she is nowhere to be found in the house, she is outside reading her Bible.

Tia Gloria's smile is warm, she calls you *amor*. She looks like your father. She does not dress fashionably, like Aunt Sara. Her oldest son Pat has cerebral palsy. Not long ago, you learned that he was born from a previous teenage marriage. Pat is always around. He speaks English, learned it growing up in institutions in the United States. You felt uncomfortable around him. You did not know what to say or how to act. As a little girl, you did not have a bathtub. Here, you took a long bath and nobody was hurrying you. You emerged with wrinkly old lady's hands and feet. When you were older, she gave you a key, so you would not have to ring the doorbell. She is always calm and still has the same help.

There are other events. Your two best friends, The Pea and Blondie, invite you to go to Houston on a bachelorette trip. You stay at The Pea's place which is all decorated in purple. You go to nice restaurants, movies and stores. They make fun of you for buying white lingerie, rather than black. Blondie organizes a lunch for ten of your closest friends. Nothing extravagant, no alcohol, all mothers except you. Aunt Sara offers you a formal shower at the Laredo Country Club. Early on, your mother's friend says: *Enjoy the whole thing, all of this is the wedding. It lasts six months.*

These rituals serve a purpose. You see the people you grew up with and review your childhood memories before entering real adulthood. You were immersed in work and forgot you are part of a bigger tribe. Your mother is proud, but Alexandra is sad. She is a single mother, living with the baby's father. You do not talk about this nuptial charade but become opposing characters in this production.

Your mother wants all the girls to go on a trip to buy your wedding dress. She is not being sensitive. It is not going to happen. Since Elliott will be paying for the dress, you go together and choose a gown. It is a plain silk organza A-line Christian Dior. Alexandra does not want to come to your wedding. You decide to call her boyfriend's sister to invite her personally. *If you don't come, he will not come. If he doesn't come, my sister will not be at my wedding.* The wedding is a full family realignment. There is a redistribution on both sides. In the public world, women come together to protect and guide the new bride. You leave the land of the single and are catapulted onto the island of marriage.

The last thing to do is to sign the prenuptial agreement. You have to hire a lawyer. He explains that you are giving up the right to anything Elliott owns or will own and advices you not to sign. *If I don't sign these papers, I can't marry him. His parents want me to prove I am not marrying for money.* Your parents do not get involved. You are videotaped signing the thirty pages to prove you are conscious.

You are still writing your editorials, doing your homework for the graduate program, building a new house in Nuevo Laredo, and being the main character in these bridal gatherings. You are the excuse to get together and celebrate.

The day comes. You avoid arguing by letting your mother-in-law and mother each do what they want. Your only request is that everything be white. For the legal ceremony, you have the American guests from Laredo and San Antonio. The tables are set outside, the white roses in the centerpieces are on steroids. Your mother-in-law dresses in black and your mother dresses in red, each expressing their emotions. Your mother-in-law is mourning her son's marriage, and your mother is thrilled to marry off a daughter. The band comes from Monterrey, the same band that will play next week. The legal ceremony commences. It is boring and people converse while it happens. Witnesses stand up to sign the papers, but when you finish signing, there is no place to sit. There was no assigned seating. Nothing matters, the saxophone is playing your song: *I believe in you and me, I believe that we will be, in love eternally, well as far as I can see.* The Catholic joke is that you are married from the waist up, but next week you will be fully married.

There is a lunch for the out of town guests on Sunday, at Elliott's uncle's house. Your dress is simple and so is everybody else's, but Elliott's mother shows up with a purple hat the size of an umbrella. It is a long afternoon, and there is a lot of alcohol served. After many have left, Elliott's mother says: *Did you hear what everybody was saying? Now it's your turn to finish raising him.* She is trying to make you feel bad because you are older. You do not know what to reply. She still cannot see that you both love him. You wonder if all mothers-in-laws are like this or is it just yours.

The whole week it rains, but the wedding celebration at the Monterrey Country Club is indoors. You pack for your honeymoon, finish your homework, the gift room is full and the list is organized. Every gift gets a numbered sticker, you know who gave what, for the thank you notes.

On your wedding day, you go for a morning walk, and it is time for hair and makeup, then the pictures: first you, then his family, then yours. Your mother-in-law's dress is red. Maybe she is a bit happy. They all leave for the church, and you wait with your father. You look up at your mountains, the afternoon blue sky is radiant. Your mother is proud to have a real wedding. Alexandra is here with her boyfriend's family. It would have been nice to have a family that was proud to have you, but you think you are not marrying them. Today you are just marrying Elliott.

As special as this day is, you are not the only bride. On Saturdays, hundreds of women all over the world dress in white to start this journey. You arrive at the church. Another wedding party is there but the service is not finished. You drive around one more time. You park and walk up the steps. The wedding organizer sets everybody up. You walk slowly and smile to your guests, listening to Mendelssohn's wedding march. During mass, you sit and stand, while your sisters fix your skirt and veil. You reach the point when you look into Elliot's eyes and say with a trembling voice: *I, Beatrice, take you Elliott, to be my husband and promise to be faithful for better or worse, for richer or poorer, in sickness and in health, to love and respect you all the days of my life.* When you leave together you walk slowly again, taking it all in. He is distressed with all the attention.

At the Country Club, you stand at the entrance of the ballroom to greet your guests. Once they are all in, you walk into the room and there is applause. You do not dance. Elliott is shy. You sit and have dinner first. There is a set of violins playing while you eat. All the tables are organized. Your mother set up table leaders to make sure everyone was seated with their friends. You have a table for two in the middle of the room, people come to greet you. After dinner, you stand up. It is time to dance: *I believe in you and me, I believe that we will be, and love eternally, well as far as I can see.* He barely moves. You enjoy the attention. He dreads it. You look your best, so does everybody else. He pulls you out of your own wedding at one thirty, while there are still plenty of guests dancing. The next morning, you leave for South Africa for a month. You have your homework to do and hundreds of thank you notes to write.

His father promised Elliott, ever since he was a little boy, that he would take him to Africa. When he realized that you were going, they organized a family trip. You land in Cape Town and stay in a nice hotel for a couple of days, but Elliott was here just a couple of months ago. Everywhere you go, he brings up family anecdotes. As they give you your room key, they call you Mrs. Theriot and you remember an older lady warned you it would take a while to get used to. After taking a nap, you go to the hotel's salon and get a haircut. You have always had short hair, your mother did not want to bother with pony tails, but for the wedding, you had to let it grow.

After time in the city, you go on a hunting safari for ten days. You stay in a camp above a hill. Elliott leaves before sunrise, comes back to eat something, and goes back until the sun sets. You have dinner together, but are alone all day. This was not what you expected. You go for a walk, but when you come face to face with a herd of warthogs, only knowing boars, you are sure they will chase and kill you. You walk slowly while your heart beats like an African drum. Elliott and the others at camp make fun of you, warthogs are almost blind. You feel humiliated. The next day, a cobra stands in front of the jeep, and your excursions get cancelled. You are trapped like Rapunzel, high on your hill.

They set up a table and chair on the terrace for you to look out, while you work on your thesis. While the wedding was taking place, you became dead weight on your graduate team. You need to work hard now to catch up. While you look at the animals drinking water and licking a big salt cube, the anticlimactic stage after the wedding sinks in. After being celebrated, supported and surrounded by all those people, now you are alone. *What am I going to do with him all day?* A friend said: *He will not be with you all day, he will leave, he'll be busy.* Whenever he is at camp, he writes a hunting journal to share with his hunter friends.

After ten days on safari, you go to Johannesburg, a big metropolitan city. Your hotel is beautiful. You walk to the zoo to see more animals. You have a reservation at a nice restaurant run by an Austrian chef. You also visit The Palace resort in the middle of nowhere. Then you go to another camp. You go on walks with the lady who manages the hunts. You all sit together around the fire in the evenings. There are other hunters. The owner has a wife and three grown sons. One is a handsome professional rugby player.

Here, you work in front of your bungalow. You are not above the countryside, but there is a waterhole outside your cabin. One afternoon, when you are reading, you lift your head to see a waterbuck. He looks at you. You make eye contact. You freeze and enjoy his presence. This connection touches your soul. It is hard for you to understand why some people enjoy killing animals.

You go back to Nuevo Laredo and set up in his parents' home. Yours is not going to be ready for a while. It is a big house. You feel like an intruder. Elliot's bedroom is full of his things and pictures of him as a little boy. His family is never home. They are always either in San Antonio or traveling. Almost all day, you have the house to yourself. The help takes care of you. You do not have to do anything. You ask and learn what detergent to buy and aroma to fill your future house. His mother is a better house keeper than yours.

Before you leave on your Christmas trip, you notice you have not had your period. You assume it is an adjustment, but check anyway. You take a pregnancy test, and it comes out positive. Then you take another one. You cannot tell if Elliott is excited or nervous or both. You thought you were never going to have babies, but you are fertile after all. As excited as you are, as sure as you are, as willing as you are to have a baby, you are petrified. You do not tell anybody else yet. It is best to keep it private in case there are complications.

Chapter 4.3   2009

Beatrice's new task at hand is becoming a United States citizen. The same lawyer that helped her get her residency guides her in the process of making the United States her new country. She carefully follows every step and does not even get a speeding ticket in three years, knowing the residency can be taken away.

She has to study for an exam and learns the answers to one hundred questions. She took American history in high school and remembers a great deal. She needs to review her representatives. She drives to San Antonio for her test. A nice, redheaded man asks her only five of the hundred questions. After she completes the requirements, she receives a notification of her naturalization ceremony.

It is a special time to become an American citizen, as the US just elected its first African-American president. The United States becomes the new world all over again. The day comes, and she shows up at the Laredo Civic Center. The ceremony is in the morning. As she arrives, she stands in line. There are a little over a hundred people. Beatrice talks to the woman standing next to her, who has waited twenty years for this day. This woman was married to an American, but he was born at home and did not have a proper birth certificate. They divorced and it took her a long time to prove his citizenship. For Beatrice, the privilege to have a new life in the United States extinguishes *what could have been*.

As they enter the auditorium and sit, Beatrice looks around and tries to imagine why all these people are here. Most of them are looking for a better life, with hope for a brighter future. Beatrice had a good life and was hoping her children would be Mexican. A woman, who identifies herself as a Daughter of the American Revolution, explains that she was born here, but they had the opportunity of choosing to be American. Beatrice was never a patriotic Mexican. In her elementary school, every Monday morning, a group of six girls marched with the Mexican flag and pulled it up the flagpole. They would sing the Mexican anthem. Now, here she is switching her patriotism to another country. She recites the pledge of allegiance publicly for the first time. She will never be fully American, because she was Mexican for too long.

She understands this ceremony matters. It will affect who she is. She reflects on who she has been, and all that is lost in translation. In Spanish, there are two verbs for the verb "to be." There is *ser* and *estar*. *Estar* is used for temporary states like: being tired, hungry or sad. But *ser* is used for permanent and essential identities like: being short, a woman or smart. *Ella es mexicana, no está mexicana.*

At the end of the ceremony, they sing their new anthem. She listens to the song. The lyrics for *The Star-Spangled Banner* are from a poem written after witnessing an attack. The poet was inspired by the large American flag flying triumphantly above the fort during the American victory. She does not sing because she has not memorized the lyrics yet, but when she hears: *the land of the free and the home of the brave,* she cries. She will now have an American family, an American marriage and American children.

Once the ceremony is over, Beatrice calls her mother-in-law to thank her and leaves a message. It was through her citizenship that now Beatrice's whole family is American. When her boys were born, she did not want to go through the process of getting them their naturalization papers, because she felt it was pessimistic. Why would they need to have dual citizenship? The security issues are forcing Mexicans from all walks of life to come to the United States. Many cannot do it legally. Recently, a friend of hers was kidnapped. It was for a day only. He moved to the United States after that. He does not talk about it, but his wife thinks it affected his self-confidence and sense of security overall.

Beatrice can see subtle differences in her boys. One day she asks Tomas: *Are you American or Mexican?* He says he is both, and she asks him why he is Mexican. *Because I like chile, Mom.* They are both Mexicans and Americans, but in a different way. Tomas is blond and has green eyes, he has no accent in either English or Spanish.

One day, Beatrice is called from school because Tomas got a pink slip for bad behavior. She shows up for a meeting. They explain what happened. The math teacher was writing something on the blackboard, and a student corrected her. She apologized for her mistake. Tomas said: *Maybe it's because you are Mexican.* The teacher is in the meeting, visibly upset. Beatrice explains to her that in her household they do not use the word Mexican in a derogatory manner, because she is Mexican and proud to be one. *If my son would have said 'maybe it's because you are French' it would have been different.* The pink slip is dismissed. She can now see that getting a passport is not going to be enough.

Spring break approaches fast, Beatrice is anxious because she will spend the holiday in the middle of nowhere with David. She is taking him to a ranch in San Andres, Chihuahua so he can see the new doctor and have his dose of the alternative treatment adjusted. The doctor studied cellular biology, neurophysiology and cognitive neurosciences. He developed a neurotropic factor cultivation to heal parts of the brain. Elliott organized for them to fly private, which alleviates her anxiousness. Beatrice is nervous. She does not know where they are going, or who will be there. They will be there for a week. She packs her computer, DVD player and DVDs, snacks, almond milk, meds and coloring books. When they arrive at the airport, there is someone waiting for them. They get on a van and wait for the others.

While David plays with his portable electronic games, Beatrice talks to the other parents to find out if they have been here before. There are people from Peru, Venezuela, Florida and other parts of the United States. Some have been coming for years. They are driven to the ranch. The landscape is arid and beautiful. As they approach the property, the road gets rough, and they can see some cows. It is a big ranch with separate buildings. They first see the tennis court to the right and a gym to the left. Higher up is the building they will stay in, it has sixteen bedrooms. Above that is a swing set and a playroom. Up to the left is the indoor pool.

They get their things and are given their room keys. She settles down and unpacks their bags. There is a king bed and a single bed. Most come in pairs with their child, either husband and wife or mother and daughter. Beatrice is here alone with her son, but she was able to fly on a private plane. Her husband shows his support by being a good provider. There is a television and a small bathroom. Meals are prepared by the help, and she does not have to do anything.

David will have three tests and two appointments with the doctor. Today he has his first electroencephalography. When it is David's turn, they go upstairs, and he sits in a chair in front of a screen. The technician places a dozen electrodes on his scalp to record the electrical activity of his brain, while he watches some images. The brain waves are printed by a special machine. In the afternoon, they are free to roam around the property. They walk to the playroom, and David gets inside a small round pool of balls. Beatrice reads *A Tale of Two Cities*.

Spending time with David is difficult because there is no language, and Beatrice loves language. They are just present together. How could she have a child who does not speak? What is the universal order that let this happen? She understands that even if he gets better, he will not go to college, drive or get married. What is his purpose? Beatrice has always been ambitious and proud. It is painful for her to accept her son as a reflection of who she is. She wants to cure him, change him and make him normal, but she cannot.

When he is done playing, they walk down the road. He finds a pond and throws rocks in it. Beatrice sits and watches him. The sunset is here. The sky changes colors and the light fades. It is cold in the Chihuahuan desert, and they have to go. He takes his shower. They have dinner. They stay in the room and she brings their dinner plates into the bedroom. After dinner, the doctor is ready to see them. His office is upstairs. It is a whole apartment. The neurologist is dressed casually, in jeans and a button-down shirt, with a blazer. Next to his desk, there is a computer screen where they can see the results of the electroencephalography. He compares it to the one they took in their first appointment in Monterrey, and points out how the brain waves are not smooth anymore. The waves are made of lines that zig zag, that reflect more electrical activity in David's brain. He increases the dose on some of the medication and lowers it on another. They receive the new bottles, and Beatrice starts giving David the new dose. The doctor will see him at the end of the week.

They go to sleep early and David wakes up early. They walk to the playroom. The mornings are cold. There is ice on the grass. After breakfast, they wait for the day to warm up and go to the indoor pool. David loves to swim and he can do it for a while. Other parents and children come later. Beatrice talks to them and hears their stories. The woman swimming with her teenage son, tells how he was born normal but swallowed a seed, could not breath for a couple of minutes and got cerebral palsy. Later, another family comes in, and their daughter is in a wheel chair and can barely move. She drools. David is strong and healthy, swimming like a fish, Beatrice feels like they do not belong. These children are vulnerable and will have to be taken care of forever. If there is nobody to look over them, they are destined for poverty, loneliness and illness. There is still a long way to go. This angel of hers is only truly loved by her. His father does not know how to deal with him, and his four grandparents are living the good life. It is too much responsibility for only one person, too much weight. Beatrice is scared thinking about David growing up. She reads *A Tale of Two Cities* to escape to another time and place.

Beatrice and David find a little routine: mornings playroom, mid-morning swimming, lunch, then computer and DVDs, swimming and time by the pond. As David spends an hour throwing rocks in the water, he looks in detail at the ripples. Beatrice becomes aware of how this boy forces her to question what she was taught to believe. She is free from pretenses. Her old problems seem irrelevant. Like other mothers, Beatrice cannot live through her children's accomplishments. This child pulls her away from the picture-perfect life she was so invested in. She has been expelled from the country club world. Her relationship to David is different. He does not know who she is. Who is she? Here they are, just present. His presence with no agenda inspires her to find a Buddhist peace of full awareness. His love is simple and primitive, as real as these water ripples that open up bigger and bigger.

The week retreat goes by slowly but finally ends, and Beatrice gets back to her busy life. Tomas spent the week hunting and bonding with his father. They went somewhere in the south of Mexico. She knows how much he loves to roam free at the hunting lodges and bond with the dogs at camp. After the vacation, Beatrice gets a call from school one morning and is asked to pick up Tomas because there was a case of *lies*. She wonders how serious the lying must have been to remove the children from school. Once she picks him up she asks what the problem is. *Your son has lice.* She is embarrassed, this never happened to her or any of her siblings. In Mexico, these subjects are private and shameful. *There are other children and they are all being asked to leave.* She takes him home, cuts his hair, applies a lice treatment to his skull and washes the sheets.

On Wednesday afternoons, Tomas takes catechism and learns about God weekly. He will have his first communion soon. As the day approaches, they attend the church where the ceremony will take place and he has his first confession. When Beatrice picks him up, he says *Mom, I think I talked to God.* She is happy and excited that he is beginning a relationship with his creator. *Mom, but he actually answered.* Beatrice has to explain what a confessionary is and how it works. *Honey, the priest is behind the screen, it was the priest who talked to you, not God.* She grew up going to a Catholic school and all these rituals are second nature to her.

For the first communion, Elliott chooses a famous hunting friend to be Tomas's godfather. They are supposed to choose a man who attends church and is religious, but for men, the first masculine child is an opportunity to network. This man does not go to church and has been divorced twice, but as a hunter, he is an advantageous liaison. He gives Tomas a hunting book. It is Beatrice who gets him a crystal guardian angel to put next to his bed. For the special day, both families are invited and they have a small lunch in her house. Most of her family comes, but from his family only his mother shows up. The others had exclusive social gatherings to attend. Beatrice sets up the tables for her siblings, nieces and nephews. The decorations are wheat branches and grapes, the symbols of the Eucharist host and wine. They take pictures before the mass. She got a nice big hat for the occasion. Tomas is wearing a white blazer and a yellow tie, with seersucker light blue pants. It is through Tomas that they get to belong and be normal.

Her sister Isabelle is engaged to be married to an American. She has been living in Washington DC for a couple of years now and that will be her home. Isabelle grew up as an only child, being so much younger than the rest of the family. She is also getting married older like Alexandra and Beatrice did. Isabelle is thirty-two-years-old. Her in-laws are simple folks, and her first bridal shower is given to her by her mother in the Industrial Club in Monterrey. Beatrice is driven by a chauffeur to attend the reunion. It is only a two-hour drive, but after the kidnappings, she does not drive herself. As Beatrice enters the room, she sees her mother's life gathered for the occasion. Her mother's friends look a lot older. Beatrice sees their wrinkled faces, some good plastic surgeries and some not so good, less hair and smaller bodies. They smile and hug her. They ask her questions, and love her with their eyes. They saw Beatrice grow up and now she sees them grow old. She is now where they were when she was a child. This time gap is a perfect design. Mothers and daughters, their lives are like a two-color knitted blanket. As one yarn comes, the other goes. They interlock in perfect loops that stitch them together.

For the last ten years, every time Beatrice comes to Monterrey, she stays for two days only, arrives on Friday and leaves on Sunday. When her boys were infants, she would hop in the car and drive herself, but the problems at the border have gotten serious, so now she comes less often and never drives alone. Today, she came just for the day. Her experience is different from the locals. They see each other frequently, bump into one another at social gatherings, but for Beatrice this is special, she does not live here. When they look at her, they are also surprised. These women's eyes make Beatrice remember her younger self. It is as if their eyes were light projectors that make her luminous with all those memories lingering among them.

Isabelle is also experiencing this. She has been living abroad for years now, first in Boston and now in Washington DC. Isabelle is getting her farewell and does not know it. The wedding is exciting and overwhelming. It will take time for her to let it all sink in, like it did for the rest of the brides. Beatrice reflects on the meaning of these female rituals. They all dress up and look pretty, but behind these wives there are tragedies and challenges. Some mothers have buried a child, some have been through divorce, others put up with cheating husbands, others cheated themselves. Women are stronger than they appear.

For Christmas, Beatrice hosts a lunch in her house. The whole family comes to meet Isabelle's fiancé. It is a big Catholic Mexican family, a total of twenty-seven members. Beatrice moves the furniture around and sets up the tables. She puts out new candles, takes out the tablecloths, sets up the place settings and has a big fresh pine tree at the entrance. She takes out the Christmas music and become Santa Claus for a day. After lunch, they all go outside and have a photo shoot. *Now, everybody will get a picture with their family.* Her mother replies: *We get a picture with everyone.* It is an awkward moment. They are just a couple now. Everybody is getting a picture with their nuclear family. There are three family sets: the immediate family, the grandparents with their grandchildren and the original family unit. When the photo session is over, it is show time, and Beatrice puts *It's a Wonderful Life* with James Stewart on television for her nieces and nephews to watch. They are not pleased to hear the movie is in black and white, but when it is finished, they are glad they watched it.

Chapter 5.1   1990

I drive downtown to the offices of the newspaper. Finding a parking spot is challenging. I go inside The Compass, a remodeled modern building. The reception is busy, well-lit with shiny gray marble floors. The receptionist directs me to the correct place. I walk around the block. In the back is a small old office, part of the building that has not yet been remodeled. The floor is polished concrete. I stand outside in line. I look different, many are applying for high rotation jobs like delivering the newspaper. It is my turn. The lady who hands out the application gives me a look. I sit down, fill it out, give it back and ask what the next step is. *We'll call you.*

I go back to finding my car and as I get in, I feel discouraged. There is a summer workshop offered by The Compass. It is their little school for training the winning team of journalists in town. I never applied.

Now, I am hoping to bypass that step. I do not have experience, but I have been journaling daily for eight years.

The paradox is I took news journalism three times, the only subject I ever failed. The first time, they were teaching us to count movable linotypes - i being half a point and o being a point and a half - to make a line. *Professor, I am sorry but when we graduate, every newspaper in the world will be computerized. This is a waste of time.* I flunked. The second time, I had a Spanish professor. He was an erudite European with body odor. Our final exam was to write an essay on modesty. He failed me. I argued my essay was good. He said: *It was not just good, it was the best of the class, but you turned it in late. In journalism that's the difference between getting published or not.* I took it a third time and at one point I asked him:

Why are you so hard on me?

I measure you with what I think you are capable of.

I am determined to become a journalist and do not apply for other jobs. Nobody knows when the next step occurs. It is my time to wait. Unemployed days go slow. There is not much to do, late breakfast, a morning walk, a good book. It is winter, the whole year is ahead of me. Recently, I asked my father for money to go on a trip with college friends, he replied:

When are you going to start making your own money?

When I talk to my friends, they tell me about their new houses, new furniture and new babies. None of them work. They went from their Dad's house to their husband's house. My mother has never worked professionally. I am navigating unknown territory. One afternoon, I am hanging out with my sister-in-law, visiting my baby nephew, and watching a movie. The phone rings, it is my mother.

They just called from The Compass. You need to call them.

Hello! I just got a call from you.

You have an appointment tomorrow at eleven.

I drive downtown again, this time wearing a suit to look older and more mature. I walk into the building, given a pass and directed to the elevator. The door opens, a small woman smiles at me.

You are in the right place.

She sees I am nervous and wonders why a girl like me is here.

I am sorry, can you explain who I am seeing?

Of course. I will be taking you to your appointments. First, you are going to talk to the head of Human Resources, then the general director Mr. Allan Reed and finally, the editorial director. You are being offered a public relations position.

Do you know what I am expected to do?

The newspaper has grown so much that we now need a person to be in charge of handling events for the staff and welcoming special guests.

I have to tell the truth: I want to be a journalist.

Today you should go to your appointments. If you are going to mention that to anyone, it should be the editorial director.

First, I meet the Human Resources director. His office has a nice window. He has glasses and a beard. He is kind and makes me feel at ease. To my surprise, he is an engineer. The appointment is brief. When I come out, I am taken to the elevator.

Have you been to the top floor?

No, I've only been to the reception.

It's the cave of Ali Baba and the Forty Thieves.

I think she is exaggerating, maybe she has not seen much. I am mistaken. When the elevator door opens, we are at the top. It is a fish tank surrounded by glass, overlooking downtown. The whole floor is composed of two big offices for the Reed brothers, with a meeting area in the back. The secretary offers me a seat and something to drink. She walks into the kitchen. Another secretary is in the mirroring waiting area. Everything looks new and modern.

When I come in, I am impressed with the size of the office. The director is on his computer, sitting behind a huge mahogany desk. I sit in the living room in front. There are Persian rugs, modern paintings and leather sofas. Mr. Allan Reed is a small man with glasses and a beard. He is the genius behind the new Compass, a brave new source of truth in Mexico. He went to college in Austin and came back determined to revolutionize Mexican journalism.

He looks at my application and asks:

How are you related to Octavio Theriot?

He is my father.

We have neighboring lockers at the Club. Why are you here?

I know I am being offered a P.R. job, but I want to be a reporter.

You can talk to the editorial director about that.

The meeting is brief. He is a busy man. He might suspect that this was a waste of his time, but I answered truthfully about my intentions. Then, I am taken to see the editorial director. We go to the newsroom, which is the whole fourth floor. As we walk out of the elevator, there is an operator directing calls. The hubbub and fast paced rhythm are electrifying.

This is nothing. The evenings are madness before deadlines.

During my entire childhood, first thing in the morning, my father walked out the door to pick up The Compass. He went to military school and was an early riser. Every morning the newspaper has its place on the breakfast table. The smell of paper and ink mix with the aroma of fresh coffee. I am standing among the people that produce that news portal. I sit and wait for the editorial director. His all glass office is in the heart of the newsroom. He is short, has a receding hairline and a sparkle in his eye. When I am about to enter his office, a banker from Laredo, Texas arrives. I know him, greet him and identify myself. *How's your Dad? Please tell him I say hello.* The secretary takes him to see somebody else. What are the chances that at this precise moment he would come in. I enter the office and sit down. It is obvious the editorial director is a force of nature, the vigilant eye that supervises this madness.

It's great that you know this man. My secretary has to show him around, and she barely speaks any English. This is why we need a public relations person who can help around.

About that, they told me you were the person to talk to. I know you have considered me for this position, but I want to be a journalist.

What do you write?

I started writing journals, they evolved into social reflections.

Come back tomorrow with two samples.

He leaves, and my day is done. I am uncertain of the outcome. I go back to the parking lot and start thinking about my essays. As soon as I get home, I read my stuff and try to choose something to give him. The next day, when I show up with two pieces, he reads them and says:

These are very good. I need to think where we can publish them. But for now, what is it you want to do here?

I think I could be a cultural reporter.

It's done. You can start right away.

He asks his secretary to take me to the cultural section and introduce me to the editor. I am excited until I see my new boss. She is wearing all black, her most distinct characteristic is her short black fluffy hair, that bounces when she speaks. She looks at me, does not smile. I can feel her rejection. She does not like getting orders from above. She knows I did not take the training workshop with Dr. Gardner and assumes that somebody made a call. This is going to be harder than I thought. She is busy and tells me to show up the next morning. When the day is done, I lie in bed and thank God for this opportunity to make my dream come true. It is not what I imagined, but it is real. I will work hard to prove I am smart, capable and a fast learner.

On my first day, my boss wants to send me to interview the head of the women volunteers of the Red Cross, who happens to be married to one of my uncles. The day before mentioning the banker went well, I bring it up. She is quiet, thinks about it and sends me to cover another event. I should not have said she was my aunt. That made her uncomfortable. She is the link to sources and controls the networking. She approaches a blonde woman. They are friends, and sends her to the Red Cross. I get a bunch of little notebooks to write in, and I get a photographer to go with me. When we get in the car, the photographer immediately asks about a little remote control hanging from my car visor.

What is that for?

It's for opening the gate in my house.

You have a gate in your house?

Suddenly, a wall is erected in the middle of the car. We are separated by it. I do not know how to handle his reaction and act as friendly as I can. We are late for the press conference, I do not know my way around some parts of the city. When we enter the room, I am ready to apologize, but they have not started. They were waiting for us. The Compass newspaper is number one and press conferences do not start until The Compass is in the room. From this day forward the newspaper is my new husband. I am his six days a week, and my name is Beatrice from The Compass. Out of thin air, I have to create a self-confident persona, that is what is expected of me. I have to ask questions with authority. The other reporters follow my lead.

Back in the editing room, someone is assigned to help me write my first piece. I am given a manual to memorize my new sacred creed: said, mentioned, explained, replied, commented, spoke, uttered, pronounced, indicated, repeated, presumed, supposed, suggested or revealed. I will use these words to express the opinions of others. I am now a clean container that will be filled and emptied every day.

The first week is intense. Every time my boss talks to me it is to scold me because I did something wrong. One morning, I get the courage to tell her that the next time she wants to correct me, she needs to make sure it is for something she has already explained. She cannot help herself, the fast pace does not leave any free time. It is hard to follow the ferocious appetite of this news consuming machine. The product is made fresh every day. We start from scratch each morning and our deadline is at seven. The international section has until eleven.

I have lunch with a friend from college and complain.

My boss hates me. I took a shortcut but I am doing the work.

It can't be that bad.

I promise you it is. I think she feels threatened by me.

Well you got in. I still don't have a job. Stop complaining.

I can't put in my resume I was at The Compass one week. I feel like a prisoner counting the days. I have to be there for one year.

As time goes by, I enjoy the job. I interview painters, writers, poets and sculptors. I go to museums, galleries, the theater, opera, concerts and conferences. Everywhere I am taken care of, I am the press. Interviews are fascinating. It is not rude to ask questions one after another. The best part is getting answers. My personal life is stagnant. Once I turned twenty-three, I became an official old maid. Most of my friends are married now, and my mother can't stop worrying.

Mom, I will never marry. Can you accept that? Please try to be happy for me, and if I change my mind, I'll let you know. We need to stop talking about my marital status as if it were a tragedy. According to her, I failed to get a husband. Now, I am forced to build a professional life. The fear of dying alone creeps into my inner monologue, but when I see my name printed on the pages of The Compass, I feel part of a bigger mission. If my American friends could see me now they would be proud.

The editorial director gave me a weekly column for my short stories. He decided to publish them in a social supplement. I chose to hide behind an alias. I am afraid to publicly show my creative side. My whole life I have maintained a façade, one of a good simple girl, and I am not ready to pull off my mask. After three weeks, three stories and three Alias, a colleague says: *You need to sign your work. People are reading what you are writing. I've been in this business for years. You need to take credit.*

After spending time with the cultural reporters and hearing their profound conversations, witty humor and sarcastic remarks, I feel a sense of belonging to an artistic tribe. Some write poetry or plays on the side. One of them has a rock band. Without consulting my parents or childhood friends, I decide to sign my work, knowing that this decision will change my life forever. My readers are confused, the short stories are written in the first person. I write about a young woman having cancer. They think I have cancer. I write about a homosexual man, they think I am gay. They figure out my style and begin enjoying the truth behind the fiction. The newspaper is the perfect greenhouse for me to blossom and find my voice.

Chapter 5.2   2000

You wake up early, cannot sleep worrying about having this baby. Your fear of not being a good mother, haunts you. You sit down to write, it helps you line up your thoughts like things. When Elliott wakes up you tell him your worries. You are in Paris with his family. The apartment is finished. It is cold and rainy. You stay in, and binge watch the whole television series *Friends*. Later in the day, you go out to a seafood restaurant for lunch. As you walk back in coats and gloves, by the side of the Seine, Elliott tells his father about the pregnancy. He is happy but advises you not to tell his mother for now. She is busy making everything look perfect for the New Year's Party they are hosting. There is great expectation this year. The threat is that computer programs might terminate on the year 2000.

You celebrate with families from San Antonio. You are older than the children and younger than the parents. When it is midnight, you walk towards the Seine. You watch the Eiffel Tower light up with winking bright fireflies all over and white fireworks fly to the sides, making it look like an opening white peacock tail. The streets are filled with people. Your secret is this is the year you become a mother.

When you go home, you get involved in the finishing touches of your modern house. The architect is your cousin Gilbert. He comes once a week to supervise the work. It is a huge statement for a town like Nuevo Laredo. Some friends told your in-laws they were worried that the walls were crooked. They did not know that is how they are supposed to look. The marble floors are cut sideways, showing a different vein. They are left unpolished. The house has an L-shape. The social area is in the front and the family area is in the back.

Your father warns you about construction workers. Once there is a roof over their heads, they slow down. He is right. One afternoon, you come to check the construction to find cards and cigarette butts on the terrace. You can still smell the smoke. The daily cost is high. You need to be done. You become the angry woman who starts giving everybody a hard time. Your mother-in-law is always gone and blames you for taking away her privacy.

The house is in the southeast of Nuevo Laredo. It is in a new quiet residential neighborhood, a few minutes away from downtown. It is the second house built, after your in-law's house. It is next to a private school. You are surrounded by the countryside. There is no garden, just dirt in the backyard. Once you move in, you hear the house crack as it settles. Being a new construction, you see scorpions crawling out of corners and even a hairy black tarantula outside. The living room is empty and will stay that way for a while. Decorating the house is challenging. You have a limited budget. You furnish the basic areas with hand-me-downs. You focus on the bedrooms and family room. The architect is demanding. You follow his instructions, obediently hoping to enjoy this beautiful space for years to come. With the first storm, the windows leak and you have to reseal them.

At night, you can hear the coyotes. In the morning, the sun sneaks through your aluminum covered windows.

You are lonely. This is not your home town and you do not have many friends. The drive to Monterrey is short. You go often. Your friend Blondie organizes a welcome back coffee. It is a bittersweet event because it establishes you as an outsider. You waited a long time to be married. Now, you are somebody's wife and still feel like you do not belong. You are building your life somewhere else, with people you still do not know.

Being a border town, Nuevo Laredo has a large floating population. The few that claim to be born and raised here, are not welcoming to outsiders. These locals, like other locals, have a tight bond difficult to penetrate and the Theriot family has a special place among them. This makes it challenging. People make assumptions of who you are.

Nuevo Laredo's nightlife is more interesting than nightlife in Laredo, Texas. The Mexican side has many restaurants and places that close late at night. People from all over Texas come to have dinner at The Cadillac Bar, your father's restaurant. They walk around downtown buying Mexican dresses or hand-painted plates. Some gringos are here to get drunk, buy valium or visit la *Zona de Tolerancia*, Boy's Town. Elliott drove you there once. It is a fenced property. The concept can be traced to the troops based along the border. A group of vendors, launderers, barkeepers and prostitutes set up next to the soldiers to do business.

The Cadillac Bar is a landmark. You have been coming here for years. When you were younger, you saw a man with a big cowboy hat stand up and scream: *I love this woman, she's my heart and soul.* It was exciting to see what people do after a few shots of tequila.

On Monday nights, you have dinner with your father when he comes to Nuevo Laredo. He just remodeled the restaurant. Alexandra, your sister, made the floor plans. When this place opened in 1920 it was called *Caballo Blanco.* After prohibition, the border became a favorite destination for Americans who wanted to get drunk. Your father told you the story of Mayo Basan from New Orleans. Basan lost his job as a waiter, and moved to Nuevo Laredo. He established a restaurant that served fine food with beer, wine and whiskey. On the menu, they had turtle soup, soft shelled crabs and gumbo. They now serve *green enchiladas, tampiqueña* and *cabrito* for the Mexican palate. The signature drink is the Ramos Gin Fizz made with gin, orange blossom and egg white. The attraction is the bar where the margaritas are hand shaken. In the back, there is a long mirror that says *Cadillac Bar* in red, flanked by a wooden high back bar. The tables have white linens. The bartenders and waiters wear white coats with bow ties. They play live music in the evenings.

The other landmark is your grandfather's house. As a child, when visiting Nuevo Laredo, you would stay there. It belonged to your aunt Sara. It was the first house built in *Colonia Theriot* in the late forties. It was known as the *Gone with the Wind* house because of its front covered porch with tall columns. The outside was made of gray brick with white trimming. On the inside there were tall ceilings, and a great stairwell with a big window right in front of the main door, which took you to the second floor. In the back yard, there was a tennis court and a large swimming pool with two diving boards. Your father as a young man, to show off his athletic ability, used the three-meter diving board. Behind the side driveway, next to the kitchen, were the maid's quarters above the garages. This big house seemed empty. The only cozy space was the kitchen. Your mother remembers how the help was the life of the house: Chevo the waiter, Chago the chauffeur, Tencha the cook, Tacho the night guard, Chelo and Sara the cleaning ladies.

The house was under your grandmother's name. When she died, she left it to your father. Your grandfather asked your father to bequeath it to his older sister. He accepted and that created tension with your mother. She said: *That's all she had to give and she gave it to you.*

Becoming Mrs. Theriot and living here brings you back to your family's past. You drive by these places, and your curiosity has a life of its own. Understanding the relationship between the two sides of the river is a challenge. *Los dos Laredos,* as it is known, is a peculiar border. Of the four American states bordering Mexico, Texas is the most Mexican friendly. It took you years to understand that the *Deep South* is about history, not geography. Geographically Texas is the deepest south.

How can two neighbors be so different? Crossing to the other side is your weekly pilgrimage. The heart of this community is the river, the living body of water that separates two countries. As you drive towards the river, on the Mexican side, the houses are painted in magenta and yellow. The streets turn and swirl, divide and collide, creating natural chaos in traffic, barking dogs on roofs. As you approach the bridge, you see stores selling Spiderman piñatas, vendors selling bobble head toys or plaster Tweety figures. You touch poverty and smell fried taco stands. Growing up with real Mexican food, you fully comprehend the insult Taco Bell is to Mexican Cuisine.

You sit in the car, idling for thirty minutes, waiting to cross into the most powerful nation on earth. It is at the bridge where the feeling of the crushing Empire is most evident. At all times, your hands are on the steering wheel. Every driver is trying to find the fast lane. When it is your turn, and the border officer looks into your eyes, you better know who you are and where you are going. While he questions you, a dog sniffs your car, while mirrors check for anything taped under it. You leave, crossing every road bump, exhaling. There it is, a real American Highway, "the yellow brick road" to the mall.

Your whole life you have come on shopping trips to Laredo, Texas. When you were younger, you would shop downtown. When the Mall opened, it became a more desirable destination. Time was limited. First, you would grab a bite with a cold grape bubbly soda. American sodas were a treat because you had home-made lemonade daily. After fast food, you would park by the Mall, and the race for bargains would begin. The excitement was intense. You had to rush to the restroom. The expensive perfume aroma would intoxicate you. The shiny bags, stylish shoes, and endless accessories would confuse you. You needed to focus on your needs, rather than impulse shop. Then came the pain of entering the laboratory of the fitting rooms. The lighting would persuade you to believe you were not deserving and increase your shopping appetite. You needed more stuff to compensate for your grotesque human flaws.

Now that you live here, you do not hunt for the right blouse, but leisurely move the hangers one after the other. You try clothes on, buy them, take them home, think about them, and come back to return them the next day. Now that you are a home maker, your new high is the home decor department. You look for the right pillow or throw, buy Easter decorations on sale in April and Christmas accessories on sale in January. You walk inside department stores, enchanted by the smell of potpourri. You become a consumer, the main character inside the American dream. Shopping distracts you from your limited, lonely and monotonous domestic life.

Americans cross to Mexico for: cheap dentistry, sombreros, margaritas, medicines, hand-made embroidered dresses, patio furniture, cheap gasoline, fresh fruits, vegetables, and to frame art. Mexicans cross for: movies, magazines, clothes, shoes, sheets and ice cream.

Nuevo Laredo was founded by seventeen families who wished to remain Mexican. They unburied the bones of their dead and reburied them in Mexican territory. Those who stayed defend themselves saying: *I didn't cross the border, the border crossed me.*

For those who live on the border, the only question is: *How long is the line on the bridge?* Nobody wants to be stuck in line for an hour. There is a local television channel dedicated to transmitting the image of the video camera on the bridge. Its daily flow is like a tide: it goes up in the morning, with children crossing to go to American Schools, and people going to work. It goes down midmorning. It goes up at lunch time, with drivers running errands and making deposits in safe American banks. Then there is a low tide in the afternoon. The last high tide is when people return home at the end of the day.

This predictable tide goes overboard during the holidays. The weekend before Christmas, thousands of Mexican Nationals return home. The *paisanos* drive in from all over the United States, to spend the holidays in Mexico. People who do not know about this pilgrimage can be caught in an eight-hour line going back to Mexico.

Things have changed since 1994, when the North American Free Trade Agreement was signed. Trailers crossing blocked the traffic both ways. First, they were sent to the west of Nuevo Laredo. Then, a highway was built for them on the east by the river. Now, trailers have their own bridge. Locals explain how trailers caught the attention of legal and illegal businesses. From being a small town with small crooks, the "big fish" swimming in bigger oceans took notice and sent their people to check out the place. The "big fish" decided to stop swimming. After all, it is easier to hide goods inside seven thousand trailers crossing daily, than to transport the product to Miami by boat, submarine or airplane.

As you understand this community, your past merges with your present. Your baby starts to invade your body. Since you have had no complications, you decide it is time to tell Elliott's mother. *How could you do this to him? The house is enough pressure as it is.* You feel rejected, like you did something wrong. You can see she is trying to protect her son, but it is time for you to protect your own. You cannot be distracted any longer, you need to prepare for the arrival of this baby.

You have a conversation with a new friend, she describes the outfit she brought her baby home in. Yes, babies are born naked. Are you fit to be a mother? How did you not know this? Elliott drives you to San Antonio to buy things for the baby: bottles, baby clothes and gear. You get a crib, diaper changer, and rocking chair, with its matching sliding ottoman, for many sleepless nights to come.

It is time to find the right help. That is a task you will have to endeavor alone. Everybody is territorial about their own maids, always afraid to have another homemaker lure them away. A dear friend, you call her "*la sabia de Rio Bravo*," (the wise one) suggests you pay for a classified advertisement and interview candidates in a public place. That is how you find your help. Elliott's mother has Eva, a small old woman who runs her house like a well-oiled machine. She has been with your in-laws for years. She is a sweet soul, having dedicated her life to them.

You find Yolanda. She is a skinny woman in her early twenties. She wakes up cleans the whole house. You get to know each other.

Who is taking care of your son?

My mother. When I was born, my mother was sixteen and my grandmother took care of me. I call my grandmother Mama. Now my baby calls my mother Mama.

How old were you when you had this boy?

I was sixteen. When I was fifteen, I wanted to leave my house and met my boyfriend, who got me pregnant.

But now you are taking contraception?

Yes. I don't have other children, but I would like another baby.

Nelly, the other girl who works in your house, grew up with her brother in San Luis. Her mother was at the border working hard to send them money. She does not know who her father is and is determined to finish school and get a different job.

First, you buy them Mexican embroidered dresses, but they are not comfortable. You then buy them khakis and white shirts as uniforms. They keep the house clean, cook your meals, and become friends. Their bedroom is as nice as the other bedrooms in the house, with marble floors and a big window. They have a big television and cable. You are not family, but keep each other company.

Two months before your due date, July 2, 2000, it is a historic day. Being seven-months pregnant, you stand in line to vote for the presidential candidate, Vicente Fox Quezada. Your husband drops you off, with a chair and an ice chest. You do not have a local voting credentials and have to vote on a special ballot, along with hundreds of people. They came from all over the United States, to make sure the opposition party PAN wins. You stand in line for five hours, talking to people, and listening to their stories. The excitement is contagious. You are proud to be here to make history. The party dictatorship has to end. It has been seventy-two years. The PRI needs to go. As your husband picks you up, and you see others still waiting, you feel hopeful for your unborn Mexican child. Mexico and you are going into labor at the same time.

Chapter 5.3   2010

One of Beatrice's new year's resolutions is to start working on a book about her grandfather's life. She wants to understand what happened. She reads a doctoral thesis written about him and a Texas Monthly article from 1987. They give her a general idea, but she wants to know more. Her father talks vaguely about his past, and Elliott's version is focused on his own grandfather.

Most people, when they talk about their grandparents, have memories, pictures, trips and many Sunday lunches they can recall. Not Beatrice. All she has are bits and pieces of her grandfather's public persona. She only saw who Chito was to the world. It was the Wicked Witch of the West, her step-grandmother, who was committed to keeping his public image alive. Most of what Beatrice finds are stories of his success as a business man. She discovers an article in *Time Magazine* called *Big Five* published on September of 1951. It is about him and his four brothers. The article referenced his passion for African safaris and hunting. Chito was the subject of this story mostly for the house he built in Nuevo Laredo. *Time Magazine* editors described the prosperity in Nuevo Laredo burgeoning from the Don Martin irrigation project, which transformed a desert land into a fertile area for cotton growers.

This blossomed land created a fine crop of millionaires that built themselves many new houses. But none of the houses is so spectacular as a palace, now building up the river at Nuevo Laredo, with seventeen bathrooms, a swimming pool, a five-car garage, and three bars. For miles around, everyone knows that the house belongs to Octavio Theriot the eldest of the five Theriot brothers, who has done more than anyone else to make the once-dry lands blossom.

Together the Theriot brothers control 69 companies, employ 11,000 workers and gross more than $50 million dollars a year (1951). The brothers got a running start on their empire, building from their father who died in 1931, leaving his sons a tidy business in cotton, cattle, soap and cottonseed.

"The business my father left" says Chito "was small and we were a large family. We couldn't make the family smaller so we made the business larger."

The brothers put up a cotton mill, soon found that to be successful they would have to finance cotton growers, and wound up owning four banks, 10,000 acres of cotton land. In partnership with Anderson, Clayton and Co. worldwide cotton brokers, they built two big cottonseed mills. When they found they had surplus of cottonseed oil, they built a vegetable shortening plant to process it.

To market the beef from their ranches, where they ran 15,000 heads of cattle, they built their own packing plant. They added a chain of wholesale and retail general stores, four Chevrolet agencies, four movie theaters, and some 20 other enterprises.

"We're doing in a hurry what it took a hundred years to do in the US." says Chito.

One of the reasons the Theriots were able to expand so fast: Mexico's laws put a tax ceiling of 333% on corporation profits and prohibit double taxation. A company's profits are taxed but not the dividends.

"It's a good way. You have to let the individual grow. After he has grown, then tax him, but let him grow first," said Chito.

It is interesting for Beatrice to hear his voice, his expressions, the way he explains things. She was a reporter. She should be interviewing people about their memories now that she is here in Laredo, Texas.

She finds another article published in March of 1971, twenty years later. It was published in the Owosso Argus Press and is titled *Private Game Preserve is Strictly a Hobby.*

The pick-up truck bounced through the thick grass its driver pointing at the zebras, buffaloes, giraffes, black bucks, Norwegian elk and llamas running over the chaparral, thorn bushes and cacti. Chaparral and thorn bushes? Right place and right animals. This is the largest privately-owned game preserve in the world. Unlike other preserves this is not run for profit or as a public service, but strictly as one man's hobby and contribution to conservation.

It is located south of Nuevo Laredo on Mexico's rugged border land, a short distance from Laredo, Texas. Hot in the summer and cold with whistling winds in the winter, but immensely beautiful. The preserve - 15,000 fenced acres- is part of an 80,000 acres cattle ranch, owned by Octavio (Chito) Theriot a Mexican industrialist from Nuevo Laredo. There are approximately 90 species and more than 12,000 animals on the preserve, not counting coyotes, bobcats, raccoons and a few pumas, plus other local varieties.

The Theriot family owns a large corporation which includes cotton gins, wheat mills, edible oil plants, animal feed plants and a bank, among other enterprises. Because of his businesses, Theriot has been living in Mexico City for the past seven years, but escapes to the ranch for weekends whenever possible.

"It sure beats watching television in Mexico City," he said with obvious pleasure as he drove his pick-up chasing a herd of black bucks. Forgetting business worries for a while, the millionaire often takes friends on a light excursion to hunt jackrabbits. He doesn't hunt his own imported animals because "it would be like destroying things in your own home." He has hunted throughout the world, but now he is basically a conservationist.

"I started the preserve in 1957, when I brought a few animals from Africa, the ones that could adapt easily to this type of climate" he said.

The animals roam free on the ranch. The fences protect them from the pumas. Visitors are impressed by the sight of healthy animals from five continents roaming together. Wild beasts and zebras are seen side by side with some Santa Gertrudis cattle kept in the preserve. Buffaloes and ostriches appear a minute later, followed by white Norwegian elk, greater kudus and Pakistani goats. Elsewhere, the visitor finds llamas, ibex, white fallow deer, impalas, Argentina horses smaller than ponies and Australian Kangaroos. There are Russian boars, Thompson gazelles, axis deer, Indian sheep, Royal Crown cranes, Oryx and many other species.

These articles are based on lists of possessions, sizes, and amounts of money. They give Beatrice no idea of where all this prosperity came from and what the family was like. She starts interviewing her father's generation. There are twenty-nine cousins altogether, and she starts interviewing the older ones first, in case somebody dies. She has various objectives: to understand his story, to meet the relatives, and ultimately to heal. She knows the reason for the 1978 legal battle was money, but she has a gut feeling that this mess derives from her great-grandfather's suicide. She buys a couple of notebooks and starts taking notes. She prepares a questionnaire and decides to focus on their most treasured memories and Sara Hortense, her great-grandmother.

Out of her grandfather's seven siblings the only one who is still alive is Alfred. He is ninety-two-years-old. He is the one who remembers the house, because he lived in it. The house became restaurant Victoria. He describes it in the interview. *The family house at 3020 Victoria was finished in 1932. The walls were ten inches wide, made with adobe, this made it cool in the summer and warm in the winter. The roof was made with metal sheet, and when it rained, the water was gathered in a cistern. A room on the side housed the kitchen, with two ovens where they cooked with mesquite wood. A pecan tree shaded the patio. Above the garages, there were three bedrooms and two bathrooms, where we the younger boys lived.*

Contacts with the next generation are interesting in themselves. When she arrives for the interview, she is taken to the living room, and the maid brings her something to drink. She pulls out her notebook and gets ready to take notes. She can feel their need to impress her and prove they are not *has-beens*. She knows this because she grew up feeling that way. They talk about their travels and want to convince her they are doing well. She can see how she is not a regular reporter. They know she writes for the newspaper, but she is a descendant herself and married to another family member. She technically represents two families. She acts as professional as she can, to make them forget that. Once they get into it, they want to talk about their childhood, siblings, and personal experiences. She listens attentively and feels their nostalgia. The older cousins are in their eighties. Some interviews are more fun than others. An interesting situation is that whenever someone does not want to tell her something, she finds out through the others. One of them got married young. When she asks him when he got married, he says *I don't remember*. Somebody else tells her, he got his girlfriend pregnant and had to get married.

Lala's family is the one who remembers Sara the best. Lala was the firstborn, and when her mother Sara became an old widow, she moved in to live with her. Lala's children grew up with their grandmother. Lala's descendants are all still married to their first spouses and have not sued each other for money. As a young woman, Lala studied at the Conservatory in Mexico City. She had a beautiful voice. That is how she met Ramón, who played the piano like a professional. The musical couple moved constantly for seven years. Sara asked them to settle in Nuevo Laredo. At first, they lived above the bank, which was not a good arrangement. When their son Pancho, the first grandchild, played with marbles, his uncle Kiko complained about the noise. Once there was space available in the house in Victoria, they moved in with *Mamagrande* Sara. Their only daughter, La Nena, became her grandmother's cooking apprentice; she learned Sara's Cajun and French recipes. Her *Mamagrande* would say: *If you want to be a good wife and mother you must learn to cook.*

Many remember Sara making chicken soup with the same chicken more than once. They all agreed Sara was strict and demanded respect with her eyes only. When her children or grandchildren borrowed money from her, when they finished paying their debt, she said: *You can borrow again.* She was a hard worker, woke up early every day. Her children were always welcome in her house for a long mid-day Mexican lunch. Once they were married, her five sons usually had lunch there and talked about business. She never got involved in that aspect of the conversation, but made sure there were no quarrels. She was generous to her daughters-in-law and supervised the distribution of wealth was fair.

Even though she became a widow at fifty-five, she devoted her life to her children and grandchildren. She focused on family, never on money. On her birthday, September third, she demanded that everybody show up, even her son Shelby who suffered rough roads to get there. Out of her five sons, four married women like her: middle-class Americans who were raised on the border, fluent in Spanish and content with being housewives and mothers. Only the youngest married a woman from Mexico City.

Sara dressed well but never extravagantly. She used to wear pastel colors, always a dress or a skirt, with gloves and hat. She had good eyes, but could not hear a thing, she was practically deaf. On Sundays, she would pick up a grandchild and take him or her to have lunch at *El Rio Hotel*. If her granddaughters showed up wearing pants, she would not take them. She always spoke Spanish. She had an American accent her whole life, but insisted on speaking Spanish at all times. Her chauffeur drove her everywhere. She traveled with her grandchildren during the summers to: Mexico City, Acapulco, and Sabinas. Her and her travel companion was another old lady. When they stayed in Mexico City, she would rent an apartment close to Chapultepec. Against tranquil blue skies, she could see the volcano Ixtazihuatl. From Mexico City they traveled to Acapulco, leaving at six in the morning and arriving at nine o'clock at night. When staying at the Marina Hotel, close to downtown Acapulco, they spent the morning at Beach Caleta and the afternoons at Hornos Beach. On the trips, she would wake up at six and have everybody up by seven. Everyone was allowed one egg for breakfast, before setting out for the day. La Nena ate very little and the others would fight over her egg. *We came here to visit not to sleep, if you want to sleep you can stay home.* When they went to Sabinas, Hidalgo, they stayed at *Quinta La Gloria*, outside the village. The children would drive into town on top of a wagon to have ice cream. They had to pass a cemetery. Fearful, they held each other's hands. They swam in an irrigation canal. When they went to the ranch, the butler would organize horse races without saddles. The elder grandchildren were the ones who had the privilege of traveling with her and getting to know her.

When these old men and women speak of their grandmother, it is with respect and love. More than one assures Beatrice that they were her favorite. She was born in 1875 and lived to be ninety-nine years old. At the root of the family's success was her labor as a frugal, hardworking mother.

Beatrice is forced to come back to the present and put the interviews aside for a while. It is time to focus her emotional energy on a family wedding coming up. Isabelle, her sister, is getting married. They are in the final stretch, attending her showers. She gets the full treatment like Beatrice did. There is a shower for her in Mexico City. After that, they have a girl's trip to Acapulco: their mother, Alexandra, Isabelle and Beatrice. They stay at Alexandra's apartment, which does not live up to their mother's standards. Beatrice is determined not to be confrontational but to make this a nice trip for Isabelle. Her body gets the message and on their drive there, she literally loses her voice. She cannot scream or argue, she must economize her whispering words. Mom and Isabelle are both high maintenance. They each get a room by themselves, while Alexandra and Beatrice share a bedroom. The first morning, as they are the ones that wake up early, Beatrice lies on her bed and tells Alexandra: *I haven't shared a room with you in so many years, I feel like a little girl.* Alexandra and Beatrice go to the supermarket and chop the fruit in the morning. They stay busy, go to the beach and eat at restaurants. At the end of the trip, Isabelle forgets her suitcase in Acapulco. She assumed that one of her three moms had put it in the car. She is fifteen years younger than Alexandra and twelve years younger than Beatrice. She never fully integrated.

Around the wedding date, there are clashes between the drug cartels, and Elliott and Beatrice argue. He says he will not go to Isabelle's wedding. *You didn't go to Alexandra's wedding because you were hunting. If you don't go to Isabelle's wedding I will not go to your sister's wedding.* The problem is the cartels are fighting for the interstates and there have been shootings on the highway between Nuevo Laredo and Monterrey. They do go, and are driven by a chauffeur. They leave early on Friday and stay at a nice hotel with Tomas. David stays home.

On Friday night, there is a welcoming dinner for all the out of town guests. Anthony, her brother, is the host and his modern house is stunning; the lighting, buffet, tables and flowers look exquisite. Beatrice feels sad because it was the same architect that designed her house, but her brother still gets to live in it.

On Saturday morning, they have brunch at the hotel, and Beatrice gets her hair done at the beauty salon. They go to her parent's house for the family pictures. After the photo shoot, they go inside for the civil wedding and then to the church. Beatrice has been to this church many times for many weddings, including her own eleven years ago. The mass passes quickly. As they exit the church, there are fireworks and even though she greets acquaintances she feels like an outsider. Her parents' friends are older, shorter, have less hair and do not hear well. Everybody goes to the Country Club. Elliott and Beatrice give relatives a ride, who are shocked when they hear her speaking in English to her son. They enter the salon and sit at their table. Tomas does not engage. He is playing on his portable Nintendo video games. After dinner, her father gives a speech in front of all the guests and sings *As Time Goes By.*

On the outside, a wedding brings social attention, guests and pictures in the newspaper, but on the inside, it brings conflict and stress. Now that Isabelle is gone, her parents should be empty-nesters but they are not. Gerard got divorced and is living with them. The family is now in the next stage and her parents are getting old. Her family has reached a point of maturity, in Elliot's family, she is still the only intruder after ten years.

On Sunday, they drive to the airport and drop off Elliott and Tomas, who are going to the Yucatan peninsula on a hunting trip. The next morning David and Beatrice leave for his treatment. They spend a week there. She reflects on the wedding and her family. Alexandra lives in Mexico City, Isabelle lives in Washington DC, and Beatrice lives in Laredo. They are all spread out. At one point, their parents got six lots for all of them to live together in Monterrey. Everybody sold their lot and followed their dream wherever it took them. Beatrice's mom is not a traditional Mexican mother. She is busy with her own life studying, writing and playing bridge. She is now studying for her second master degree and thinking of completing a PhD.

Earlier in the year, Beatrice saw the movie *Temple Grandin*. Temple is autistic, a professor who studied the behavior of cows and designed cattle chutes to keep them calm. The autism community in Laredo organizes a yearly conference, and they bring Eustacia Cutler, Temple's mother to the meeting. Beatrice attends eagerly to get inspiration from this new role model, the mother of an autistic child. Eustacia is tall, elegant and in her late seventies. When Beatrice shakes her hand, tears come into her eyes, and she thanks Eustacia for giving "special mothers" hope. Eustacia gracefully replies: *Think of me as your future*. She is an amazing woman. She went to Harvard, wanted to be an actress and singer but sacrificed her personal goals to raise her children. Her wealthy husband wanted to put Temple in an institution, and she divorced him to prevent that from happening. In her presentation, she explains that autism is a family disorder because it affects the whole family. Beatrice now learns there are no answers only choices.

Chapter 6.1   1991

The reporters at The Compass cultural section hear about a job opportunity at the brewery's art museum. Everybody wonders who will get it. After completing a full year at the newspaper, I get an interview. One of my fantasies is to blend in the art scene. For the interview, I dress for success, the art world thrives on refinement. My costume: an ivory suit and the obligatory pearls.

The brewery is the heartbeat of Monterrey. San Pedro is just a by-product where big families had their country homes. Everything was built around it. Driving into the industrial heart of old downtown, it becomes clear why northern Mexico is frugal. In this desert land, food was never at arm's reach.

Monterrey and the brewery were founded by families who were Jewish and converted to Catholicism out of fear. Isaac founded the brewery in 1890, and of his eight children, Eugene and Robert prospered. They were both graduates of Massachusetts Institute of Technology and expanded the business into other industries. The seeds of manufacturing developed to feed the needs of the brewery: glass and carton for the bottles, metal for the caps. This is where the "Monterrey Royal Family" comes from.

I have been to the brewery's art museum many times with my mother. I park next to the entrance and look at the nineteenth century red brick building, a testament to the city's history. It is partly covered in ivy and has a dignified air. In the reception area, there are two gigantic copper brewing kettles. Their round form and shiny surfaces are sculptural. Having a few minutes to spare, I walk into the exhibition galleries. Some have wood parquet floors and others, Saltillo tile. The columns and ceiling expose the industrial bones of the building. The space is quiet and solemn. The Mexican modern art on the white walls awakens my pride and admiration for the country's natural beauty. Dr. Atl's landscape *A Plein Air* takes me to a corn field overlooking the blue valley mountains. I feel the fresh crisp air and step on the dry corn leaves. The white clouds float by. I look at my watch, it is time to go to the offices.

The entrance is hidden like a bat cave, behind a white wall. There is a long corridor. The library is to the left. The reception has a small living room. I wait a few minutes. The director's office is full of art books. He smokes constantly and has an ashtray that sucks the smoke from his never-ending cigarette. He looks at my resume and explains the job offer.

We have a group of volunteers that help us with the guided tours, but we need to improve that. I will attend to the VIP guests, but if needed you'll help. There's also the organization of exhibit openings and other events like concerts or conferences.

This is my dream job! I will be studying the exhibits with the volunteers, give guided tours and organize parties. When he mentions the salary, I control my smile to hide the hilarity inside. I will have a real salary! They paid me little money as a reporter.

I wait for the call. When I get it, I am thrilled to leave the newspaper. A year of learning and humbling myself, of being aware of all that I do not know. Leaving the newsroom is bitter sweet. I will not be creating a world view, but I will not be filling empty spaces with recycled ideas about daily needs either. My first day, I am convinced the staff in the museum has chronic depression, the pulse is a dead flat line. I start working on creating a manual for the volunteers. I sit at my desk and do research. The background: collections and the *Wunder Kammer*. Then, a quick review of museums in Europe and the United States. I summarize the history of the brewery museum -directors, exhibits, the permanent collection- and present the basics of art education. The work gets done fast. I come from a place where everything was due today.

The biggest chunk of my job is focused on coordinating the volunteers. We have a little class on Monday evenings. This group is a human zoo. Like Noah's Ark there is two of each. They all have special reasons for being here: a midlife crisis, divorce, death in the family, or an empty nest. It does not take me long to figure out that the head of the volunteers is having an affair with one of the ladies, the one with big hair and noisy jewelry. They leave together, and the husband calls Tuesday asking questions.

We have various teachers. They give us sessions on art history and aesthetic appreciation. On rare occasions, we have an artist explain his work in detail. If the artist is dead or too famous, the director instructs us. During the day, I get time to read and write my weekly column, my remaining connection to the newspaper. I enjoy my role at the weekly meetings. The spine of the museum is made of four vertebrae: conservation, curation, marketing, and public relations. Other resources come and go. When I finally feel part of a well-oiled machine, a big art museum opens next to the cathedral, in front of the city's main plaza. It's a massive colorful building designed by the modern Mexican architect *Legorreta*.

We all await inauguration night. A successful marketing campaign has built up expectations. I have been working in the art museum for only three months. It is the beginning of the summer. The reception is a formal black-tie affair and I borrow one of my mother's evening gowns: a purple silk chiffon dress that looks like a Greek toga, with matching purple shoes. I have a color period like Picasso. My date is a handsome man who will look good in the pictures. The reception is filled with elegant guests, an army of waiters offering *hors d'oeuvres*. I can hear English, French and German spoken in the hallways. This is unprecedented in Monterrey. There are hordes of people. The museum is so big it feels empty. At the center of the building, there is a patio filled with water. The biggest masterpiece of the night is the building itself. It's a magical event, a milestone that will change the art scene forever. The next morning, the dream team has a "pity party." We make fun of how the paintings look like stamps on those monstrous walls. The large dove sculpture outside has a small pond. We laugh hysterically when the director points out that the disproportion makes it look like the dove just peed. We then go to our offices and reflect. It hurts to be eclipsed by such a bright star.

I do not daydream about last night. Mixing with the players makes me feel like entourage. The *has-been* wound creeps into my psyche. My grandfather was a visionary leader who led his family into extraordinary wealth in the fifties. When my grandmother died, the Wicked Witch of the West came into our lives. She was an American seductress who had the bedroom keys, hypnotized my grandfather and spent his fortune. It has been five years since he died, and we are still waiting for an inheritance that vanished into thin air. These thoughts are watered like a weed when I come close to the jet set. This pain swells when I have to entertain new collectors. They are old men who parade their Italian suits and Hermes ties, while showing off their second wives' silicon boobs and their multi-carat pendants. Their simple minds offend. Their boring lives, supported by possessions, fired by ferocious social hunger, bite and chew on the artist's heart.

When we organize our events, my biggest challenge is the guest list. The golden portion of the list is *The Family*. I know the genealogy tree on both sides: the pretty and the smart. The museum belongs to the pretty branch. I do not know my own roots, but it is hard to survive in Monterrey without rendering tribute to *The Family*. Now that I work for the brewery, I am aware of them at all times. The director here is a gorgeous woman, widow of *The Family*. She is glamorous and bright, but one of her daughters asked in an art class if cubists came from Cuba. This daughter gives me constant instructions for *the list*. Being around the royals is bad, but seeing the director pimping the artists is unbearable. The guided tour that makes me feel like a cultural courtesan is when I show our biennale to the Mexican president's brother. His nickname is Mr. Ten Percent, because in all the businesses he gets his ten percent cut. I explain the art while a secretary follows us. When he says *I like this one*, she writes down the information of the painting. Later on, these pieces will be bought for his country or beach house.

What makes it all endurable are the times when I sit alone in the exhibit galleries and stare at the art in sacred silence. I visit imaginary places. The artist's brush takes me into other realities. These rectangles are portals to other worlds, a testimony of sites that have become ruins, a proof of some hidden past or painful memory. Knowing the artists is a privilege. There is an exhibit by a young sculptor. He explains his pieces to us on a Monday evening. There is fire in his eyes when he explains the process of gestation. Some of the pieces are large marble monoliths with encoded astronomic messages. Others are soft stone knots and bows. He lets some visitors touch his work and this license becomes transcendent when a group of blind men touch the marble and know it is black.

Little by little, I find my tribe. Behind the pretensions, there is a clan of sensitive, smart and sophisticated souls trying to find answers to big questions. The museum, like church, brings out our connection to divine wisdom. The guided tours give me the opportunity to see the eureka spark in the children's eyes. In the Robert Motherwell exhibit, we discuss abstract expressionism.

How do you paint sadness?

You paint a man crying.

A man crying is a man crying.

Sadness is grey. A boy screams in the back.

What is wrong with this woman?

I ask about a photograph titled Blind Woman.

She is blind. A little girl says.

Seeing the art is rewarding, but nothing is as powerful as making it. I make a contribution when I write. It does not matter how good I am, as long as I surrender to the process and tap into the source of providential creativity. By exposing this artistic side of me, I feel vulnerable, but the connections I make are more honest.

The better my professional life is, the worse my personal life gets. The cultural scene is overrun by homosexuals, making it difficult for me to meet any prospects. I become friends with a man who looks Italian, with big green eyes, curly hair and tan skin. He is handsome and always impeccable. I jokingly call him *Son Altesse Royale*. He is a fearless young collector who has invented himself from scratch. He has an apartment in Manhattan and knows gallerists and collectors in New York. His branding and marketing intimidate. He is hungry for social validation and is careful to associate with the right people. I can tell he is cautious. He introduces me as somebody's granddaughter. It is my grandfather who is famous in the New York jet set, not my father. As I become part of the artistic entourage, I get included in his gatherings. The first time he invites me I ask: *Son Altesse Royale is it going to be in the Grand Palais or the Petit Palais?* I am referring to his parents' house and his bachelor's apartment.

His family lives in a new development at the foot of the mountain. It is painted black. The structure is mostly triangles, with pointy edges that reach for the sky. There are a couple of living rooms with incredible art, a real *Chagall* in the center light. The waiters walk around offering drinks. The hostess is wearing a black and white Chanel suit with gold chains. I am not wearing any brand, just a little black dress. My escape is to the guest bathroom, I need to check my make-up and give myself a pep talk in the mirror. Above the toilet there is a copper plate urinated into by Andy Warhol. I come out ready to mingle. The action is on the terrace overlooking San Pedro. It does not take long to join in the conversations. They all revolve around art: making it, buying it, looking at it or exchanging it. There are collectors, gallerists and artists.

The Sunflowers was sold at Christies for forty million... To think he sold only one painting in his lifetime... He is the ultimate case of the misunderstood artist... He became famous because he cut his ear off... He painted the sunflowers to decorate Gauguin's bedroom... I believe there was something "off" with his vision... You can see the madness in every stroke.

Behind *Altesse's* shield of glamour is a damaged soul who needs art like oxygen. He gathers a peculiar tribe of wounded veterans that find peace in coming close to aesthetics. It is he who assembles the art clan. In this industrial desert, patronage is the first sign of evolution. In this sensible circle, I meet other gay men and enjoy their witty conversations, but our friendship has a frontier, and we compete for male attention.

My social life is not fertile ground for romance. These feminine men are neither prospects nor acquainted with possible candidates. I am about to turn twenty-five, and my determination to marry a virgin is now heroic and senseless. Any idiot can marry a virgin at nineteen. My work gives me a sense of satisfaction, but I feel forced to contemplate the possibility of having a physical relationship with no strings attached. I have nightmares of dying a virgin and having the worms eat my hymen. In therapy, I analyze my plan to give up my virginity before it is too late. When is too late? It is hard to know.

I recently read *The Fountainhead* where Ayn Rand wrote *"There are two things we must get rid of early in life: a feeling of superiority and an exaggerated reverence for the sexual act."* Determined to get this done, I buy the pill, take it for a month, and choose my victim. I choose Tarzan, an athletic specimen with no grey matter, making it impossible for me to fall in love. After a few dates, I build up to the encounter, and when it happens it is a huge disappointment. It is a meaningless animal experience that has no effect on me. It is mostly painful. We are on a quest to open a trail between closed hills. There are two huge insights: understanding that every man has this equipment hanging from the whole, and that I now have an empty space at my core. No wonder they are so detached! The tool is outside their being, while we surround the invasion. I have now compartmentalized my intellectual, emotional and physical needs. I have just risked becoming damaged goods for many Mexican men, but I pray I will find a man who is more evolved than that. From this day forward, I am navigating uncharted waters.

Chapter 6.2   2001

For the last five months, you have not traveled much because of the baby. You brought him with you to Austin for a weekend. You are staying at a nice hotel. They set up a crib and a diaper pail in the room. It is early in the morning. He wakes up happy. Today, five months to the day, is the last time you breastfeed him. After you have room service, he takes a morning nap. You leave him as Elliott is plugged into his computer, and go out for a walk by the river. It is a clear winter Sunday morning, there are a few people jogging. Now that you are not a walking human refrigerator, you recover your mobility. As soon as your feet start moving, your brain is turned on. Looking at the blue sky and the smooth undulations in the river, you recall the sequence of events, how motherhood hit you like a truck.

It all started at dawn. You check your bag for your pretty hospital gown, the baby's clothes and toiletries before leaving for the hospital. No nail polish and a full shower, patient manners. You get there and are given an enema to clean you inside out. Then you wait under that bright hospital light. The process of inducing the baby begins. You can see your baby's heartbeat in the monitor. He is not distressed, but you are. The nurses make you comfortable. The doctor comes and goes, contractions come and go. After seven hours of hoping to dilate, the executive order of the C-section is given. You do not want to go through with this, but the baby has to come out. They clean you, take you into the operating room. Elliott stays outside with his mother, who just drove in from San Antonio. The doctor thinks Elliott might faint. The anesthesiologist starts a conversation to distract you, then comes the big injection and you are gone. When you awake, you see your purple and greasy baby. They take him away to be cleaned. Later, you wake up in your room. You can hear people talking outside. Your brother Anthony and his wife are here for a visit. You cannot concentrate on visitors, your wound hurts. You cannot move your legs. The anesthesia is still working. When the nurse brings the baby, she helps you plug him in to your left breast. It is unpleasant. He felt enormous inside you and looks tiny outside. He is a blonde pink little rat.

Next morning, you wake up, and the nurse helps you bathe. You cannot walk well. You start crying inside the shower. Your stomach is still big, with a deep wound underneath, seven layers of tissue butchered. There is no chance of fitting into your jeans anytime soon. After getting cleaned, putting on your pretty gown, and a bit of makeup, it is show time. Your eldest brother Octavio comes to see you. Your father-in-law arrives with a friend. It is Friday, and your parents are conspicuously absent. They preferred to go to Mexico City to attend an artist's cocktail party.

Knowing you were not getting any help, you hired a nurse for the first three months. Your friend Blondie helped you get her. They call her Yayita. She is a refined old white woman. She looks youthful for her age. Taking care of newborns keeps her young. She agreed to work with you because her niece lives in Nuevo Laredo. You leave the hospital with Yayita, Elliott, and the baby. You arrive and set up downstairs in the baby's room for the next forty days. Yayita is staying in the next room. Elliott is upstairs in the master bedroom. The nurse teaches you how to feed him, burp him, dress him, cut his nails, change his diaper, clean him, bathe him and wrap him up like a little *taco*. You have a journal where you write when he eats, evacuates and sleeps. He hates the water. Bathing him is torture. When he cries, you cry.

The first two weeks, Yayita does not take a day off. Finally, she leaves to spend the day with her niece. It is Saturday, your first day alone with the baby. You are anxious and so is he. Elliott is leaving on his three-week hunting trip to Africa and a sadness overcomes you. The crying begins, like a faucet that is broken and cannot be closed. While the baby sleeps you call your doctor.

Hello, sorry to disturb you at home, but can I speak to the doctor?

It's no bother, but he is out on his mountain bike with friends. He should be back in a couple of hours. Maybe I can help you. I have been married to him many years.

Well, I am embarrassed to say, but the thing is that, well, you know, the truth is that I can't stop crying.

The exhaustion is building up. Try to sleep when the baby sleeps.

I just ruined my life. I don't think I can do this. I can't stop worrying about him and his future: What school is he going to go to? Who are going to be his friends? How am I going to keep him away from drugs?

You are not going to take care of a newborn forever. He will grow. When he is older, you will face each challenge, one day at a time. Watch a comedy to take your mind off things.

At three in the morning, I feel overwhelmed thinking I am the only living soul going through this.

Every mother goes through the same process, but it will pass.

You watch a comedy on television, the only problem is that the laughing hurts your wound.

The few friends you made come and visit. A small group of wives come to see the baby. Your question to them is:

Just explain one thing: How is it possible that there is a single woman on the face of the earth who is willing to have a second child?

It gets better. You will forget.

No. I swear, I will never ever forget.

What all these people do not know, is that your mother-in-law has kept her distance, and it takes your mother and father a whole month to come see the baby. You did everything right, got married in white at the altar, had a legitimate child, and still your parents had better things to do. When Elliott leaves for Africa, they come for a couple of days. When they leave, your sister Alexandra comes, then Anthony and his wife come visit. You do not know what you would have done without the help and the nurse. Your whole life you have relied on them. This time is no exception. When you breastfeed him, you have a sense of completion you cannot recognize. This daily ritual is concentrated tenderness fueling him to be propelled into life. Every time this creature is hungry, he gets milk with a soft loving container that wraps love around him. During breastfeeding, you stay calm and concentrate on him.

After burping him, you just stare at each other in full presence. He looks into your eyes without blinking and you look into his. You know baby zebras lie next to their moms to memorize their stripes to recognize them in the herd. This baby is memorizing your face, looking at you with such intensity. He is sweetly reminding you that his survival is your responsibility. His glance is divine, pure and holy. He is a being who just landed in this reality, *welcome to the world, little one.* Rebirth makes sense to you now. Looking into his eyes, you realize he came from another dimension.

It is time to think about a name. You consider different options and research from those around you. You know he is a Leo. He was born on a hot summer day in August, at 3:05 in the afternoon. This fact will come in handy when you get him his astrological birth chart. You do not know at what time you were born. Your mother remembers it was on a Wednesday afternoon around three. The doctor played golf on Wednesdays. Most people know their time of birth because it is on their birth certificate. Yours is not a reliable source. Your father was the one who registered all of you, and he did not pay attention to details. When he registered your sister Alexandra, he forgot to write down her middle name. In your entire family, she is the only one that does not have a middle name. In Mexico, when the first girl is born, she is named after her mother. Your grandmother died a few months before your sister was born, and she was named after her. She looks like your father's family. It was natural that she got a paternal name.

Your brother Gerard was born between Alexandra and you. Your mother wanted another girl. When you were born, she was happy to have a pair of girls. You were the fifth and youngest. Your name comes from your maternal grandmother. *Beatrice* means bringer of joy. One Mexican tradition is to be named after a relative, the other is to use the saint's designated name for your birthday in the *Santoral*. If you had chosen the saint for your baby he would be Eusebio.

In Mexico, married women used to keep their maiden name and add the husband's name with a "de" to signal possession. American married women adopt their husband's name and become somebody else. Most girls are not named after their mothers. It is confusing. Women's first names liberate them from the lineage yoke. Firstborn men get their father's first and middle names, adding Junior or the third at the end of their names. Your father and eldest brother are part of a long line of Octavios. Your nephew is the seventh Octavio Theriot.

Your second brother was named Anthony, after your maternal grandfather. After his mother's death, your grandfather Anthony started a career as a diplomat in New York. This is the grandfather you knew. Your only memory of him is touching his almost bald head and feeling his smooth skull, and all that soft white small hair around the sides of his head. He had beautiful green eyes and thin lips. He spoke fast, and it was difficult to understand what he said.

Both your grandmothers died before you were born. Alice and Beatrice were both daughters of political men involved with journalism. Alice's father founded the Laredo Morning Times. Beatrice's father was a lawyer and poet, part of a group of bohemian writers of poems and essays in journalistic publications. His most famous poem describes the emblem of Monterrey, *el cerro de la silla,* the saddle mountain. In perfect rhyme, he explains how the sun climbs out behind it, delaying the sunrise, and reflecting all the colors of the rainbow. Violet peeks among clouds, blue wrapped in foggy mornings, emerald green in sunny afternoons and the sun burns in the sunset right before twilight.

One peculiar thing your parents have in common is that they are both ghost children. They were born after a baby died having their exact name. Your father's brother lived for three months because a nanny dropped him. Your mother had a pair of twin sisters who lived for only a few days. Just looking at your baby, you cannot imagine the pain. Both your father and mother probably came into the world with a depressed mother, who when she looked at them, realized the dead baby would never be replaced. You cannot imagine how your mother felt having five children in six years. As you enjoy your baby, you try to imagine how when you were a baby, there were two toddlers and two infants around you. Your mother had plenty of help, but she still gave birth to all of you herself, with her tiny little body. She confessed to you that she only breastfed you for a few weeks and that your whole first year of life you were looked after by a nurse. You did not have that intimate gazing moment with her. She could not love you more. After she had you, she decided to take the pill, in spite of the fact that it was a new product and had high hormonal levels. She was raised by nuns in a boarding school from the time she was six-years-old, but she was willing to go to hell not to have any more babies.

As you finish your walk, a switch in your brain is turned off. You return to the present and head back up to your room. The baby is awake playing with Elliott.

I love that you love my baby.

He's also my baby.

In the beginning, he was all yours.

Back in Laredo, you adjust to your routine. Now, you have more freedom, you do not have to run back home to breastfeed. You are proud you did it. It only takes a few days for him to get his first cold. They warned you that as long as he had your antibodies, he would be safe, and so he was. It is winter, and when you go out, you do not make eye contact with strangers. You do not want people to touch him. You are rude enough to request: *Please don't touch him.* Still, they grab his hands. That is probably why he got sick.

Once winter is over, you take him out on walks. You live outside Nuevo Laredo in a new residential area. During your daily morning walks, at 9:15, you see an airplane take off, the only flight to Mexico City. Your walk consists of going to your in-law's house and coming back. It is serene and quiet. You enjoy the fresh air. Tango, your Jack Russell Terrier is ecstatic. When you get back, you sit Tomas down to watch a little video called *Baby Einstein.* Now that Yayita is gone, the maids help you take care of him sometimes. The sleeping is better and your body is healing. Your parents just sold their condominium in Laredo, Texas, and you get more second-hand furniture. The living room is now furnished. You have new fences. Your dog Tango can run in the backyard. Your mother-in-law is visiting often. Tomas becomes her baby too.

Your in-laws campaigned for the family name, your triumph is that Tomas, his middle name, it is only his. He will not be yours or his father's. He will be himself. They insist that he gets his American passport. The day you take Tomas to the consulate, your mother-in-law shows up, looking sharp, in her Chanel suit, Hermes bag and Gucci shoes. She knows the effect she has on others. She is the American-born citizen and is here to make sure her grandchild gets the right treatment. You do not think it necessary to get the American citizenship, but your father-in-law insists that living on the border you need to keep your options open. You want to live in Mexico and have Mexican children, but this is giving your children the opportunity to choose. The reason you accept is that the dual citizenship is an option. Your boys do not have to choose to be American or Mexican; they can be both or so you believe.

Before spring ends, you fix the backyard and plant grass and trees. The house looks finished. The gift closet is upholstered in velvet. The custom-made wooden children's closets are finished. The outside deck and swimming pool are built. Gilbert, the architect, just got two national architecture prizes for your house. You still go out to department stores hunting for special objects to give it a personal flair. After taking a *Feng Shui* class, you go to the beach and buy three prosperity fish at a kite store and hang them on your terrace. You spend a weekend in Kerrville and while Elliott hunts in a nearby ranch, you find patio furniture for the terrace downstairs.

You are used to your new normal. Your baby can sit, eat, and play. Buying stuff for the house is done. The thrill is gone. You can now see motherhood is not intellectually stimulating. You feel unchallenged. A friend invites you to attend a seminar. A speaker from Mexico City comes to give an introduction to the theory and practice of Buddhism. He refutes New Age beliefs that surround eastern cosmogony and disseminates true Tibetan culture and spirituality. The workshop begins on Friday afternoon. This crowd is culturally curious. In casual conversation, one of the attendees tells a joke: *When an individual has an imaginary friend you call him crazy, but when a group of people have an imaginary friend, you call it religion.* This commentary is earth shattering to you. You grew up talking to your imaginary friend daily.

You are invited to join a group of Buddhists for dinner on Saturday night. The hardcore Buddhists warn you about how the ending of the first seminar given in a new city is usually magical. On Sunday, when you are having your final meditation, the windows are whipped open by strong winds. As soon as you leave, the winds calm down. You feel grateful for having a new practice to calm your crazy mind.

Two days after that, it is September 11, 2001, your second wedding anniversary. Elliott is in Africa. You wake up, and your sister Isabelle calls to tell you to turn on the television. Two airplanes just crashed into the Twin Towers in New York City. Nobody knows who did this or why. Other crashes are reported and air traffic is brought to a halt. Elliott calls:

Are you OK? We are watching television, and as we were watching the news, we saw the second plane crash.

We are OK. How about you? How will you get back home?

I am not leaving for another two days. Hopefully, I can keep my flight, but I'll send you an email letting you know.

The conversation is brief, and he hangs up. He calls back to say: *I forgot to say Happy Anniversary.* The rest of the day you are glued to the television and the phone. Nobody understands what is happening. The worst images are of people jumping out into the abyss to escape the flames.

You choose to write about the subject for the newspaper. You explain this event is unprecedented and cannot be called anything. It was not an aerial attack, a kidnapping, or a failed attempt. Two planes full of people were used like missiles to destroy the biggest emblem of New York City.

You remember your first trip to *the city that never sleeps.* Your parents took your brother Gerard and you to have dinner at *Windows on the World.* When you got to the World Trade Center, you had to use a specific elevator, and the ride was long, all the way to floor one hundred and six. You had a nice dinner overlooking the city down below. You were almost in the clouds. It was the first time you tried New England clam chowder. You remember because the next morning you threw up.

Nobody knows how this will affect the world, but you know traveling will never be the same. Sure enough, it only takes a few weeks to see the difference at the International Bridge. The crossings take twice as long and extreme measures have immediate repercussions. At the end of October, the newspapers talk about George Bush signing the USA Patriot Act (Uniting and Strengthening America by Providing Appropriate Tools Required to Intercept and Obstruct Terrorism). Americans decide to trace the money going out of the United States to make sure it is not funding terrorism. This will surely have an effect on drug dealers. Drugs will continue to go into the United States, but the money will get stranded. It is hard to imagine what the consequences will be when money stops flowing smoothly. You ask your imaginary friend for guidance and protection.

Chapter 6.3   2011

The conflict between the cartels continues on the border. There is collective psychosis in the community; distrust has poisoned the city wells. Everyone who used to live in Nuevo Laredo has moved to Laredo Texas. In Mexico, the cartels are destabilizing society, and in the United States, the real estate bubble has burst. Elliott's family takes drastic measures. They sell their family ranch. *Now that we don't have a ranch, what are we doing here?* Elliott buys a smaller ranch close to San Antonio, that is only his, where he keeps his exotic animals. For years, Beatrice has made her daily effort to be happy in this town. They never thought they would leave.

They make an appointment in a military school Elliott went to in San Antonio. They dress up and drive. While Tomas spends the day with other students, they take a tour and walk around campus. They see the classrooms and high tech electronic boards. Tomas will have to start over, once again. Tomas said to a boy: *My parents are making me come here, but I like it.*

Beatrice has complained about living on the border, but the border is not Mexico, and it is not the United States. It is a breed of its own, where you get the best and worst of both worlds. She knows most residents in her neighborhood, and Tomas has many friends. Beatrice can find him wherever his bike is parked. She has help every day of the week, and David is well taken care of. They have a big backyard and a swing set. Beatrice has friends to keep her company while Elliott is on his hunting trips.

Spring is the best time to put a house on the market. Most people like to make the move during summer, when their children are out of school. Elliott and Beatrice put a sign in the front yard and try to sell the house themselves. The first day, a man calls saying he wants to see it. Elliott recognizes the name. He is the front man for illegal business in Nuevo Laredo. He is not a dangerous man, but a powerful one. They call him *the unnamable.* For political events, his name is never on the list, but he is always included. Elliott decides they have to let him see the house. Before he comes, Elliott and Beatrice argue. She does not want to let this man into her home, but they agree they will not sell the house to him even if he wants to buy it. It is a Sunday afternoon, and *the unnamable* parks his Cadillac SUV.

He is fair, slim, well dressed and polite. As Beatrice shows him the house, she gives a few explanations of what they have done to it. She can tell he is disappointed the house is not more luxurious. Most people in this town assume things about the Theriot family. There is not enough granite. The curtains are not custom made, and there is no fancy electronic equipment. They have tidy closets, comfy couches, a well-tended garden, with a dog, and a swing set. There are little hand prints on the windows, height marks in the master bathroom, toys, stuffed animals and family pictures. Before he leaves, Beatrice explains apologetically that when the boys are older, they will remodel. He listens, but the tour has had an effect on him. He looks at her in the eye and says: *This is a home and there's no money in the world that can buy that.* There is silence after that. They pause and walk towards the door. Beatrice looks at him as he takes a last glance. At that moment, she sees him for the human being he is and feels sorry for all that he has lost in his journey to power. As they close the door, Beatrice feels gratitude for her home. As he drives away, Elliott explains that one of the man's children died in a car accident, and that he had a bad divorce.

With the recession and the burst real estate bubble, there are no offers. They have to be patient with the sale of the house. Elliott tries to convince Beatrice to live in a trailer home in the new ranch, outside San Antonio, while they build the house of his dreams. She refuses and tells him that between living in the countryside and staying in Laredo, Texas, she would rather stay. They agree on finding a townhouse.

San Antonio is a big city. Elliott's parents have a house in the Heights, and that is where they look. David will go to the Heights public school. The children are familiar with the playground. Beatrice had brought the boys on weekends when she visited her in-laws' in the summer. The Special Education teacher, Ms. Auburn, knew from an early age she wanted to be in Special Education. She is young, enthusiastic, beautiful inside and out.

Once Elliott and Beatrice know their children's school, they look for houses inside the school district. Beatrice drives to the Heights and makes appointments to see options. They are expensive compared to Laredo. After a dozen visits, they choose a new condominium. The market gives them the opportunity to buy it half off. The process is complex; after the real estate debacle, there are strict new loan restrictions.

During the summer, Beatrice drives back and forth between Laredo and San Antonio. She brings her Waterford crystal glasses and places them on the kitchen shelves. She has to go over all their possessions, one by one. Half their belongings stay there and the other half go. The condominium has three floors and an elevator. After living in an older house in Laredo, it is nice to have big closets, and a new kitchen. During the summer, while they can still enjoy fulltime help, Elliott and Beatrice escape to San Antonio to buy containers, hangers and drawer liners. This move is not forced.

While all of this happens, Tomas is at a summer camp in Orca's Island, a camp Beatrice went to as a child. She goes to pick him up, while Elliott is hunting. She flies to Seattle and takes the ferry to San Juan Islands. She looks out into the different bays and hears the cry of the seagulls. The last time she was here she was twelve-years-old. She gets off the ferry, rents a car, drives in the woods to her bed and breakfast and has dinner by herself, looking at the sunset. The next morning, she drives into camp. She walks around and tries to recognize the place. She sees the humongous tree house on top of a tall tree next to the main lodge. She asks and walks around until she finds Tomas laughing. He is happy to see her. Beatrice hugs him tight. Every summer when he leaves, she misses him like oxygen. They walk by the shore, follow some trails in the forest, reach his cabin and grab his stuff. They head back to Seattle and spend a couple of days there. His clothes are dirty and smelly, Beatrice takes him shopping for t-shirts and jeans.

They land in San Antonio, and Tomas looks at his room all set up. His clothes are in his closet. His desk has his things on it, and he is starting school soon. David has a hard time accepting the lack of backyard and starts having behavior issues. He hits his head on the walls out of frustration. When he runs around, it sounds as if there is a horse on the third floor. They all prepare for a new life, buy school supplies and find their positions. Tomas has to wear a uniform, and David takes the bus. His teacher insists he needs to become more independent.

San Antonio has cooler weather, tall trees and better radio stations. There is free jazz and classical music all day. The hardest thing to adapt to for Beatrice is not having live in help. She has to organize her time better. She gets a cleaning woman and a nanny. Elliott leaves on Mondays for Laredo and comes back on Thursdays, when they have their date night. They talk on the phone in the evenings, but he drifts away slowly, like a boat pulled into the ocean.

Beatrice is determined to integrate and becomes *Yes Woman*. Her mother taught her that when you move to a new city, you go where you are invited, no questions asked. She finds herself a book club and joins a yoga studio. Elliott and Beatrice belong to the right clubs as non-residents and now become resident members. Beatrice gets a newspaper subscription, a pediatrician, a dentist, a physician, a gynecologist, a hair salon, a dry-cleaners, and a seamstress.

When they have been in San Antonio for a month, as Beatrice sits and waits with David for the bus, she opens up the newspaper. The cover story is that the homecoming king for Heights High School is a boy with Down Syndrome. The article shows him wearing his crown and explains he only takes it off to go to sleep. Beatrice cries tears of joy. This inclusive community is theirs now! David will have a better life. As David blossoms in his special education class, Tomas withers. The academic level in his school is too high. The military culture is foreign to him, and he is having difficulty making friends. The boys were welcoming the first weeks but gravitate towards their kindergarten gangs. Suddenly, he does not want anybody to know he speaks Spanish. The other challenge he faces is his height. He is much taller than his peers and continues growing like a plant. In just one year, he grows six inches.

Beatrice's need to blend in and make friends becomes urgent, but she cannot penetrate the locals' circle. They protect their bond with spiky shields. It does not take her long to single out the alpha female mom in Tomas' grade. Beatrice calls her and leaves her messages, but is ignored by her. Her mother-in-law organizes lunch dates with her friends and their daughters, but they are younger and so are their children. Beatrice cannot make plans with other kids. They are older now and make their own plans.

Someone recommends her for a volunteer position in David's school. She is supposed to be training to chair an event. In Mexico labor is cheap, and there are always extra hands for support. Not here. The night of the event, Beatrice is late because the nanny is late. She does not bring her kids, fearful of David's behavior. Her reputation with the mother mafia is ruined.

A family friend invites Beatrice to participate on boards of different causes. Again, she fails miserably. To be a member of a board you either give money or get money. The money is not hers to give. Elliott's donations go to hunting and conservation. Beatrice refuses to call strangers asking for money. It is not a good way to start relationships. Attending those meetings gives her the opportunity to see firsthand the wheel of American philanthropy.

The only group that grounds Beatrice is a foursome of women from Monterrey who live at Heights. She is the one who calls them to set up lunch dates. One of them is a royal who came here because her bodyguard was shot. The other is a yogi married to a Mexican politician, and the third is a colorful hippie healer who escaped insecurity in Mexico. The healer is doing energy work and needs to practice. She asks them to be her guinea pigs. Beatrice is *Yes Woman* and say yes to becoming her patient. She does it to make friends. They talk about nutrition and learning disabilities. Now that Beatrice has access to high quality food, she refocuses on David's diet. There is a whole aisle for gluten free foods in the local supermarket. Beatrice connects to a health coach and improves her pantry with super foods and vitamins. She researches new options for healing autism, but the challenges with David multiply.

Before the heat ends, Beatrice takes David to the Country Club for a swim. While she is putting her things down in a chair and extending her towel, David jumps in the pool, takes off his swimming suit and poops in the water. A woman notices. Beatrice gets him out, the other children get out of the water. She leaves with her son like a thief. The pool closes for the day, and she never takes David to the Country Club again.

All their doors have inside locks, but in the evenings, when Beatrice picks up the afternoon mail, David escapes and runs around the condominiums. The police show up to see what is going on. Beatrice is defensive. The officer approaches her to ask if she needs help. She is embarrassed but the officer says they are trained to deal with these children.

The biggest challenge is taking David to the dentist. Just for a cleaning, someone has to come out in the parking lot and give him a pink liquid that will knock him out, so he can be taken inside. Then, with laughing gas, they keep him still enough to clean his teeth. One of his molars is stuck and needs to be pulled out, a procedure that with a neuro-typical child would be uneventful. David gets scheduled for full anesthesia at the Children's Hospital.

Beatrice does not talk about these incidents to anybody. She isolates herself, and the resentment towards Elliott builds up. He sleeps in Laredo three nights a week and continues with the hunting trips. They cross the fine line where he is gone more time than he is home. When he comes home, the complaining begins. He does not want to hear it.

At the end of autumn, Tomas has behavior issues at school and is asked to leave. Beatrice goes to David's public school to demand a space, but they do not have any. When she mentions that he is fluent in Spanish, they decide to place him in the language immersion program. Tomas is much taller than everybody else. His first day of school, he pretends to be a teacher assistant. His height becomes a problem. A boy in school tells him he is deformed. To give him a different perspective, Beatrice researches until she finds an article that proves that tall people are happier.

As hard as Beatrice tries to pretend they are normal, she cannot keep it up. Autism is a family condition, and they are affected by it. She is supposed to be the only one that knows how to deal with David, but she doubts herself. To escape her life, she becomes involved in Facebook. She starts looking at other's people lives and reconnects with friends from Monterrey. This becomes a new form of association. She lives under the illusion that she recovered lost friends. Facebook is a window to the world, but it is closed. In this newsfeed, Beatrice provides nice family pictures to share and does not have to explain that David is autistic.

Her last attempt to be normal is getting a family portrait done by a local photographer. On an autumn Saturday morning, with the perfect white crisp bright light, they are all dressed in jeans and white t-shirts. As soon as the photographer arrives, David becomes anxious, and everybody gets stressed. They work hard to get him to sit. They decide to ignore him and take Tomas' photo. They go to the master bedroom for the family picture. It catches the morning light perfectly. They sit on the white bed and struggle to get David to look at the camera.

Beatrice is tense. They have to do this! She needs this picture for the Christmas card she sends every December. She needs to have a picture of them looking normal, like everybody else. She needs proof that they are a real family, and can sit together, and hug each other, and smile, and have the dog on their laps, and put their shame aside, and look into the lens with pride, and have a sense of belonging to humankind. If they can do that, they can do other things. This family picture is a beacon of hope, her proof of normalcy, her passport into civilization. She needs this picture to keep believing that it is all worthwhile, that all these years have a purpose, that the image of this family is good enough to stand on top of any fireplace mantel shelf, among other Christmas cards. She needs to capture this moment in time as the pinnacle of a long journey, before her boys lose their angelic soft skin, before they are embarrassed to hug her, before they realize she does not know everything, before they turn into teenage beasts, before their childhood ends, before the beginning of the end.

Chapter 7.1   1992

Women are like gas. We fill the space we are in. There can only be one grown woman per household. When my sister Alexandra graduated, she moved to Mexico City and has been living with friends ever since. Now that I have real income and have tasted independence, the friction with my mother grows.

The first thing I get with my own money is a good stereo and many CDs. My room has been orange and yellow since I was a child, colors for a kitchen and food, not rest and sleep. The first step is getting rid of the orange carpet, which is replaced by a neutral almond tone. Then, I buy two white and blue hand painted Japanese vases, take them to an electrician and turn them into lamps. Next, I get an all-white comforter, new curtains with white and blue paisley print, and the final touch, I paint the wall behind my bed in a bright cobalt blue. When my bedroom looks the way I want, Alexandra comes to visit.

What happened here? This was our bedroom.

You said it yourself 'was.' I told you about it over the phone. You've been gone for five years now.

I know. I just didn't think about what I was going to feel when I saw it. Now, I don't have a space to come back to.

Are you coming back?

No. You don't understand. I pay a rent and live with friends, but this is my home. This change makes me feel evicted.

After her visit, my parents invite a married couple and offer them my suite, thinking it is theirs to offer. It is useless, this will never be my space. I am a grown woman and like gas invading my mother's house. None of my friends ever lived alone, but Alexandra does. She has made fun of me for being a spoiled princess. I need to prove her wrong.

San Pedro has plenty of apartments for college students, a constant floating population, who have a bad reputation as tenants. Some places require a three-month deposit. The newest apartment buildings are up on the mountain, but you have to wait for someone to die to get one. After looking at the newspaper, I make appointments. I find a small guest house in the backyard of a house. I go shopping to buy pots, pans, cutlery, glasses and plates. It is a small space with one bedroom, a small living room, one bathroom and a small kitchen. The front door is inside a gated micro patio, and on the side, there is space for the water heater and washing-center. I am getting what Virginia Woolf calls *A Room of One's Own*, to turn the short stories that were published in my column into a book. I sign the contract and move into my flat. The space is limited, but it is all for me. I will not go shopping in a while, my closet is small. The last acquisition is my answering machine. Once I get it, I become a modern independent woman.

It is winter, the first night that I sleep in my apartment. I hear cats mating. As I lay my head on the pillow, a sense of satisfaction comes over me. I did this all by myself, the blue lamps, the paisley curtains. This is a space of my own.

I have lunch with my parents, my mother hugs me and cries:

This is not the way it is supposed to be.

Mom, please stop acting like this is tragic. You should be proud.

I don't know anyone who has a daughter living alone.

Alexandra lives alone.

She lives in Mexico City. You moved out here, in Monterrey.

My best friend tells me that her mother said decent girls do not do this. These commentaries make me anxious. I make an appointment with a therapist I used to see as a teenager. His office is downtown. The moment I sit down it all pours out.

What brings you here? I haven't seen you in a while!

I moved out of my parents' house to finish my book.

Congratulations!

Most people react like I am jumping into the abyss.

San Pedro is a conservative society. Women are treated like girls.

I have a good salary, and I am tired of taking care of my mother's life. On the weekends, I pay the maid's salaries, pick up my teenage sister from her dances and feed my hungover brother Gerard.

You should help out because you live there for free.

Now that there is no juicy inheritance, my parents are keeping their lifestyle and throwing us under the bus. I need to start my life.

Is that what you want to do?

I don't have any other options.

Like other women, you could stay home and wait for the right man. You know what, let's pause. Let's do real work here. Where is this anger coming from? Tell me about your mother.

My whole life, I have wanted my mother's approval, and now I have failed her. But I don't want her life. I hate her life.

Maybe you are not failing her, but doing what she wished she could have done.

Maybe, the problem is that in the life she chose, her friends' daughters are married, and I am not.

Let's back up. Please describe your relationship with her when you were growing up.

I was my mother's favorite. I would go with her to run errands. I sat next to her in the passenger's seat, and watched her drive her blue Ford Galaxy. She held the center of the big steering wheel with her three fingers, wrapping her pinky around the edge. She always used the same coral nail polish. I would look at her, and she was the most beautiful woman in the world: her pale skin, green eyes and beautiful blonde wavy hair. She's not even five feet tall but always wore the highest heels she could tolerate. She was a master at dressing up. When she went out in the evenings, she wore Private Collection from Estee Lauder. Even after five children, she still had a tiny waist. I have a picture of her when I was a toddler, and she is wearing a bikini. I remember her gymnastics class. The group of women in their black leotards down to their hips and their pointy breasts from those firm brassieres. The teacher would clap and count as they repeated sets of exercises.

What else do you remember?

When we went shopping I asked if she liked certain shoes or a dress. I needed to understand what was pretty or ugly, elegant or tacky. Her approval was important to me, and I understood good taste was a matter of survival.

Why were you her favorite?

I was pretty, but not any kind of pretty, I looked like her. We are both short, have a straight nose and green eyes. Alexandra is pretty but she looks like my father's side of the family. When I was born, my mom was exhausted. She told me once, that when she was pregnant with me, she just wanted to shoot her stomach. My mother went to Catholic boarding school from the age of six, but she started taking the pill after I was born.

What did you do together? How did you relate?

She was busy with her friends, on the phone with her sisters, or playing bridge. She didn't cook or do chores. We had two live-in maids. In the afternoons, she would take naps. What I remember doing with her was watching television at night. She loved to watch detective shows like Columbo or Ellery Queen. The place where we have a sacred bond is the theater. She would take me to concerts. My dad would never go.

What is your most treasured memory with your mother?

My first trip to New York. When we were about to land, she made a drawing to explain streets and avenues. Her father lived in New York as a young man and took her for the first time when she was thirteen. She was excited to show us around. We went to touristic sites, museums, Central Park, but the most special thing was seeing 'A Chorus Line.' I was thirteen when I heard the song 'Hello twelve, hello thirteen, hello love.' My entire childhood, I took dance lessons and felt that that song was about me. It was the first time I understood what art could do.

Are you still your mother's favorite?

No, I am not. Two things changed everything forever and they happened at the same time. In the summer of 1978, my brother Gerard and I were sent to a summer camp on Orca's Island. My mother was having a baby girl, twelve years younger than me, and eighteen years younger than my eldest brother. When I came home after camp, I woke up from a dream. Fantasy died the day I carried Isabelle. I wanted a baby sister, but not a real one that pooped and peed. Alexandra and I became the helpers. On Sundays, the maids were off. We would take turns putting her to sleep. We became allergic to romance. No boyfriends for us, no kissing or holding hands. Sex made real babies.

How did this change your family?

I was dethroned, but I wasn't the only one. My eldest brother had to give up his room. The three of them shared one room and one bathroom. Shortly after Isabelle was born, Octavio left for a semester in Mexico City. Anthony, the second oldest, found a girlfriend and was always at her house. Alexandra went to a boarding school for two years. When she came back, I left. We were separated for four full years. My mother was always stressed out. The peace was gone. Isabelle was a sweet baby girl. It was like she had seven parents total. We all took care of her.

You said there were two things. What was the other one?

That same summer, my father lost his job. My grandfather, the entrepreneur, was fighting his brothers. When he became a widower, he started seeing the Wicked Witch of the West. They married when I was two years old. I never met my grandmother. The witch was a glamorous spender that built a thirty-five thousand square foot house and had jet set parties. The family didn't like her. When my great-grandmother died in 1975, the fighting began. There was a criminal complaint against my grandfather, my father, my aunts and their husbands in 1978. My father didn't know about it. My aunts and uncles escaped the chaos and spent a month in Colorado. My father drove to Nuevo Laredo as usual and was stopped at the checkpoint and taken to jail. He was there for a month. My mother never explained anything. She would wake up early and talk to lawyers on the phone all day. We didn't know what was happening. All we knew, was that we were not supposed to talk about this to anyone. That is when the prosperity ended.

How did this affect you?

It's affecting me now. My parents are not saving for our future or planning to leave us an inheritance. I am paying rent, while my girlfriends are given houses just for getting married.

But you are not married yet.

A friend of my mother's dad died. He gave his inheritance to his son-in-law instead of his own daughter. He thought if he left the money to her, she would have marriage problems, so he left everything to her husband. That is medieval.

Parents have the power of the purse. They use it to reward things they believe in. They are not rewarding your independence. They don't agree with what you are doing.

Let me explain to you the gap I am in. Milan Kundera wrote: Men are looking for a woman that doesn't exist anymore and women are looking for a man that doesn't exist yet. Men might say they want modern women, but fathers don't want modern daughters. How are we supposed to make the transition happen?

I don't think this is a collective issue. Let's talk about your father. How do you see him?

My father is a lord. He is handsome, strong, athletic and a man's man. He hunts, plays tennis and golf. He dresses well, always. Brown shoes before six and black shoes for the evening. He knows about wine and cigars. He has traveled everywhere twice.

What is your most treasured memory with him?
Well, let me think. We don't do much together. He is gone a lot.
Was he on the New York trip?
Yes, of course.
What do you remember about him?
He would run in Central Park and buy fresh fruit for breakfast.
Was there a special moment with him?
He took a nice picture of me having lunch at Tavern on the Green.
Let's try something else. What has he taught you?
If I exercise, he smiles, if I don't he frowns.
You need to be pretty to be loved. His love is conditional.
Everybody's love is conditional.
Does your mother make you feel the same way?
No. I don't think so. Well, she likes smart people.
Does she love you whether you are slim or not?
She is a woman. When I am fat she worries I will not find a man.
Are you dating anybody?
I see a handsome young prince who doesn't take me seriously.
Does he take anybody else seriously?
Not really. He's never had a serious girlfriend.
Why do you like him?
He is handsome, fit, sophisticated, well dressed.
Like your father?
Now that you mention it, yes, just like my father.
Do you see a pattern here?
I don't see anything.
Don't get defensive. The first man in your life is your father.
I know that. Do you think I am stupid?
Does your father do anything with you?
I told you he is busy.
There are other fathers who make time for their children.
They are losers who don't have better things to do.
Just share one treasured memory you have with him.
I have to think. Give me a minute.
Our time is up. I see two contradictions you need to think about.
You say you hate your mother's life but complain about not being married.
You are accomplishing more than just finding a man to take care of you,
you are taking care of yourself and following your dream of becoming a
writer. On the other hand, you think your father is wonderful, but besides
him being handsome, you can't come up with one special memory the two

of you share together? Relationships are about making connections not just looking good.

As I sit for a minute in the parking lot, I feel worse. I don't like this therapist. I am not coming back. Who the hell does he think he is? He is jealous of my father because he is ugly. His conclusions are simple, and I don't like the way he makes me feel. It's none of his business how I relate to my father.

Chapter 7.2   2002

After the attack, the border adapts to a new routine. Everybody schedules more time to cross the bridge. The interrogations are slow. You just got back from Morocco. You were there for two weeks. Everybody else canceled their travel. You got a tour guide just for you. There were few westerners in view. Before sunrise, you could hear the loud speakers from the hotel, calling Muslims to prayer. After that, you spent a few days in Paris. When you left Charles de Gaulle airport, there was tension. You had to take your shoes off. Before Christmas, a man attempted to detonate plastic explosives concealed in his shoes. In airports, people are not friendly anymore. Everything takes longer.

You go back to your routine after the long trip. Tomas can have his usual food. He had diarrhea for the entire trip. His little butt was red from the constant cleanings. You used up all the diaper rash ointment. Looking at the pictures, you see that the highlight for him was when you were riding camels in the desert. He was crying. You were singing to him. When you got off the camels, he realized it was all sand and started playing. It was a moment of pure joy.

For Christmas vacation, the maids left and did not come back. They were married to brothers and quarreled. Elliott makes fun of you for not handling the help better. You have a Masters in Organizational Development, but the strategies taught are directed at professionals. The woman who is helping you now is from the south of Mexico. She assures you that she can do all the work herself. You want to get her a visa to take her to San Antonio. It is not an option, because when she left her house years ago, her mother took her identification away, preventing her from leaving. You think it is too much work for one person, and she is lonely. You buy her a needlepoint kit. She spends the afternoons in the kitchen embroidering a grey fountain with birds. She mentions her sister is not happy at her job. You suggest she can come work for you. A few days later, the sister's employer calls screaming and accusing you of being a maid thief. These border women are tough.

As you spend time with your maid, she confesses that she is from Guatemala. She has not seen her son in years. She cannot go back. She came into Mexico by wrapping drugs on her legs, underneath her skirt. She cannot get a visa, because she is also an illegal immigrant in Mexico. She is a hardworking woman. Eventually, she leaves to work with her sister.

Now that Tomas walks around everywhere, you enroll him in a little Montessori school. Twice a week you sing, clap and play. He loves to see other babies, and you are desperate to talk to other mothers. He is more independent. Elliott and you talk about having another baby, because you want them close in age. Before spring begins, you are pregnant with your second child. It is April first the day you find out the gender. Elliott could not come to the appointment with you. For years, he plays pranks on you on April fool's day, this time you get him.

So, which one is it a boy or girl?
Honey, they're twins.
Oh shit!

He acts upset, but has to admit it is good. He plays the same prank on his father, mother, your father and mother. When you can talk about it you tell him: *It's a boy because I have worked most issues with my mother. I think you have more unresolved brother issues: first your grandfather and my grandfather, then your father and uncle, now you and your brother. We'll see what this pair of brothers have to teach us.*

People start asking you if you will try to have a girl and you reply: *I am not having any more babies period.* Motherhood does not come naturally to you. The move left you with no support system. You feel like those tropical plants with aerial roots that grow on trees and your roots have not reached the ground yet.

You go to the pediatrician to take Tomas for a regular check-up. Sitting in the waiting room, you get complimented for your pretty son. You feel obliged to say *Likewise,* even though you do not think the other baby is pretty. It bothers you the way his parents lovingly stare at him. You observe your thought, a gift from Buddhist meditation. Being pregnant awakens your own feelings of unworthiness, making you undesirable. You are jealous this woman is here with her husband and you are not.

You have been writing a local editorial on Sundays, mentioning Nuevo Laredo's shortcomings. Your criticism is constructive, and you use Monterrey as an example of how things can be improved if citizens get involved. You question the use of resources, but the level of honesty here is lower than where you come from. You complain about not having good universities and the limited cultural opportunities. The hate mail is overwhelming. You tell the owner of the newspaper, either they stop publishing the letters, or they stop publishing you. Once they stop, one of the local socialites pays to have her letter published in the other newspaper. You go to pick up your unpublished hate mail and sit in the parking lot crying. This bitter anger directed at you is hard to understand. Elliott suggests you call the person who wrote the meanest letter. You find her name in the white pages and call. *Hello! May I speak to the lady of the house?* It is easier to attack a faceless person than to attack an individual. You have a civilized conversation. She agrees that the contrast between Nuevo Laredo and Laredo, Texas is undeniable. Having the exact same weather, the filth and dust in Nuevo Laredo has to be attributed to bad government. You are tired of people attacking you for pointing out the obvious. You write an editorial with bigger words, intimidate the readers and the hate mail stops. They criticize you but read you. The proof is that you recommend a tiny Italian restaurant, and see with your own eyes how the owner closes the door in the Mayor's face. She cannot handle the demand created by your recommendation.

The one thing that simmers in your mind are the mixed feelings towards the Theriot family. All that hate is aimed at your last name. Nuevo Laredo is grateful to the family for creating businesses, but they look up to you as the responsible problem solvers. Somebody wrote to you: *You don't like the restaurants? Then open one yourself.* People assume things they do not know. Your resources are limited, in this family women never had a chance.

There are incidents that awaken your curiosity about your background. One day, you call a local store that sells Mexican crafts to ask about wood furniture. The woman who answers the phone calls the owner and says: *Don Chito's granddaughter is on the phone.* How does she know who you are? You only gave her your name. You know so little about your own genealogical tree that you married a third cousin.

Elliott mentioned there is a PhD thesis written about your grandfather, and you get a copy. It is written by Betsy Link, your grandfather's lawyer's wife. You ask your father if he knew about this document and he says: *It is all wrong.*

You read it. The title is *Spirit of Entrepreneurship: O.L. Theriot and the Twentieth Century Mexican Experience.* You dive into an unknown past. Mrs. Link worked with thirty file-drawers, litigation papers, depositions, financial statements and tapes. She interviewed forty subjects. The thesis starts with the historical background tracing your genealogical tree back to your great-great-grandfather, who was a merchant. Your great-grandfather came to Laredo, Texas, which was booming after the arrival of the new railroads in 1881. He first worked for the Volpe family and then started his own business in Nuevo Laredo selling sugar, rice and wheat by the sack. He met your great-grandmother Sara Hortense Rentrop, whose family came from Liberty, Texas. They moved to Nuevo Laredo because her father suffered from asthma. They got married in 1900. A few years later, during the Mexican Revolution, they moved to Laredo, Texas. Your grandfather and his brothers were sent to Peacock Academy in San Antonio. When things settled down, they moved back to Nuevo Laredo. Their big break came from a brewery distribution, and an ice plant they installed to provide ice to all the bars serving alcohol to Americans during Prohibition. With all that gain, they established a bank built in 1925. Then they had an oil mill and a soap factory. When they were building a new house on Victoria street, loans were not paid back, and your great-grandfather committed suicide on January of 1931, dying intestate. That is when your grandfather took over. He was a talented entrepreneur and made business grow. The family was united and wealth was distributed fairly until your grandmother died in 1963.

As you read about this distant past, the numbers and dollar values bore you. You want to know about people's lives, mostly the women, the unsung heroes, giving birth, rearing children and managing households. As you reflect, your belly grows. Elliot's grandfather died recently, you hire one of his nurses to help you with your second son.

You take Tomas to the Montessori Center in the mornings. It is located next to the Cathedral, which your grandfather built. You drop your baby off, for just an hour. You walk next-door and visit the church. It is white, a beautiful modern structure with a tall colorful stained-glass window in the entrance. The floors are black, and the benches are heavy and simple. There are six white sculptures on each side and more stained windows in between. There is a giant dove structure representing the Holy Spirit on top of the altar. You walk outside to the plaza covered with pecan trees. On the other side is your grandfather's grey brick mansion, a testament to time. Now here you are, living your life with your baby.

On the third day, you regret your decision.

Maybe this was not such a good idea.

I promise you he cries for two minutes. How are you doing?

I miss him so much. Your eyes get teary. Your bond is strong, and it is hard to let go, but he needs to have things to do and you need to prepare for the next baby.

Moving around gets harder with an infant and a big stomach. You understand that soon your proportions will go back to normal, but you feel deformed. You still visit Monterrey frequently. During the summer, when Elliott is hunting, you spend time at the beach. You are making a few friends and join a book club. It is refreshing to read literature. You have been reading journalism for years. You forgot literature is timeless, personal and slow. The first book you discuss is *The Picture of Dorian Gray*. It makes you homesick for the urban sophisticated lifestyle. You will now have a chance to read the books you did not read in high school. When commenting on certain parts of the book, two conversations sprout. There are those who read the book and those who saw the movie. You must be patient. Through this group you get invited to participate on the board of the new cultural center that is going to be built soon.

Now, two older women help you with the housework. One of them is studying to be a nurse, and the other used to work in a textile factory. The one who worked at a factory is in a relationship with her married neighbor. She is divorced and came from Guadalajara. She did not have any support and would leave her baby alone in her house to go to work. One day, she came back to find her baby on the floor. These are everyday border stories. A friend of yours, who has a dance studio, volunteers at the Nuevo Laredo prison. She tells you it is full of girlfriends or wives of criminals, most of them doing favors, ignorant of the fact that they were smuggling drugs across the border. Corruption chews on budgets for parks and education. This town is filled with those who are hunting for the American Dream.

As the summer comes to an end, you have lunch with your in-laws at a new restaurant. Tomas is obsessed with *Toy Story* and jumps from a chair with a hand in the air saying: *To infinity and beyooond!* Your mother-in-law says: *To think that now Tomas will be the big boy.* What is she talking about? He is your baby. You do not understand what she is saying.

You are scheduled for another C-section, and the birth day is chosen. This time you got the good room in the hospital, the one with the waiting room outside. Your mother and father come. Now you know what you are in for, but there is a new ingredient, the betrayal to your dear firstborn. When you come home from the hospital, you bring a gift to Tomas on behalf of the baby, as you were told, but your little boy has been dethroned. You will love the newcomer as much as you love him, but it hurts to see your bond bleed. Now, you understand why he is the big boy, he is huge compared to your newborn.

Tomas lives with his father upstairs for forty days, and it is a bonding time for them. Elliott's maternal grandmother dies and he takes Tomas to San Antonio for a few days. Elliott loses his three living grandparents and brings two children into the world. It is the circle of life. You live in the baby's room, and the nurse comes early in the morning and lets you rest. You breastfeed him, but your mother insists you do not have enough milk. You complement with formula to make sure he is not hungry. This baby is different. You do not have gazing moments. As soon as you are finished feeding him, you can put him in his crib. He is not as interested in being held. At night, he lies there and does not cry. His gaze is absent. The one thing he loves is water. He loves to be bathed. When you are in the dark exhausted, you know this too shall pass. You repeat a Buddhist mantra: *Everything changes, moment to moment, instant to instant, nothing lasts forever. Everything changes, moment to moment, instant to instant, nothing lasts forever. Everything changes, moment to moment, instant to instant, nothing lasts forever.*

The nurse is much older than you. She worked for Elliott's grandfather and has seniority over the maids. She is tall, heavy and wears eyeglasses. She arrives every morning at seven. She is a good cook. Elliott calls David *the attachment*; she is always carrying him. She changes the dynamic in the house, and there is another adjustment with the help. You now have Lety from the state of Hidalgo and Mine from the state of San Luis. These girls are both bilingual, they speak old Mexican dialects. One speaks Nahuatl, the other speaks Zapotec. They make a good team and last for a while, giving your home stability.

Now that the baby sleeps in the crib, Tomas is in a bed with rails on the floor. You tell your friend Blondie about your exhaustion and wanting to please Tomas. At night, you lie next to him, and when you think he is asleep, you slip out of his bed. He says: *Where are you going?* You get back in there and reply *Nowhere.* Blondie recommends a book called *Obedient parents, tyrant children.* The book has examples of parents like you. You try to set some boundaries. The first time you spank Tomas, he spanks you back. He is tough.

You have a small baptism for the baby. His name is David, which means beloved. Your family is here as well as and Elliott's family. Your house looks good, and you enjoy having people over. Now that you are done with the reproductive phase of your life, you can go back to being a normal person. What worries you is that David doesn't have daily bowel movements. The pediatrician suggests a suppository and syrup in his milk. They do not work.

Tomas is such a beautiful boy. You fear David is not going to be as beautiful. They are good looking in different ways. David is fair, has dark hair and blue eyes. He looks like a cherub. At night, after his bath, which is his favorite time of the day, you love drying him and covering his smooth pink skin with lavender lotion. Your breastfeeding ritual is not sacred anymore. Tomas is always around, demanding the same attention as always.

You now have some free time, you continue reading about your grandfather. The thesis explains how, when your grandmother died, he changed. He was invited to events by himself and did not include his brothers anymore. Many of his decisions were risky, and he started borrowing money faster than he could pay it back. His siblings were worried. He would go visit his friend Maurice in San Antonio and stay in his house. That is how he became involved with the Wicked Witch of the West. She had great taste and helped him with the design of the cathedral in Nuevo Laredo. She was twenty-three-years younger and married, but that did not stop him from pursuing her. According to this thesis, he had a five-year love affair with her. When Maurice divorced her, she looked for him, and they got married in March of 1968. She moved to Mexico City, leaving her children behind.

Your father never talked about this, probably out of shame. Once your grandfather became a widower, he broke free and decided it was time to play. By then the businesses were entangled. There were documents that proved it was all his, and documents that proved that the five brothers owned everything in equal parts. That was the Mexican way of doing business. When there was risk involved, he would take it in his own name, but when there were good earnings, they were distributed fairly among them. When he built *Casa Arabesque*, the family grew apart. It was a thirty thousand square foot mansion inside a three-acre lot built at the top of a hill on Bosques de las Lomas, the most exclusive residential area in Mexico City.

Chapter 7.3   **2012**

Elliott and Beatrice have been members of an organization for young CEOs for ten years. They offer small support groups called Agoras. A few years ago, Beatrice helped organize a lunch for the spouses' Agoras in San Antonio. She could not join them, because she was living in Laredo. Now she can. Beatrice works with the administrator: they get a list, make calls and gather a group of women to go over the norms. They get trained by a moderator and have a rehearsal of how the meeting is supposed to go.

The Agora consists of women from different backgrounds. The one thing they have in common, is that they are all married to type A successful men. Most of them were not born in San Antonio. They meet for four hours and follow the communication protocol: ask questions and share. There is a confidentiality agreement which allows them to share experiences as they build trust. The women feel constrained, but these restrictions make the conversation efficient. Beatrice cannot tell them what to do, judge them, offer advice, give guidance, or cheer them on. She can only ask questions or share. They observe themselves and learn this new form of communication. When there is an opportunity to present a personal matter, Beatrice jumps at the chance. She needs guidance on how to deal with her autistic son for the summer. There is another mother with a special needs child, and she shares her experience. She feels their support without judgment. They learn to be active listeners.

As they build bonds, they talk about things that matter. In their group, there are two locals who struggle with trust. They know the same people. Being an import gives Beatrice the freedom to reinvent herself. Nobody has preconceived notions of who she is supposed to be. Beatrice discovers the more they share, the more their similarities come through. They worry about the same things: health, love and money.

Beatrice's book club also meets once a month. This group is made up of local women who have known each other for years and have the same network. Their children go to the same schools as well. This is Beatrice's first opportunity to enter people's homes. Every month there is a hostess who suggests the book and has them over for breakfast. When Beatrice arrives, and the door is opened, she feels part of an American movie. She has seen these red brick homes in films her whole life: the plant-framed walkway to the white door, the windows with shutters on the sides, the wood stairway, and the den next to the kitchen.

The reunion starts with anecdotes, personal cautionary tales. Beatrice cannot interrogate. She is socially blind. Through observation, she figures out who the natural leaders are. Everything else is hard to decipher. Their communication is polite, and their comments are politically correct. When they gossip, Beatrice does not know who they are talking about. The subject matter is the same everywhere: death, corruption or love scandals. Beatrice cannot jump this rope. The beat is staccato, detached, no drama, no details, to the point. There is a repetitious phrase said again and again: *Bless her heart.* Beatrice cannot tell if this is mercy or mockery. She participates but she does not know if she is saying the right thing.

As she hears these women talk about their families and recipes, their dedication is overwhelming. There are no full-time maids in this community. These mothers do it all themselves, with part time help. Where are the college drunken-skinny-whores from the movies? It must be a seasonal beast who inhabits sororities and becomes extinct after graduation.

After half an hour of updates, they talk about the book, the island Beatrice likes to swim to. Books are the excuse to get to know each other, the hook to talk about things that matter. Beatrice is usually an avid reader, but these books are not only in English, they are American. The language is not the problem. It is the subject that is not familiar to her. She is *Yes Woman* and reads with the intention of understanding. The writing is direct, casual, colloquial and blunt, but the realities are foreign. Beatrice tries to blend in, take part in the discussion, but fears her observations are too different. She is a foreigner, an outsider. She grew up hearing American music, watching American television shows, and now she gets to read American books, but she has an accent. When books are recommended, her suggestions are off. A book list is a pulse difficult to read. They choose their own kind. Beatrice is an observer. When the conversation flows toward politics, one of them says: *The best way to figure out what is happening in politics is to watch Saturday Night Live. The first sketch determines the political course.* Beatrice needs to watch the show to understand Democrats and Republicans.

After feeding her sense of belonging, working her tolerance to this new transition, she finds the strength to go to the next stage with David. Beatrice has been following a British doctor, Andrew Wakefield, known for the Autism MMR Vaccine controversy. *Thoughtful House* in San Antonio was his original organization. They focus on gastrointestinal research. Last year, they became the Johnson Center for Child Health and Development in Austin. The doctor is gone, but they are committed to the gut-brain connection. David gets an appointment.

Beatrice drives David to the new clinic in Austin. They are given a comfortable room. While David plays, Beatrice fills out a long questionnaire as quickly as possible, afraid he will wander around. A group of experts comes. They see him play and ask more questions. The nutritionist gives her a list of approved gluten free products and educates her on the kinds of food he can have. They will follow the diet. Beatrice drives back feeling like a good mother again.

The next Saturday, she gives David a magnesium supplement until his stomach is emptied out. They start a twenty-one-day antibiotic treatment for his gut bacteria and then follow the diet like a new religion. He gets a bright red rash behind his knees. Beatrice calls her friend the healer to be assured this is good. When the body is detoxing too fast, the expulsion concentrates on armpits, inner elbow and behind the knees. It is as if these gut fungi had a colony inside his stomach. Beatrice is proud for kicking these bacteria out of her son's intestines.

As winter ends and there is no threat of another freeze, Beatrice fixes her micro front yard. The gardener cleans it up, takes out what froze and plants roses and a sago palm in the corner. With all the stairs, their miniature old Pomeranian's knees are hurting. *Bolita* belonged to her sister-in-law. They got her when she was a nine-year-old dog and now she is thirteen. She walks with Beatrice in the mornings and enjoys the fresh air. They keep each other company during the day. Her night coughing is getting bad. When *Bolita* gets her hair done, she looks like a little lion.

Once a month, their old Mexican nanny hops on a bus and comes to help with the boys for a weekend, so Beatrice can get away with Elliott. Tomas and David miss her, but Beatrice misses her the most. She worked with them for six years and left a void, forcing them into a new family dynamic. Taking care of David is challenging. Beatrice has not been able to find the right help to feel at peace. He is not small anymore, and now that he runs out the door, she gets nervous. He still wakes up in the middle of the night. One Saturday morning, after being with him since four a.m., Beatrice falls asleep, and he escapes. After a short nap, she wakes up to find out he is gone. Elliott did not notice that he had found the keys, opened the door and left. Beatrice finds him a block away. A police car is there. She gets a dirty look from the woman who reported him. Beatrice feels judged for being a careless mother. She walks back home with David. The officer comes inside and sees the family pictures that prove this is his home.

During the recession, educational programs were cut. David does not get to go to summer school. Beatrice researches options for summer vacation. She finds an occupational therapy center with a swimming pool. Maybe there they can teach him not to take his swimming suit off. It is expensive and can only take him for three hours in the afternoon. It is far away and takes up her whole day. The first day, when she picks him up five minutes late, the robust woman at the front desk says: *Do you see that clock? Starting tomorrow, you will be charged two dollars for every minute you are late.* She is never late again.

Beatrice visits her parents in Monterrey for a weekend. Now, she has to fly home. She waits for her flight and looks at sunglasses in the duty-free shop. She notices a couple of women, a mother and daughter, speaking Spanish loudly. When she approaches the cashier, she cannot tolerate their obnoxious volume and asks them to keep it down. The daughter turns and screams at her: *You don't get to hush us. This is a private conversation, and it is none of your business.* Beatrice replies: *If you want to keep it private speak softly. The whole store can hear you. You are not in your home. This is a public space.* As an American citizen, Beatrice is embarrassed by these loud Mexican women, because she is not one of them anymore.

While in Monterrey, Beatrice spends an afternoon with Blondie. She picks her up at her parents' house to go to the Country Club and have lunch. As they drive, Blondie notices the car does not have any gas.

We can go to the gas station, it's ok.

Absolutely not. These men are just sitting there doing nothing. I am not supposed to know if my car has gas. Blondie tells her guard to come with the chauffeur and pick up the car, fill it up while they eat and drop it off. This incident would have gone unnoticed by Beatrice, but now she cannot see this as normal anymore.

As they eat, Blondie dives into the local gossip, but Beatrice cannot follow her train of thought. She has forgotten people's names and faces. She has not lived here for twelve years now. The waiter brings her freshly squeezed lime juice for her club soda, and she thanks him enthusiastically. Blondie suggests she should not exaggerate. It is inappropriate. Beatrice tries to talk about her life in San Antonio, but Blondie gets distracted. Beatrice does not talk about her flawed child. The less she speaks of him the more normal she feels. Blondie brags about her perfectly developed and socially functional children. Beatrice listens. As Beatrice hears Blondie talk about her life, a life she knew well, it dawns on her that she is becoming an American. Beatrice's family is American, and this is not temporary. She looks at her friend and feels sad. They are different now. This friendship is like a balloon that she holds onto because it makes her feel young and hopeful. If she lets go it will float away.

When Beatrice goes back home, she gets the local hangover. As soon as Elliot goes to Laredo and the boys leave for school, she loses her anchor again and fantasizes about being a local somewhere else, in another life, in another time. She knows she is not the first to come and start from scratch. Her great-grandfather came to the United States to find a better life. Her grandfather went back to Mexico to build a bigger business. Her father grew up in the United States and left, escaping the Korean draft in 1950, and met her mother. Beatrice came to a boarding school in New York. Back and forth, back and forth, back and forth. Other immigrants cannot do this because of the distance, the language, the cost. It is not until Beatrice experiences this uproot happening inside her, that she suffers a deep transformation taking place.

On a Wednesday night, they go as a family to have dinner at a Mexican restaurant. They eat *antojitos* while listening to romantic Mexican music. She drops off Elliott and David at the house. It is the Fourth of July, she drives Tomas to see the fireworks. She parks close to downtown, where they can watch the colorful explosions in the sky. That is when it hits her. She starts crying. Beatrice has celebrated the Fourth of July many times, just as she has celebrated Bastille Day on July the fourteenth. This time she feels the abyss. Her son is celebrating his Independence Day, and she is not. The Mexican Independence is on September sixteenth. Mexicans celebrate by screaming: "¡Viva México! ¡Que Viva! ¡Viva México! ¡Que viva! ¡Viva México! ¡Que viva!" Patriotism can only be taught once. The second time is betrayal.

She is ashamed of the Mexican-Americans who do not speak Spanish or English well. She makes an effort to stay fully Mexican and fully American without mixing them up, but this is schizophrenia. In Mexico she feels American, in the United States she feels Mexican. She now appreciates those years stuck on the border and the sense of belonging she had.

At the end of the summer, their house in Laredo, Texas is sold and they can now look for a house in San Antonio. Beatrice searches on the internet. Real estate and interest rates are at an all-time low. She has to stay in the same area because of the schools. Most houses are traditional and old. There are affordable houses in a lower price range, but her dream is to find a modern house, like the one they built in Nuevo Laredo. She finds one and makes an appointment.

The house is on an acre lot, with two gates facing the adjacent streets, one in the front and another in the back. It is modern, all off-white, limestone floors and grey doors, windows and awnings. When Beatrice enters, she is intimidated by the décor. The house, shaped like a horseshoe surrounds an interior patio with a swimming pool. The curtains are custom-made. The kitchen is full of light, windows everywhere and an endless yard in the back. The master bedroom has His and Her bathrooms. The boys' bedrooms share a bathroom, and the living area by the kitchen is spacious. As she drives back home, she gets excited thinking of David having a private swimming pool where he can swim naked, and a huge backyard for Tomas's new dog.

A month goes by, and Beatrice gets a call from the real estate agent saying the price was lowered again. She is bold enough to say: *We are only interested in it if she takes our townhouse.* The magic word is the name of the architect. It was the same architect who remodeled the modern house and built the condominiums. They make a deal and swap houses.

The move is set for December, two days before the world is coming to an end, according to a Mayan Calendar. For the swap, they get a moving truck, the carpets get washed, and the refrigerators are cleaned with Clorox. Beatrice gets twenty minutes alone and following the advice of a healer, she blesses her house. The three previous owners left in the middle of a divorce. She consoles herself thinking they were all second marriages. She will be fine, she thinks. She opens all doors and windows, rings a bell loudly in every room to move the energy around. She sets an intention: for the dining room, family times and good food; for the bedrooms, quiet and restorative sleep; for the swimming pool fun and safety. As she closes the doors and windows, the movers come in with their furniture.

After only twenty-four hours, Elliott's sister comes in with an expensive remodeling proposal which Beatrice rejects. It bothers her that Elliott's family perceives this property as part of their domain. The boys are thrilled with their new space, and they get ready for the arrival of a Jack Russell Terrier. They are invited to a Christmas party to meet their neighbors on the block. They are welcoming. Beatrice is eager to meet the couple next door, Spanish speaking doctors.

Beatrice wants to understand the commotion over the end of the world. She researches the myth. The first theory is that the world is finishing the fourth Mayan sun, a five-thousand year-long cycle. The final sun is made of clay and the beginning sun is made of gold. The second theory is that on December - for the first time in twenty-six thousand years - the sun rises to cross the galactic equator, with the Earth aligning itself with the center of the galaxy. Beatrice prays that whatever lies ahead, she can accept what is and find the courage to change.

Chapter 8.1   1993

I am sitting in my office at the museum, going over some material for the volunteers, and my secretary tells me I have a call from The Compass. It is one of the owners.

Hello is this Beatrice?
Yes, hello. To what do I owe this honor?
I have been reading your column and I have an offer.
I am flattered.
When can you come over to talk?
You tell me.
How about tomorrow at 10:00. Does that work?
Yes, it does. See you then.

I hang up, bursting with happiness and walk to my colleague's office to tell her about the call. During the day, I call my sister Alexandra to share the news. I wonder what kind of opportunity he is talking about. The next morning, I go to The Compass. It has been a long time. When I enter the office, I see it is just as big as Mr. Allan's office but looks to the west. Mr. Randolph Reed is a short, older man, with white hair, a big tummy and a kind smile.

Come in. Nice to meet you. Take a seat.

Likewise.

I write the daily editorial and could use some help.

You want me to help you write the editorial?

We would collaborate. I would train you.

I would be honored, but I have never written editorials.

I need new angles, somebody to bounce ideas off with.

How often do you write? I have a full-time job at the museum.

The editorial is published five days a week.

What Mr. Reed writes is the opinion of the newspaper. It is published in the upper right corner of the opinion page, and it is signed by *Ombudsman*. My father reads it every morning, and when he has lunch with his friends, they talk about it. I am a twenty-five-year-old woman and was chosen to collaborate. There is a big audience.

Every day, I read the editorial. Most of the time, he questions decisions made by the authorities. The subjects are out of my league. What can my contribution be? I decide to make a pitch. I suggest we write about how during the winter many old relatives die. Mr. Reed likes the subject, and I present a draft. He edits it, and it gets published the next day. Then, the following day, we need another big idea and then the next. We schedule appointments over the phone, and I ask questions. In the beginning, my questions are simple, I don't know how the government is divided and what each bureaucrat does. Mr. Reed knows these people and has lunch with them.

I have noticed the most successful writer in the opinion page says he has four readers and you say you have two. Why do you make that joke?

It started a long time ago and I kept it.

I don't think it fits. The other guy, fills his space with jokes, you are more serious, it doesn't match your style. After that conversation, he never mentions his two readers again. That change reassures me. Mr. Reed reads what I write and one day he calls.

Something about your writing bothered me, and I couldn't figure it out, but I got it. It's your punctuation. All your sentences and paragraphs are the same size. You rarely use exclamation points or other forms of punctuation. You should try changing it. It will improve the rhythm and make your text visually attractive. This feedback makes me see my texts differently.

As I get more involved with the editorials, working for the museum becomes less important, and my patience with the volunteers evaporates. Our writing team work is improving. and I feel confident enough to immerse myself in this ghostly existence and resign from the art museum. This is now my only job. My income and responsibility increase. I move to a two-bedroom apartment at the outskirts of the mountain, with a splendid view of San Pedro. I use one room as an office. The calls change to meetings. I could not possibly be up on the top floor of the newspaper, with the Gods of Olympus. I am given a space in an office outside the newspaper. I learn more tricks to ignite ideas. The starter is quotable quotes. When there is a subject to tackle, we rely on millenary wisdom to make a statement. The pseudonym *Ombudsman* is appropriate: it is the voice of the people, and arguments are presented the way a lawyer would debate in court. Sometimes there is not much to say, and the space needs to be filled anyway. We need to elaborate and elaborate, without being boring.

It is amazing to see Mr. Reed's mind at work. It is a blank page ready to be filled. We choose a subject and make a statement by building one thought at a time. It is not a tennis match. I am a wall he plays against. I bounce his own ideas back to him. He thinks out loud, and I interrupt his thought process and ask the things that are unclear. My participation begins to matter. One time he says: *If you don't get this, nobody will.*

Mr. Reed's mind and information are a big knot that we undo one string at a time. I am the filter that distills his complex understanding and translates his ideas into simple language. The hardest part is to figure out what we think. The cheat sheet is today's paper. We choose a piece of information or a politician's declaration. That is the starting point, but the goal is finding the right angle. The conversations are intense, and we find the thesis in the exchange.

For months, I don't call Mr. Reed by his name. As time goes by, he insists I use his first name. At first, I do not know anything about him and get few glimpses of his personal life: pictures of his children, ends of phone conversations, travel plans, lunch confirmations and complaints about politicians. It is surprising to learn that he is the older brother. Mr. Alan Reed is the public persona, the face of The Compass, but Mr. Randolph Reed likes his anonymity. When we finish writing, he leaves early.

This is an exciting time for the Compass. Their dream team has such synergy that one newspaper is not enough for their talent. They create a new publication for Mexico City. The secret to their success is their education. Both brothers went to the University of Texas and learned journalism the American way. In Mexico, there are restrictions. The State controls the paper supply. If a newspaper publishes a story they are not supposed to, there is no more paper. The Reeds are about to change journalism in Mexico City.

As the new publication hits the streets, newspaper carriers' union refuse to deliver it. The owner and writers get out and sell the paper on the street themselves and get all the free publicity they need. Our pieces are published in Mexico City while they figured out the right writers for the new product.

When I became a journalist, I believed that the press was the fourth power, after legislative, executive and judicial. Press conferences reinforced that idea. The more I write, the more I see it as entertainment. We are not making decisions. We are putting words together to fill a space day after day. Politicians and business men make plans, turn them into a reality and then share them with the press. We do not touch the creative process. We quote statistics, studies, old ideas, but we do not make anything new. We are not sources. We follow reality wherever it goes and describe it.

There are rare occasions when I have the feeling that we are changing the course of people's lives. I feel proud of arguing something meaningful when NAFTA is being negotiated. There is a proposal in favor of changing the legal name of the Mexican United States to only Mexico. I suggest we compare this to having a name and a nickname, and how it is good to have a proper name for formal introductions. I get the privilege of hearing somebody use this argument in conversation.

I did not understand why Mr. Randolph was not excited to have this privilege. Now, I see why he is tired. Every morning we start with nothing. It does not matter how we feel, or if we have something to say or not, we have to come up with an idea and develop it. It is a blessing to have my ideas published, but it is also a curse. I am an invisible buffoon. The word yesterday or tomorrow does not exist in journalism; there is only today. We create the illusion of a unique product, but there is nothing new under the sun. We repeat the same ideas over and over, give out old information disguised as new. There are occasions when we get to participate in something that matters. We sit in our pulpit and express an opinion with eloquence. There is no science, no research, no authority. We scratch the surface and create the illusion of depth.

With time, being a ghost writer is not enough. I am not supposed to tell anyone what I do. I suggest to Mr. Randolph writing something in the editorial page with my name on it. To make me feel confident, he complimented me. Now, he insists I am not ready and he needs to review what I write. He gets the fame, the glory and a life: wife, children, house and business. Being close to fifty, he has made the big decisions but feels confined by them. I can tell he envies that my life lies ahead, but he does not know uncertainty fills my days with anxiety. I am not going to be here much longer. My bag of tricks is full, my hunger for recognition is a gut grumble.

Mr. Reed has a comfortable life but is not free. He has to write the column daily and is tired of it. He is included in important gatherings but is just one of many leaders in the community. When I was in the newsroom, we would joke saying there is no life after The Compass, it is a media emporium. I have no options.

My personal life is like a treadmill. I walk endlessly facing a wall headed nowhere. I go out with a couple of guys. Among journalists, my name is getting out. A local news anchor asks me to dinner. At the restaurant people recognize him. I make fun of how he is always posing, assuming people are looking at him. As he turns I say: *Camera two!* He is also notorious for going out with lots of different women. I call myself *Miss Summer* and he corrects me: *My dear you are Spring.* He is implying his rotation level is faster; I will not last until summer.

Swimming three times a week, I spot a couple of eligible young bachelors at the pool. I go out with Frank, but he leaves for a Masters in Los Angeles. There is an anthropologist who asks me out, but he was misinformed about my family's economic situation and leaves to pursue a real heiress. I see a computer genius once in a while, but he is a workaholic. There is a guy from Mexico City here for a couple of months and he takes me out, but eventually leaves.

As a single person, it is hard to know when options deteriorate. I have an older cousin who is popular. She explains the dilemma. *Many of my friends had one or two options, and made a choice. I had four or five options and thought more would always come. One day, the options dwindled.* I am already there. All the single guys are now a gang of men set in their ways, not willing to share their life with another. I am beginning to consider dating divorced or younger men.

Whenever I see the reporters from The Compass, they make subtle comments about my ability, suggesting that the opportunities I get are due to my background or looks. I resent the implications. Mr. Randolph chose me before we met. My background does not help, it actually interferes with what I do. When I was a reporter, a woman I know would ask that I not be sent to her press conferences. She felt more comfortable dealing with the other reporters. Why is it that people who were not born into privilege always assume that true talent can only come from shortcomings?

The news anchor invites me to participate in a televised debate he moderates on Sundays. When other participants see me, they assume I am there as a special guest. When I finally speak up, they are impressed with what I have to say. I do not see why brains and looks are mutually exclusive when it comes to women. My looks can be threatening in my professional life, and my brains are a menace in my personal life. Other pretty women are smart, but they hide it. I stopped doing that a while ago.

My working relationship with Mr. Randolph happens mostly on the phone, but I have noticed on days when I am dressed up, because I am doing something after work, my appearance is distracting to him. I will not complain. I have heard my mother explain how men have stopped looking at her; that neglect brings her pain. I struggle to understand why it is hard for men to take pretty women seriously. Still, I would not dare look ugly; the idea that my appearance determines my value is deeply ingrained in my reptilian brain.

My work has become a dead end, so my boss gives me a break. Every year, he gets invited to the State of the Union. He has been there dozens of times and this time sends me to represent him. For years this happened on the first day of September. This year, it takes place on the first of November. It is a Mexican ritual in which the whole nation renders tribute to the President. This report needs to be given to congress, but nowhere does it specify that it has to be read.

The day comes. I fly to Mexico City early in the morning. A car picks me up at the airport and takes me to congress. There is an army of bodyguards. I am given a special pass, go in to find my seat. It is madness! Both floors are full of suits. Every single powerful sector of the population is here, a diverse entourage. It really is an homage to Mexican presidentialism, a reign of six years. This year is special because it is the fifth report Carlos Salinas de Gortari is giving, and it is time for him to choose his successor, which he will announce next month. Once the successor is known, the whole system is put into place to make a safe transition. The moment when the crown and scepter are handed down is the vulnerable period of the system. It is the dictatorship of a party. Power is absolute but ends after six years. Today, we salute the present king, but in a couple of weeks the crowd will scream *Le roi est mort, vive le roi!*

A journalist, sitting close to me, asks which newspaper I represent. When I say it is The Compass, he asks for my name. I feel like I was caught cheating on an exam. It is not me who should be sitting in this chair, but there can be no empty seats in the King's court. I feel uncomfortable. I am not the only one who was sent to substitute for somebody. A woman sitting to my left falls asleep. The reading of the report is long and boring. I take notes to summarize the content, trying to find the right angle.

As soon as it ends, I go out to find my chauffeur, drive to the airport to go back to the newspaper to write. While on the plane, I review the event, and reflect on what just happened. My suggestion is to do something creative. Halloween just happened, I suggest we refer to the report as a costume party. Mr. Reed loves the idea, and we play with it, make up costumes, giving some a treat and others a trick. He supplies the context and information.

No matter how hard we work or how good the piece, the product has a lifespan of twenty-four hours. It only matters today. Tomorrow it is used to line bird cages or clean windows. Whatever is on newsprint, is not published to last. What we do is misinform. We talk about what is visible, measurable, and scientifically provable, but that fades. What is timeless, what matters is the subtext, the essence of any experience. Journalism is transient and can never get deep. It is not meant to.

Working with Mr. Reed has given my self-esteem a boost. He appreciates my ideas and values my opinion, - a true mentor and teacher. He has taught me not just to think but to reason. One day he says:

You are really special.

You are too.

No, there are many like me, but not many like you.

His comment might be based on my determination to become a writer. He was born into journalism and joined the family business.

In order to become a writer, I need to believe that what I have to say matters. Coming up with ideas, hiding behind somebody's reputation makes me feel safe, but it is suffocating. I cannot do this much longer. The networking is not mine, and a lot of the information is not accessible to me, but I have learned the craft of the editorialist. I would rather do something mediocre and sign it with my own name, than continue to be a ghost. This space will never be mine, and I will never get the credit.

Chapter 8.2   2003

There is some economy in having a second child. You had the crib, the changer and the rocking chair, and you were already in this business of having a nursery. What does not work well for you is that both boys want your attention. You still have help. They keep the house clean and the meals coming, but you have two hands, two eyes and two ears, and use them in unison. You cannot divide your attention in perfect halves.

Your household reaches a high efficiency level. The curtains are installed, even the ones in the living room. The garden is growing and the backyard does not look abandoned anymore. Most rooms have furniture in them. Your dream was to have a house in Monterrey, to catch up with your peers, but it will never happen. Another world is evolving one hundred and fifty miles away. They are at another stage of life.

You continue to have experiences that give your last name a new meaning. One of the ladies in your book club tells you: *Here in Nuevo Laredo you are the highest form of royalty.* This statement isolates you. You were vaccinated against self-importance at fifteen in your boarding school. When you met real blue-blooded east coast Manhattanites, your sense of importance vanished for a lifetime. You understood that outside of Mexico you are *a Mexican,* and it is not something to be proud of. There are layers of royalty. If you are at the top of this pyramid, it has to be a small triangle. This imposed status separates you from others.

In the afternoons, before you sit to write, you drop off your two maids with your two sons at Nuevo Laredo's country club. The locals sit together and chat. Their judgmental eyes follow you. Some may assume you feel superior for not staying. You do it because you do not know anybody. You are desperate to make friends. Your brain analyzes friendship. You met your childhood friends in school. You studied together seven hours a day, five days a week, for eight years. The first hypothesis is that friends do things together. You know that is not enough. What seals the deal is friends belong to a group and have friends in common. You cannot decode local gossip. You do not know the protagonists and cannot follow the stories. Strangers' scandal is not juicy. The other ticket in is having a local husband, which you do not have.

You observe the locals in Nuevo Laredo. The majority of women have only a high school education and few have jobs. Their hair is longer, they wear skirts or dresses in brighter colors. They love to talk about cooking recipes and their children's accomplishments as if they were their own. It took you years to decipher belonging codes in Monterrey, now you have to start from scratch. Belonging to the local royals is not a bridge but a river.

You do aerobics in the mornings and try to network after class. You attend a weekly meditation session and chat afterwards. The only group where you are an insider is your book club. You find the fastest relationships are built by reading the same books. Your authority grows as you read, take notes and research authors. You meet once a month in someone's house. There is tea and coffee, cake and cookies. The conversation starts with gossip. Strange things are happening in Nuevo Laredo. The new Mexican president has ignored organized crime. It is becoming a parallel force, like ivy on a wall. The small-town crooks were killed and after almost ten years of free international trade, there are more trailers crossing the border every day. Groups of masked men are seen in dark cars at odd hours.

A friend took her baby to the emergency room in the middle of the night. She was stopped by armed men who said this is their town at night.

My son went out to get some tacos and had a horrible accident. There was a chase, someone crashed into him and turned his car over.

There is a house in my street filled with men only, they could possibly be from the Pacific Coast. The new mafia is not from here. They are coming from other places, and they have no respect for us.

Topless joints and bars have to pay a share to stay open. If they don't pay, they run the risk of having their business burned.

There is a new student in school whose mother drives a Jaguar. His father owns one single Blockbuster. The numbers don't add up.

Do you remember that new sushi bar they opened with bells and whistles? It was burned down last week. They were laundering money.

Speculations multiply. This dark force invades the city, a strange gargoyle that comes alive at night and crawls back into a black hole as the sun comes out.

You sit on the terrace, around a teak table outside your room. The spring breeze blows your hair. The tall bamboos whisper in the wind. The ivy begins to climb the ashlars inch by inch. A pair of swallows work hard to build their nest with twigs and leaves for the summer. You are like that mother swallow, working hard to establish this home for your husband and two boys. You improvise, uncertain of what course to choose.

With time, you understand. Your lack of belonging is grounded in your family. As you go about your business in Laredo, Texas having lunch, walking in the mall or at the country club, you meet the Theriot clan. After reading about your grandfather's life, you can see how greed cracked all bonds. You had hoped that marrying another Theriot would heal the situation, but it worsened it. The sharp edge that cuts the deepest is Elliott. He is not fully embraced by your family and neither are you by his. You are the most affected party, now that you are here. The biggest fight was between the two lions, Elliott's grandfather and your grandfather. His own fraternal commentaries pop up: *My father has real money not like yours.*

Marrying a Theriot, dressed in white in a church, having a nice house and two pretty babies was not enough to win your mother's approval. After years of writing for the newspaper, your mother still does not read your editorials. You cannot share your accomplishments, they make her jealous. You cannot share your challenges, they make her worry.

You are reading literature. This awakens your soul. You can leave this town, this place, this motherhood jail and go to Macondo with Garcia Marquez, to India with Arundhati Roy and to the British countryside with Jane Austen. When you read a good book, everything is real. It is the synthesis of what is true. Human interactions are built with small talk, glass bridges. In books, writers address issues that matter. You had read the news daily for years. Now, you see how they misinform by packaging events. As you read *Hamlet* you see how an heir escaped his responsibility, just like your father. Years ago, when you sat at the movie theater with your mother watching *The Lion King,* she sobbed. Disney based this story on *Hamlet.* Simba and Hamlet are royalty. Their uncles took over. Their fathers died. They were sent away. They fought their uncles, but Simba had a happy ending and Hamlet died. While books penetrate human stories lived and relived through plot, conflict and resolution, newspapers are a factory of blocks stamped with names, dates and places.

Your source of belonging comes from your little boys. Tomas is getting funnier. He mispronounces things. After his shower, when you brush his wet hair you tell him: *You are so handsome.* The next morning at breakfast, his father carries him, and he grabs his dad's face with both hands saying: *You are so handsome, Dad.* While he watches a bear movie, he places his air rifle next to him, to feel safe. Elliott does not like to go to the movies, so you build a good DVD collection. You have nature, adventure and science films: *The Great Barrier Reef, Dolphins, Blue Planet, The Living Sea,* and *Africa The Serengeti.* Tomas watches them over and over.

Now that you have two boys, instead of one, you lose mobility. Your regular visits to Monterrey are not as frequent. You still meet your friends monthly for lunch at a hip restaurant, hear stories about their teenagers going off to boarding schools. With laser vision, you scan their fashion statements to update your attire. Your conversation is not clever. Your observations are outdated. As you sit with the right group at the right restaurant, a childhood friend passes by and asks: *What are you doing here?* With an accusatory tone, she suggests you are now taking a place that no longer belongs to you. You are like a child sitting on the beach sinking into the sand, determined not to move.

There is a new routine at home. You all have breakfast together. You drop Tomas off at his morning Montessori school, then walk with David in the stroller and the dog by your side. While you revise your "to do" list you look at David. There is a corridor next to the kitchen. The sliding glass door overlooks the outside deck. David sits there, on a little rug and plays with his toys. He has a plastic spiral tube with five colored balls. He does not drop them through the tube, he bounces one, over and over and over. That gesture makes you anxious. When you sit him in the den, he grabs the ball and bounces it over and over and over. You can recognize that as autistic behavior. When you were a teenager, you watched a movie about an autistic child called *Son Rise* on public television. The film told of a mother determined to engage with her autistic son. As he bounced the ball obsessively, she sat by him, mirroring his motion. When he spun a plate, she spun her plate. She locked herself in the bathroom for hours, determined to connect with him by doing what he was doing. These images are crisp in your mind, and fear invades you. You hide the balls. Out of sight, out of mind. When it is time for David to go play, clap and sing in the afternoon classes at the Montessori school, his behavior is different. *Every child is unique* you hear from other mothers. He crawls. There is no glimpse of him trying to stand or walk. He has few words but he is normal. You show him cards with images and repeat the names. He is distracted. *Don't worry about it. He'll do everything eventually.*

You feel disconnected from Nuevo Laredo, but your children help you carve out a place for them. Through them you meet other mothers. You pray for a good friend and find her. You first see her at a museum conference, then at the Buddhist meditations, and then at the Montessori School. You approach her: *We should have coffee sometime.* One day, after dropping the kids off, you have breakfast together. You talk about books and know your friendship has a strong foundation.

You feed your soul with walks, books and meditation. In the spring afternoons, you tend to your new garden, watering the young trees. In the patio, you have three blossoming camellias in big pots. Inside the living room, there are two tall corn plants, their buds give the space a sweet spring scent when blooming. Outside the living room, there is a trio of sago palms, and a screen of tall bamboos. Outside your bathroom there are three ponytail palm trees. On the terrace by your bedroom, there are a couple of yellow and green crotons plants that barely survived the winter. Behind the television room is a row of purple agapanthus. In front of the main door, there is a small pond filled with water lilies and a pair of orange koi fish.

Your father-in-law brakes his shoulder in a skiing accident, and your summer trip is canceled. This gives you the opportunity to join your family on a cruise to celebrate your father's seventieth birthday. You leave the first week of August. Before you board the ship, you hear the news of a confrontation in Nuevo Laredo between the cartels. It happened in the middle of the night, on a main avenue. Bazookas were fired. The conflicts have been escalating.

The cruise is a perfect place to be with a group. You gather for meals and wander on your own. As you sit having breakfast, you observe your siblings with their husbands and wives. Each couple has become a unit, they look alike, dress alike and are synchronized. You can see how your clan is at a different stage. It has transformed into a new creature. In Elliott's family, you are still the only intruder. You participate in excursions and rebuild your bonds during dinner. On your father's birthday, Elliott suggests the family sit together, and the in-laws sit at the other table. You look around as they eat. They are all getting older. They are spread out: Alexandra in Mexico City, Octavio in Laredo Texas, Gerard in Nuevo Laredo, and Isabelle in Boston. When dessert arrives, Alexandra and you sing a song from *Pippin* called *No time at all*. You have known it since you were teenagers. You played the record so many times, that you remember the part where the needle skipped and jumped over. The chorus is: *Oh, it's time to start living, time to take a little from this world we're given, time to take time, 'cause spring will turn to fall, in just no time at all.* As you sing, your father smiles, and you all surf on the sound waves of this song into the deep ocean of family nostalgia. There is such joy that the man at the next table asks what they are celebrating and says: *When I am seventy, I'm coming back with my family.* You cherish this moment as a pinnacle of becoming.

As the trip comes to an end, you are eager to see your boys but saddened, as you and your siblings drift apart, pulled by your own children and daily routines. Going back to Nuevo Laredo is depressing. You are still an outsider, and your place in Monterrey is becoming smaller.

You are being expelled from the productive world and relegated to the sub world of motherhood, where moms convince each other that what they do matters. Your nest gets prettier, twigs and leaves turn into shiny golden bars, which in turn become a golden cage. The bait that lured you in were the four hundred thread Egyptian cotton sheets, rugs and pillows but ultimately the promise of a happy marriage. The professional terrain does not coexist with diapers, strollers and high chairs. Family-friendly places are in the periphery of society. Children are set aside like cute domestic animals. You lose your passport to adulthood and get deported into the land of the small people, where the conversation revolves around green tables and red chairs. Your brain goes into hibernation mode and is frozen into a long winter that will last a decade. When you want to address this issue, it is treated as irrelevant. You feel resentment towards the women at your bridal showers for not fully explaining what was about to happen. You have joked about fairy tales and the happy ending as an ellipsis. Why doesn't anybody explain how mothers are thrown into the dungeons of society by taking care of the little people? Your voice fades into the choir of pedagogical techniques and decoration advice. In all those years of being single, you did not even smell dissatisfaction. Women, like other powerless factions of civilization, are Oscar-deserving actresses, pretending to each other that this is all they ever wanted. You did want to have children, but at the entrance of this jail, you left your civilian clothes. Men pretend mothers are behind the scenes, but mothers are the hidden iron rod inside the pillars of society. When you hear other mothers, you witness how they all support their families. They manage the emotional patrimony of the world. They create Christmas from scratch. From stuff found on sale in stores, they make homes. They do not build equity, there is no return on investment or profit. Their allowances are hugs and kisses, smiles and cuddles, lullabies, and bedtime stories. The male conspiracy claims all of this is priceless, but there is no dollar value set on a woman's work and dedication. Mothers become like children themselves, taken care of by the male adults who run the world.

Chapter 8.3   2013

Beatrice's new modern house compensates the one she lost in exile. They have come full circle. The right house in the right city. Elliott lost interest when they left Nuevo Laredo. Now, he is willing to invest resources into their home. There is so much space. They buy new furniture and get rid of the hand-me-downs. First, they buy the outside iron furniture, to have sitting areas on the patio. His parents buy them a tall and heavy antique commode and a golden chandelier with crystal for the entrance. They get new white sofas for the living room and antique dining room furniture. They fix the sprinkler system, the gates and the swimming pool pump.

Behind the pool area is a jungle of plants. Beatrice spends a whole weekend pulling the weeds with her own two hands until she gets blisters. Behind the jungle there is a rotten fence. They replace it. They hire an electrician and install a dozen hanging lanterns on the patio tree. When the pecan trees bloom, winter is over. They can plant. She plants roses outside the kitchen window, that she can see when she cooks. Outside David's room, she plants yellow *Esperanzas,* and outside Tomas's room she plants Golden Dewdrop as a hedge, to hide the air conditioning unit. She gets rid of the custom-made dark, heavy curtains that hung from wall to wall. There is natural light everywhere, and they can see the flowers.

They get a new dog, Max, their fourth Jack Russell Terrier. He sleeps with Tomas for a few weeks, while he is still a puppy. *Bolita,* the senior Pomeranian, is nervous around him. He starts sniffing her and tries to hump her. He ends up living outside on the patio. There are two hanging bird-feeders. The birds keep him company.

Keeping this six thousand square foot house beautiful is a full-time job. There are five air conditioning units that need maintenance twice a year. They hire a swimming pool and garden service. The cleaning lady comes three days a week. Elliott is proud. The boys have space to roam free. In the afternoons, David jumps on the trampoline, swings and swims naked. Tomas invites friends over on the weekends. During the fall, he starts playing football.

Beatrice is a professional wife now. She has come a long way learning about nutrition, cooking, decoration, ornaments, cleaning supplies, plants, and gardening. The obsession with big houses in her family comes from her grandfather's thirty-four thousand square foot house *Casa Arabesque.* The only time she ever slept there was when she was eleven years old. It was the Christmas of 1977. The year before the legal battle among the brothers. The house was at the crest of Bosques de las Lomas, an exclusive residential neighborhood her grandfather developed. He had a three-acre lot, surrounded by a tall wall. The entrance to the lot was on the corner. Once they opened the gate, the car could turn right to the other corner tracing a lake with exotic African birds, or turn left to park in front of an entrance to the house.

Driving in, the monumental stairs became visible, with two big sculptures of lions on both sides. The entrance hall was like the lobby of a hotel, with a black and white marble floor. To the left was a ballroom with a white grand piano. It was carpeted all in pink, from wall to wall, and surrounded by a built-in white sofa. There were Moroccan pillows, wooden tables with mother-of-pearl carvings and metallic carved lamps, all gifts from Moroccan King Hassan II. On the other side of the hall was a dining room that sat forty-eight people in six round tables for eight. There was a huge tapestry hanging on the wall. Beyond the Ballroom, there was a black bar with dozens of African trophies from the more than twenty safaris her grandfather had taken with friends and family.

There were bathrooms for ladies and gentlemen, three toilets in each one. The wall at the end of the hall created a division between the public and private spaces. Behind this wall was the informal dining room, which sat eighteen people. There were three round tables with white camel bases holding glass tops. There were three kitchens. The maid's quarters were in the basement. In the center, there was a white marble indoor swimming pool, with a retractable skylight. At the front of the swimming pool, there was a human-sized happy Buddha, Beatrice remembers rubbing his stomach for good fortune.

To the right side of the pool, there were three guest bedrooms each decorated with an exotic theme: Asian, Mexican, and Moroccan. Each one had two king beds, spacious full bathrooms and closets. On the left was the master bedroom, which was like an apartment inside the house with a small kitchen, living room and office. The bedroom was painted all in black with no windows, a dream man cave. They had his-and-her bathrooms and closets, a barber's chair and a sauna. Her closet looked like a small boutique. Her bathroom was all hand-painted like an underwater ocean, and the bathtub was a big shell. Beatrice took a bath in that tub pretending to be a mermaid until she had wrinkled hands. The Wicked Witch of the West gave her oil pearls to put in the bath. Behind the master bedroom was their baby girl's bedroom. This room was all in white lace, with satin pink ribbons, and porcelain dolls. Next to the girl's bed there was a doll bed in fine wood. Beatrice remembers this room the most, because she was jealous. In the backyard, there was a green house and a tennis court. This house was first opened in 1973, the year the family business declared bankruptcy. They enjoyed it for five years and then moved to San Antonio. Twenty years later it was sold for the lot only. It was torn down and turned into an exclusive gated community of ten houses.

As Beatrice's house gets prettier, her home becomes less functional. They have this house thanks to Elliot's father, but his mother becomes invasive. Every time she comes in the house, she moves things around. She has exquisite taste, but Beatrice struggles with boundaries. When she leaves on a weekend to visit her parents, she comes back to find her books thrown onto her closet floor. She learns they should not be displayed because they are paperbacks. Elliott's mother sets up his hardcover hunting books in the living room. Then, she generously buys plants and pays a decorator to arrange the bookshelves, all for a party they must host. When Beatrice sees the books, she cannot figure out the order, the subjects are all mixed up. After close observation, she realizes the decorator grouped the books by color.

The price of making a dream come true is waking up. This is the house of Beatrice's Mexican dreams, where she would have full time help and cheap labor to maintain it. She always thought she wanted to be a professional wife, but it is an endless goal. She has to take care of this house herself or manage the people who fix things. The plumber comes to clean the clogged toilets David fills with wipes. The carpets are washed frequently now that *Bolita* is almost blind and has accidents. David continues hitting his head and leaves marks on the walls. Tomas keeps bringing Max inside. He chews on things. The bird food is creating a problem with cockroaches. The repair list never ends. When a friend from Monterrey visits, Beatrice jokingly says: *This is my beautiful golden cage.*

It does not matter how big and pretty the house looks, David still wakes up in the middle of the night, *Bolita* is still coughing, and Tomas's acne is a full-blown issue, making him painfully shy. The house was just a distraction. It brought weight into her life, making the lightness of being bearable.

Beatrice finds out there is a rumor, among real estate agents, that her house has a spell. Every couple left here divorced. The last three divorcees were second wives. She convinces herself she is immune to the curse because she is a first wife. She is determined to make this their shrine of peace. In front of the windows, overlooking the patio, she sets up her orchid hospital. Her mother-in-law used to throw her orchids away, and now Beatrice brings them back to life. She bought clay orchid pots, cut off the plastic bags that strangled their roots, water them once a week and let them listen to classical music. At least half of them are always in full bloom. But it does not matter what she does, Elliott still leaves on his hunting trips. She is getting used to him not being here. They are living separate lives.

Beatrice's life feels empty and shallow. She cannot live for this house. It is not challenging enough. A friend invites her to a bible study. She accepts the invitation to go once. Her first time as a guest she arrives early. There is singing. she grabs the hymnal and follows along. They are singing *Amazing Grace.* She has heard this song in movies, but never listened to the lyrics. *Amazing grace how sweet the sound that saved a wretch like me.* As a teenager going to church gave her joy. She is a shy singer. The older ladies have beautiful loud voices. *I once was lost but now I'm found.* She sees the stained glass behind the altar and sees her God, the one she grew up with, her Jesus. She feels safe, uplifted and hopeful. *I was blind, but now I see.*

In the fall, she gets a call from her Bible leader and gets invited officially to a study group. She warns the leader: *I am not ready, still coming out of an atheist period, but I will fake it until I make it. I am coming because I saw all those happy ladies, and I want what they have.* After the disappointment from the Legion of Christ, she is skeptical of organized religion, but this group is non-denominational. They just want her to read the Bible.

When she was a teenager, her aunt Gloria gave her a Bible, with her name engraved on it. There is a page in the front for her family tree. At some point, she was going out with a divorced man and thought it would look bad to write his name in it. He had children from a previous marriage. In it she wrote her husband's name and her son's names. She never thought she would read it because it was in English. Now she is reading, underlining and using it like a life manual.

Beatrice has read many books, but not the Bible. The Catholic church prohibited Catholics from reading it on their own until 1963. This Bible study is thorough. It involves four steps: first read, then then discuss, then listen to a sermon, and finally read notes that explain the lesson. When she first tries to do her homework, she cannot find the references. There are more than sixty books in it. She has to check the index.

Many of these ladies quote the Bible with ease. Their faith becomes evident when Beatrice sees their network. They take care of each other's kids. The older women help the new mothers, army mothers, or single mothers come to hear the word of God. The first months, Beatrice is uncertain, but the more she hears anecdotes of doubt, and stories of domestic madness, she stops feeling isolated. They have petitions. The leader prays for them and Beatrice learns to pray a different way.

When she was growing up, prayer was a mantra she repeated like a parrot. Rosaries, *novenas*, asking, asking, and more asking. Here, they have manners, they begin with gratitude. When they are going to ask, they are taught to be specific. When Beatrice prays for David, she has to go to the bottom of the problem. She starts with: *God may David be healthy.* He is healthy. *May he feel loved.* He feels loved. *May he be happy.* He is happy. Then, she realizes what she has wanted all along, from the day he was diagnosed, is for God to make him normal, and that is not part of His plan. From now on, she prays that He helps her accept David for who he is.

This year they are reading Genesis. The subject that stands out for Beatrice's is the relationship between brothers. The first set of brothers is Cain and Abel. Cain killed Abel because God accepted Abel's offering and not his. Abraham had Ishmael and Isaac. Ishmael was the son of a slave and an only child for sixteen years. Because he was teasing his half-brother he was expelled from Abraham's family. Isaac and Rebekah had twin sons, Esau and Jacob. Esau was Isaac's favorite and Jacob was Rebekah's favorite. When Isaac was dying, Rebekah deceived him, and Jacob got his blessing instead of Esau. Esau wanted to kill Jacob, who fled to save his life. He then became the father of the twelve tribes of Israel.

This gets Beatrice thinking about her grandfather and Elliot's grandfather. They were only eleven months apart, and her grandfather was the apple of their mother's eye. Elliott's father has an older brother who was also the favorite. Her own two brothers are eleven months apart. Again, it is the second one who has dedicated his life to proving his worth. Elliott is the firstborn and carries a lot of responsibility. His brother feels overshadowed by him. Now, Beatrice has two boys. She can see how the firstborn possesses a space that is not open to anybody else. He can be proud because of it. At the same time, he gets no buffer, no shield, and a lot is expected of him. Beatrice hopes her two boys will break the spell of the greedy fights. David is not part of the competition. In Exodus, they talk about generational curse, *I the Lord your God, am a jealous God, punishing the children for the sin of their parents to the third generation of those who hate me.* Her boys are entangled in this lineage on both sides. Only God knows how David's autism has come to teach everybody a lesson.

To be able to travel with Elliott, Beatrice gets one of David's special education teachers to stay with him for a weekend. The teacher does not follow the prescribed diet, Beatrice comes home to a boy with an upset stomach. She looks for other options where he will be taken care of and in the company of other children. Another mother shares a respite care facility. David stays there on Saturday nights. He has a hard time sleeping at first, but she hopes he enjoys being part of something. Now, Beatrice has Saturdays off and can sleep late on Sundays. Being a special mother limits her capacity to be a good professional wife. She feels frustrated by not being both.

As Beatrice becomes familiar with the Bible and the group, she finds a problem. Many of these women believe what they read is a fact. She does not. The other problem is the undeniable male dominance. The Christian God is a father, and he has a male son. After appearing at the temple as a child, the most important historical figure in the world disappeared, until the wedding where he turned water into wine. No one knows where Jesus was for eighteen years?

Beatrice researches the Bible for the first time. She finds out there are one hundred and forty women mentioned in the Bible. Most of them are wives. The description of *The Wife of Noble Character* is in Proverbs 31. There are also: daughters, mothers, concubines, queens, sisters, one princess, three prophetesses, two midwives, two handmaids, a grandmother, a granddaughter, a mother-in-law, a daughter-in-law, and a sister-in-law. Not much is revealed about them.

Beatrice knows Eve was created from Adam's rib as a helper, fit for him. She was the first sinner. What she did not know is that there are two books about women. The book of Ruth is about a woman who married into the Hebrew family and was a faithful daughter-in-law. The book of Esther tells the story of an orphaned girl, raised by Jews, who marries King Xerxes and saves the Jewish people.

As Beatrice becomes familiar with other books in the Bible, she learns that there are three women briefly recognized for individual merit. In Judges 4 there is Deborah, a female judge and prophet, who led a successful counterattack against the forces of Jabin, King of Canaan. In the same book, there is the heroine, Jael who killed Sisera in order to deliver Israel from the troops of Jabin. In 1 Chronicles, there is mention of Sheerah who built three cities: Lower and Upper Beth-horon and Uzzen-Sheerah. She built three cities! No more information is shared on the subject.

What catches Beatrice's attention in the New Testament is that Christ's first recorded disclosure of His identity as the Messiah was made to a woman from Samaria. He asked her for water. The only woman disciple was Mary Magdalene. She travelled with Jesus as one of his followers. What stands out is that in the four Gospels, she is named at least twelve times more than most of the apostles.

After being raised in an all-girls Catholic school, Beatrice is surprised to find out *Song of Songs,* written by Solomon, celebrates sexual love. It honors the voices of two lovers who praise and yearn for each other, and rejoice in their sexual intimacy.

Beatrice was raised Catholic. She praised Mary not only as Jesus's mother but her mother. Mary is a female figure who intercedes for her children. She is a human woman and the mother of the son of God. Beatrice hits a wall, there are many questions she cannot answer through pure devotion. In psychology, humans are fully responsible, in the church, God is in control. She continues going to her Bible study for support.

Beatrice wonders: if the Bible has no reference to women as individuals, they only exist in relation to men, what about all the women who do not have a man? Surely, she is more than somebody's wife or mother? As hard as Beatrice has researched her ancestors, there are few stories about the women before her. What did they feel? Did they have dreams? What happened when their children were grown? She can now see how her mother has fought to have a life of her own, and her children resent her for it.

After feeling stuck, believing there was no life after the newspaper, I hear of a reporter who is working for a news agency. I call, ask about her experience, contact her agency, fly to Mexico City, have an interview, and get hired. I pack my life in boxes and take it to my parents' house. I surprise my boss by saying I am leaving. He is sad to see me go, but being a ghost writer is turning me into a ghost woman.

A few days after my twenty seventh birthday, I land in Washington DC to be trained as a correspondent. I check in at a Days Inn downtown. I cannot sleep. The city jungle noises are syncopated. The next morning, I show up at the office to meet my new boss. His name is Ignacio. He is seven feet tall, has a beard and long hair. When he walks towards me, he bows when passing from one room to another, to avoid hitting his head on the ceiling divisions. This man is a legend at the agency. He has lived in thirteen cities all over the world.

Did you have a good flight? Slept well?

More or less, thanks. I checked out and brought my stuff.

You'll be staying with Jackie.

He is two feet taller than I am.

Here you will learn to write concisely and fast. Let's do a quick overview to make sure we are on the same page. Keep in mind the news agency is the first source of information. It feeds radio, television and newspapers. Radio and television have two deadlines, the midday and evening broadcast. As you know newspapers have one deadline, at the end of the day. Don't forget we are a corporation that sells news. We sell our news mostly to Latin-American countries. The three global news agencies are: the French AFP, the American, Associated Press and the British, Reuters. They have offices in most countries. We are smaller and are controlled by the Mexican government. We edit and always protect Mexico's interests. I know you are used to expressing opinions. Here you will not do that. You are taking over the office in Los Angeles. It is a delicate time. Some California citizens created Proposition 187 to take away medical and educational services from illegal immigrants. If this law passes, three hundred thousand children will be out of school from one day to the next. This week you'll accompany Jackie to watch her work. We'll let you write some news pieces and review them before they go in the feed. Remember, we are always sending something. If there is an earthquake, you have twenty minutes to send a few lines.

I meet the rest of the team and follow Jackie all day. In the evening, I take my suitcase to her studio. As generous as she is for letting me stay with her, I feel uncomfortable. I am sleeping on the floor. Her space is tight and has one small window. She is a self-made woman who economizes her income. We come from different backgrounds. While we are having dinner, she tells me how in her house the best piece of meat was always for her brother, but it was she who got out and made something of herself. Once I get the hang of it, my flight for LA is booked.

Like in the movies, I have a one-way ticket to Los Angeles. But I am not an aspiring actress. On the plane, the woman sitting next to me is black, has short blond hair and natural, long, decorated nails that look like bear claws. On long flights, I like to guess who is going home and who is traveling for play or work. This woman is definitely an *Angelena*. We are approaching our destination and fly over LA for half an hour before landing. I was here visiting Frank a couple of months ago. I have known him since we were kids. We were dating before he moved to do a graduate program. When I was offered the job, there were three cities to choose from, I chose LA with the hope of picking up where we left off.

As soon as I land, I get a taxi. We drive on the six lane highways, and the cab fare is seventy dollars. The urban landscape is familiar; Los Angeles has been filmed more than any other city in the world. I have seen these palm trees and colonial houses in movies and television shows my whole life. I check into a weekly rental called Oakwood suites. When I read my contract, a paragraph says I agree not to eat the asbestos on the ceiling. Welcome to the bureaucracy of the American lawsuits. The next morning, the roller coaster begins. I have two weeks before the person in charge of the office leaves. I have to: rent a car, hire a secretary, process my social security card, find a furnished place to live, get a driver's license and attend the press conferences.

As soon as I have time, I call Frank. I did let him know I was coming. We plan on having dinner. He gives me his address. I get there faster than he thought, because I follow my Tomas Guide LA Atlas. I wait. He is ready, and I am happy to see a familiar face. He has soft honey eyes and wavy brown hair. He has always been a great athlete, first as a soccer player, and after his knee injury, a great swimmer. Seeing him in a bathing suit was something to look forward to, made my swimming training bearable. He hops in my car, and we have dinner in his Beverly Hills college world, surrounded by country clubs. While he is doing his homework – on daddy's dime - I am attending press conferences and conducting interviews.

After seeing a couple of apartments, I choose to rent at *Los Feliz Manor*, not far from downtown, and close to the Hollywood sign. It is an old building that once was a boutique hotel, guaranteed to survive earthquakes. Last January, there was a big one that was felt all the way to Las Vegas. Frank told me how he had to jump out of bed in the middle of the night. My apartment is a studio. The bed comes out of the wall, but I get to choose from the original antique furniture that they have in storage. On a clear day, I can see the ocean from my window.

My days are long. I wake up at six-thirty, hurry to the office, plan the route at eight. But it is already late; it is eleven in Washington. Most days, I hang out with the Mexican correspondents: Charlie from *El Universal*, William from *Excelsior* and Zully from *Para Empezar,* a morning radio show. They are my mentors. I follow them around and pay attention to their questions in press conferences.

I spend hours isolated in the car, surfing the pavement, anxious about missing my exit. Los Angeles is flat and extended, goes on endlessly. Highways are big, knotted, grey arteries. Angelenos' casual conversations always revolve around traffic and alternate routes. Manhattan is tall, tight and cozy in comparison. When you descend into the streets, you enter a river of people, bump into others and feel close. The biggest difference is the weather. It never rains in California, people get a tan and surf through life. I find it hard to sit and think without cloudy days.

Hollywood is omnipresent. Aspiring actors show up unexpectedly. I have lunch at *The Ivy,* sitting on the terrace on a beautiful afternoon. While reading the menu, the waiter comes to recite the specials of the day, and I am astounded. He is a vision. The sunlight illuminates his perfect face, making his turquoise eyes glow. Beauty standards in LA are Olympian. When driving around, I see cars with cameras hanging on the sides to film car dialogues. On many evenings, the downtown area is closed for film shoots. Parking lots are infested with armies of extras with their wardrobes. Sometimes at night helicopters fly over the buildings for action shots.

I do not see Frank often. I buy tickets and invite him to see *Allegria,* a new show by a circus called *Cirque de Soleil,* in Santa Monica. Then, we go see the ballet *Sleeping Beauty* at the Dorothy Chandler Pavillion. Sometimes, I call and hang up, but he calls back to tell me he knows it was me, thanks to this new thing, Caller ID. I do not call anymore. It is useless. He does not even keep me company.

A reporter from The Compass is in town. We have lunch at the Four Seasons, after his press conference. He came to the premier of

Legends of the Fall. They are introducing a new actor named Brad Pitt. My colleague makes fun of his hair tossing gestures.

I get to hear Carl Sagan, interview Ricardo Montalban and attend an event with Carlos Menem, Argentina's president. I eat, breathe and sleep Proposition 187 and miss out on Hollywood action, even the launching of the new film studio, *Dreamworks*.

The day the O.J. Simpson trial begins downtown, I have to go to the LA AIDS project. They are making a five thousand donation against the anti-immigrant proposal. The press conference takes place in a small auditorium, where twenty people have gathered to hear the news. As the announcement is made, the speaker says:

We would like to know why this nice young lady was the only one who thought this donation was more important than the O.J. Simpson trial. He is talking about me. I am the only journalist here. I speak up and ask about the implications of this law.

I am representing the Mexican News Agency. Are you aware that if this proposition passes, everyone will have to prove citizenship when applying for medical services? Some patients might not use their real names when testing for AIDS.

There is a naturalization ceremony for fourteen thousand people, mostly Mexican. They have it at the Los Angeles Convention Center, no other venue is big enough. We, Mexican correspondents, rush to interview as many people as we can.

Why did you decide to become a US Citizen as a senior?

I've lived here for forty years, hoping to go back to Mexico, but that ship has sailed. I decided to become a US citizen to vote against Proposition 187 and Pete Wilson. We feel more American than those born here. We chose to become American.

This side of LA is not portrayed in the movies. It is an army of gardeners and maids that keep Tinsel Town bright and shiny for the world to see. The west side is filled with blond surfers, pretty skinny girls and fashionable crowds sipping lattes at high-end commercial centers. East LA has purple *cholo* cars with drawings of flames coming out of the back tires, pure devotion to the *Virgen de Guadalupe*, sweet smell of *churros*, and curvy sexy Latinas with heavy make-up and noisy jewelry.

There are a few personal experiences that illuminate this issue further. The owner of the *Los Feliz Manor*, Mr. Huntley, takes me out to lunch with his waspy Angeleno friends. They are all voting for Proposition 187. At the end of the meal he asks:

So, guess where she is from? As if I were a rare species. They say Italy, France, and Spain. When I tell them I am Mexican, they are surprised. Their reaction makes me uncomfortable. I am not one of them and not one of the others.

I invite Huntley to a Mexican wedding at the Ritz Carlton in Laguna Niguel. He drives me in his Jeep SUV wearing a tuxedo. I am eager to show him other Mexicans like me. He cannot believe the quantity of fresh white roses covering the gazebo where the bride and groom take their vows. After the reception, we walk barefoot on the beach and look at the full moon. He does not get a kiss for being in favor of Proposition 187. We drive back in silence.

I hang out with the guy who sold me my used white Volkswagen Golf. His name is Lars. He is Danish and lives in the United States illegally, but possibly because of his European looks he has not been a target of discrimination. He has witnessed how Mexicans are racially singled-out and is outraged. This proposition is not against him. It is against a stereotype. He never feels threatened about his migratory status.

There is a protest in late October. The team of the Fantastic Four - Charlie, William, Zully and I – come to the rescue. We are at the newly named Cesar Chavez Avenue. To see the magnitude of the event, we climb a water tank. There are seventy thousand Mexicans walking a four-mile route from East LA to Downton. There it is, an ocean of white T-shirt enthusiasts, waving Mexican flags, mariachis, images of the *Virgen de Guadalupe,* even *charros* on horseback. Many hold signs stating *No to racism. No to illiteracy.* The next morning, the front page of the Los Angeles Times says: *If you like Mexico so much, why don't you go back?*

American hypocrites! It is the army of Mexicans that builds the houses, keeps gardens manicured, cleans bathrooms and picks up the trash. It is those Mexicans that cook with passion and make food an adventure. Those Mexicans push the strollers to the park and tuck those pretty blonde children in bed at night. The cleaning lady, the nanny and the housekeeper are devoted because they are Mexican and believe in God. I know because I was raised by them. My mother was never home. It was these brown women whose warm-heart and tenderness made me bloom. Am I the hypocrite? I tried to hire a cleaning lady, when she said she charged fifty dollars for one morning I thought: *In Mexico, I can get a maid for a whole week for that price.*

My brother's wedding is November fifth, and the election is November eighth. My boss does not want me to go, and I tell him: *You don't understand. If I have to choose between being at my brother's wedding and this job, I'll resign.*

I fly home on Saturday, go to the wedding and come back on Sunday. Even after such a big occasion, when I land in Los Angeles, I feel at home. Tuesday morning is a big day. Jackie was sent here as back up from Washington. A guy from Mexico City is sent to be my new boss. He does not speak English. The ballots are open. People are out. There are signs everywhere. The mood is tense. It has only been two years since the riots after the beating of Rodney King. The Mexican Fantastic Four drive all over town to try to capture the scene. The Republican Pete Wilson and the democrat Kathleen Brown are head to head.

I am in shock, Proposition 187 passed! Another busy day ahead. The SOS initiative, known as the *Save Our State*, was approved. This would prohibit illegal aliens from using healthcare and public education services. It is challenged in a legal suit and found to be unconstitutional by a federal district court. Not even their supporters could throw the first stone. Senator Dianne Feinstein and Michael Huffington have tough policies against illegal immigration, even they have to reveal they hired illegal immigrants for housekeeping and childcare.

After spending the day in court, my Washington boss calls and says that the new guy is going to write the piece. I am livid! After three months of eating, sleeping and breathing Proposition 187, on the final stretch, somebody else takes over just because he has connections in Mexico City? I swear I will never work for the Mexican government again. I call Washington and tell my boss I know the agency does not declare taxes in the United States and threaten to file a complaint. They back off, but I cannot work with this guy anymore. Being in the office is torture. I think about my options and call my ex-boss to find out if there are any opportunities for me. He suggests I become the Hollywood correspondent for The Compass. As much as I love the Oscars, I have to think about this.

In Mexico, things are not going well. NAFTA is launched the first of January, and the same day, the Zapatista Army of National Liberation declared a defensive war against the Mexican state. In the spring, Luis Donaldo Colosio, the candidate chosen by the sitting Mexican president, was shot, destabilizing the system that had worked for sixty-five years. Six months later, in September, the president's brother-in-law was shot. I am tired of knowing more about national events than about my own family. I look at the other correspondents' lives and feel discouraged.

My parents come to visit for Thanksgiving. It is a break from it all. I show them around and get spoiled by them. We have lunch at the Ivy and Drew Barrymore is sitting in the back. When we wait for the valet to bring our car, we bump into Mr. Link, who was my grandfather's lawyer in the big legal battle among the five brothers. He invites us to have lunch at the Los Angeles Club. There are not many days left, my parents are leaving soon. We meet the next day. Mom and Dad are staying in a hotel downtown. I have to work, my office is not far, but the parking is twenty dollars an hour. I join them. The Los Angeles Club was once only for men. The hallway has cathedral ceilings, leather furniture and lots of fine wood. The dining room is also grand. As we have lunch, Mr. Link narrates how the Theriot brothers came to a conclusion after a month of negotiations, and my father was brought out of jail, like the sacrificial lamb. I know that one day I will use my journalistic skills to understand this puzzle. After that highlight, my parents leave.

Determined not to work with a man who does not speak English and will use me as an information retriever, I resign. Before I go, Frank spends the night over one more time. We have dinner. The next morning before he leaves I get the courage to say: *It's a shame you were defensive and reacted as if I had come here after you.*

I don't think you came here after me. We'll talk in Monterrey.
We never did.
While I pack my life in boxes, I get a call from an old flame.
I am calling to ask you to marry me.
But we don't have anything to talk about.
That's fine. We buy two televisions, each of us gets a remote.
For real?
I guess not all marriage proposals are created equal.

Chapter 9.2   2004

After five years of marriage, two toddlers and a fully decorated house, you are confident enough to call yourself a housewife. The pond at the entrance of the house is filled with waterlilies and koi fish. The pantry is organized. The grocery list follows the floor plan of the supermarket. You know how to plan the menus of the week, and your two maids wear uniforms. The garden is beginning to blossom, and your boys have daily routines that run like clockwork.

Mornings start with your daily walk in the countryside. After dropping off your eldest son, at his Montessori kindergarten, you strap the little one in his stroller, put the leash on your dog and go out to get some fresh air. You are outside Nuevo Laredo, in a sprawling residential neighborhood developed by your father-in-law. Your house is the second house to be built and stands out for its clean, modern, sculptural forms.

In the past five years, you have been working hard to fit your job description. You keep your house impeccable, your children clean and healthy, your help well-trained, your suitcases ready for the next trip, and your serving trays and china ready to host the next gathering. Your goal is to make your mother and mother-in-law proud and to prove to them you are a fast learner. It does not matter how hard you try, there are more balls in the air, and they are getting more difficult to juggle.

This last Christmas, you went on a family trip. You packed appropriately, included snacks for the boys, toys for long flights and enough diapers to last a week. In the airport madness, you missed your connection and your cruise. When you got on the boat, it took David, only a day to throw up in the elevator. You left the scene out of embarrassment. You only gave him bottled drinks but your beginner's mistake was the ice, which is local frozen water. He had terrible diarrhea, you ran out of diapers and wipes. In your small luxury cruise ship, you were the only mother with toddlers, and for that you got a myriad of dirty looks. Running a nursery is best done at home. You did get the right shots - of the Tahitian overwater bungalows - to put in picture frames for the living room.

Upon your return, you go back to your routine. You are faced with the dilemma of choosing a school for Tomas. Your options are limited, living in a border town. You want to explore the alternatives, so you talk to mothers with older children. The present concern with David is his developmental delay. Most toddlers begin walking at twelve months, but he began taking steps at sixteen months. The phrase *every child is different* is an aspirin that doesn't numb your anxiety anymore. In your car, you play educational songs with small words every day, to reinforce his language. You know them all, but David is not talking. You hug him and caress him, but there is an impenetrable fog between you.

In the afternoons, while you sit down to write for the newspaper, Tomas and David go visit their grandmother, who lives a mile down the road. While the maids walk, Tomas pedals his tricycle, and David enjoys being pushed in his stroller. Their grandmother has a sandbox in her garden. She calls it "grandchildren's bait." During Spring Break, while Elliott is on a hunt, you take them to the beach. They both love the ocean and playing in the sand. You are not saving the world or finding a cure for cancer, but somebody has to supervise the growth of human beings. William Wallace wrote a poem that states, *the hand that rocks the cradle is the hand that rules the world.* You do not rule anything. Being a mother is a lonely job. You still remember that for a whole decade the fear of not marrying kept you up at night. Now, you are married and feel more isolated than ever. This is not the life you envisioned. Your elusive husband is either working or hunting, preparing for working or preparing for hunting. He is a reliable provider, but he is emotionally absent. The little ones are not real company. When they yell *Mom,* they mean: *I am tired. Carry me. Feed me. Change me.*

To reach out to other adults there is the resource of hosting. A friend's birthday is a day after yours. You plan a tropical party for the summer, where all your guests will dress in white, and you'll hand out *leis* at the door. The party date arrives and you are set. You serve fresh salads with mango and jicama. You decorate with tropical flowers and play soft music. You set the air conditioner to full blast, but when the guests arrive, the room warms up. The air conditioner machine does not have the right tons per square foot. You are a novice hostess and not Martha Stewart.

Your great distraction from domestic life is holding on to vestiges of your professional life. Your editorials are published in Monterrey and Nuevo Laredo newspapers. Your column, after much resistance and abundant hate mail, is getting rave reviews. You have carved a space in the community. You cite the dirty streets, the lack of green spaces, the excess of cables above crossroads, the poor landscaping and remind readers that the budgets assigned for city improvements are not spent. You have followers and have taught citizens to complain. You are approached by a local official who offers you a minor political position. Your husband prevents you from accepting, and warns you about the threats in a town where organized crime extends its tentacles to every corner.

To face your readership, you occasionally give talks. On Women's Day, you are invited to make a presentation. You choose to talk about how media affects the way we perceive reality; you talk about how women are trained to feel the male gaze at all times. As you hear your own voice, you become aware of the contradiction of your own life. You are a blind follower of the consumer cult. Marketing nurtures irrational expectations of what your house, children and appearance should be. Every time you sit in front of the television set, hypnotized by images, your gamma brain waves swallow the shopping orders, and you become a consumer soldier. Every time you go to the gym, or grab your makeup brushes, you follow your training to fit a visual image. Marketing is a form of induction into the lines of blind obedience to the consumer creed. You speak in front of these people and discuss *Ways of Seeing* by John Berger, which analyzes how women models pose for male painters. You yourself are a victim of this theory. Your outfit today is a costume. You are a professional Barbie wearing a suit. Dressing dolls as little girls is part of the training. The attire to please men is sexy. Armor selected to outdo other women, fashion logos, weapon of status. The heavy artillery is jewelry, nuptial karats are the finest code of rank.

Your professional and personal lives are at odds. You write about strong women with personal goals, but the day you had children, you became a cave woman and got chewed up by motherhood. One day, having lunch with friends at the country club, the mother of a single child says: *I have to go. We have a math exam tomorrow.* Who is we? You already took math, and were terrible at it the first time around. Are you condemned to relive your childhood again? The typical "helicopter" mom rules and bullies. Modern kids do not know how to share. You shared a bedroom, bathroom, television and hand-me-downs from your older sister. The bar is raised high enough to turn you into Olympic pole vaulters. The result twenty years down the road, an enraged woman screaming: *I sacrificed my life for you, ungrateful brats.*

As fall begins, the director of the Montessori school approaches you. *I think you should have David checked. There is something off in his social behavior and playing patterns.* She recommends a doctor in Monterrey. You fit the appointment into your next trip home. The doctor does a general evaluation and cannot make a formal diagnosis. *Maybe you should get an appointment in Houston.* You try that. There is a yearlong wait. Your father-in-law calls a friend in San Antonio. You get an appointment for January. That is the best you can do. As long as there is no diagnosis, you hold on to the idea that this is temporary, and it will pass. When he was younger, he did have language. He would say water when he saw it in a fountain, a pool or the ocean. Your dog's name is Spot, and he called him *Oc.* He ate all kinds of food and had great appetite. Now, he is a picky eater and suffers from constipation.

This is the only issue pending. You are moving forward. First, you got the husband, then the house, then the children. Once David starts talking, everything will continue its course and go according to plan. You have evidence that he is normal. The memory of him smiling at a woman during his first birthday lunch is clear in your mind. He has shown social skills, awareness of his context and connection. This drifting off is temporary, and you have nothing to worry about.

Elliott's family opens a car dealership. It is your elder son, Tomas, who cuts the ribbon in the opening ceremony. You are dressed up, have drinks and nibble on appetizers. As you mingle, Elliott's uncle asks about your children, and you mention that David is not talking. When he walks away, your mother-in-law reprimands you for sharing that information. You feel ashamed, and this need for secrecy drives you towards isolation. This is the life of the housewife, to live inside a prison of silence and pretend it is all going well.

To distract yourself and have something to look forward to, you host a lunch in your house with a few friends. You set the white tablecloth, take out your *Limoges* china and *Christofle* silverware, pull out your Waterford glasses and buy fresh roses for the centerpiece. Your biggest challenge is cooking. You are not a great cook, but you give it a try anyway. Your friends compliment your table when they arrive. You feel proud. When the food is served, you are mortified. It has no flavor. They are gracious guests, but when they put the spoons in their mouths, your compassionate Buddhist friend immediately says: *Thank you so much for having us over, you are too kind.* That is how bad the food is. She felt the need to excuse your bad cooking by recognizing your effort. After you finish, you sit in the living room, and you approach the greatest cook of the group and address the issue. *We are all happy to be here. If we wanted restaurant quality food, we would have gone to a restaurant. Don't beat yourself up. What matters is that you had us over. You'll get better with practice. The desert is good, how did you make it?* At least one thing was a culinary success.

As you obsess over your hosting abilities, more incidents occur in Nuevo Laredo. Before, the victims were distant and unknown. Their reputation was questionable. The day comes when you hear stories involving honest, hardworking people you know. The first event happens in a nearby ranch. The bad guys show up armed, wearing ski masks, and tie the employees. They go deer hunting with machine guns. The second assault you hear about happens at a friend's house. In the middle of the night, his parents are held at gunpoint in their home. They were fourteen armed men. Their business is a currency exchange bureau, and one of the employees was laundering money.

One day, you are on your daily morning walk, pushing David's stroller and holding your crazy Jack Russel Terrier by your side. You walk all the way to your in-law's house and back. As you return, in the countryside, in the middle of nowhere, there is a line of seven parked cars. You stop and ask: *What is going on? What happened?* A man informs you that they found a woman's burned body.

Next Saturday morning, your lazy quiet day, you sleep in and have breakfast in your room. It is late autumn, the light is bright, the sky is blue, and the breeze is chilly. On your balcony, your three Chinese prosperity fish-kites are swimming in the air, swallowing the wind through their round mouths. The maids are downstairs, taking care of the boys. Your husband and you sit in your pajamas.

You can't go on your walk anymore.

But we live in a small town. There's not much to do. The thing that I enjoy the most about living out here is nature. If I can't go out walking, I do not see the point of us living here at all.

Things have changed and we need to understand that. We need to start looking for a house on the other side of the border.

We have been in this house for only four years. We've been fixing, painting, planting, finishing every detail. Next month, we finish paying for the plant generator to lower the electricity bills, and the river-stone garage floor will be done soon. We will not enjoy any of those things.

Like everybody else, we are leaving Mexico.

It is heartbreaking to give up your house, your city and your country. The war on drugs is a war like any other. It compels many to relocate.

On the weekend following Thanksgiving, on Saturday afternoon, you go look at a house across the border, that you found on the internet. You drive around a nice neighborhood and find it. It is a one-acre lot with mature trees. The woman of the house is riding a lawn mower when you arrive. Her older children are visiting from college. She shows you around her twenty-five-year-old house. She built it with her husband, chose the lot, and hired an architect, like you did. She tells you the story of when she brought the oak in the back and planted it. That oak is now a tall tree that covers the whole patio. The cement slab surrounding the oak has her children's little footprints for posterity. You are posterity.

The house is cozy, but it is somebody else's home. There are traces of the life this woman lived here, her younger daughter's porcelain dolls look at you from the shelves. Her life has ripened, and she is ready to move on to the next stage. You will not have what she has, the satisfaction of giving closure to a mature life. You are about to be uprooted and rerooted. Your tender little family will have to be strong and adapt to American soil.

You make an offer and close the deal in a week. You hire construction workers to make some changes. The house gets painted in an off-white tone. The carpets are changed. Brick walls are covered with stucco. Your closet is expanded. You plan to move in at the beginning of the year. You start looking for schools for the boys.

You cannot sleep thinking about the changes, the furniture, where things will go. As the year comes to an end, you prepare for Christmas. You are getting ready for dinner with Elliott's family. You bought a scarlet taffeta evening dress on sale. Elliott wants you to wear it. As soon as you arrive, you sense your mother-in-law's disapproval. There is an invisible threshold of adornment that you have crossed. You have been married for five years, and it is just now, wearing this dress, that you understand that you will always be an outsider. Your role here is to make your husband look good, not make yourself look good. Every Christmas you have your picture taken and there is always the picture of only them. In these past five years, you have given your mother-in-law many photographs of your family, and she only exhibits the ones with her grandchildren. Not a single picture of you graces her house. After dinner, you go home, but Tomas stays overnight with them.

It is almost an omen. The next morning, everything is covered in snow. You get snow maybe once a decade, and this time you got it on Christmas day! You are told by your in-laws that when Tomas woke up, he opened the curtain and said: *It is all white.* The magic lasts for a couple of hours, the sun comes up and melts the snow. You are packing and forget to take a picture of the white cloak covering the ground.

The next day, you leave for New York. The first day you have lunch at Tavern on the Green and David has an upset stomach. You have to get up more than once to change his soiled diaper. You go to Radio City Music Hall to watch the Christmas show. David took off his shoe in the taxi, and you did not notice. He keeps taking his shoes off. He falls asleep and misses the whole thing. You feel guilty for the relief it gives you that he sat still during the performance. You cannot take him anywhere. You try to eat at a place called Hamburger Heaven. The line goes around the corner, the waiting time is an hour. Elliott is frustrated with the Christmas crowds and offers to stay in the room with David. You go to a convenience store and buy sandwiches and fruit for all. It is hard to entertain David. He does not play with his toys. He lines them up. He does not watch television either. He is a picky eater and gets an upset stomach every other day. On New Year's Eve, you have lunch at the 21 Club. David wanders off for a minute, and you get reprimanded by the waiter. *You need to supervise your child. We have clients who are a hundred years old, and they could trip over your boy.* After that, you sit in the bathroom lounge with David during most of the meal. In the evening, when you go to a Broadway show. David sits quietly for ten minutes. Elliott has to take him out. Times Square is madness, no taxis available. He has to walk back to the hotel, with David on his shoulders, in the freezing cold.

The climax of the trip is the International Debutante's Ball. Elliott's sister is one of the debutantes. Her other brother was the escort in the two previous debuts. Elliott is her escort tonight. You meet the babysitter the hotel provided for the evening, and leave everything as best you can. You are worried she will not handle the situation, but you have to go. Your hair and makeup are off, but you are wearing a queen dress, silver and black brocade skirt and a black velvet top.

You gasp when you enter the ballroom. You see beautiful girls in their haute couture white evening gowns and long white gloves; men in tuxedos; yards of luscious fabric draping the ladies. Twenty-two years ago, you were in this room, a debutante yourself. You were only sixteen-years-old. You are stressed over the babysitter, you had no time to understand where you are and what is about to happen. Your mother-in-law asks you to sit next to her. This is unusual. When the show is about to commence, they dim the lights, and ask former debutantes to stand up. *Stand up! Stand up!* she says. If your mother were here she would stand up with you. She was also a debutante when she was sixteen. A deep nostalgia invades you, emotions slide out of your eyes and nose.

Chapter 9.3   **2014**

Beatrice's children are older, and she is better organized. She feels the need to do more, but getting a job is complicated. Newspapers are disappearing, and it is difficult to become a journalist in another country. She knows it would be hard to hide her ignorance on many subjects. A friend from the book club invites her to be a board member in an organization for writers. Their motto is *Help Tell the Human Story.* The official invitation takes place over lunch. Beatrice meets a professional writer, and as they eat, she tells the story of how she had to leave Nuevo Laredo. The writer insists she has to write this story. She starts thinking about it.

Her boys are doing better. After prayers, tears and conversations, Tomas now accepts his brother for who he is. Beatrice gets an email from a teacher:

I am new at the Junior School. I've been teaching Special Education for ten years. This morning, when I got to school, I saw your two sons walking into the building together. I want to let you know how touching it was to see your older son be so kind and caring to David. I was overwhelmed with how genuine and loving he was towards his brother. You must be doing an amazing job at home.

This mail soothes Beatrice's mother guilt and gives her license to pursue something for herself. She has lunch with a writer friend, and they agree to meet every other week to share their essays. At first, they do not meet their deadlines and reschedule. The first essays Beatrice writes are journalistic. They take a writing workshop and meet another couple of friends. The writing group extends to four members.

The other three are locals, Beatrice is the only one that did not grow up in the Heights. Each one has her style, but the other three women describe the same landscape. In the first few meetings, Beatrice does not say much. She has to learn from them. The technique is to read with pen in hand, make notes on what they like, what works and what is confusing. Their support gives Beatrice the courage to write more. She feels safe and starts writing about personal stories. The writing awakens a self-awareness that was dead. She sits down to write on Saturday afternoons, when David is in respite care. As she writes, her memories crawl out of the corners of her mind, like shy small creatures.

It is on a spring Wednesday morning, Beatrice wakes up to find two missed calls from her siblings. There is one voicemail. Today Elliott is leaving for Africa on his twenty-seventh hunting safari. She hears the message: *I am calling to let you know our nephew had a motorcycle accident last night, and he died.* Her knees bend, and she falls to the ground. Elliott takes a cab to the airport, and she heads to her brother's house. He is alone. Her sister-in-law is in Mexico City. He is on the phone talking to some doctor about organ donations. There is a painting of her nephew surrounded by flowers and candles in the living room. The twins are upstairs. She goes up and talks to them. They are crying and narrate what happened last night. A policeman came in the middle of the night, to let them know about the accident. While they go to the airport to pick up their older sister, Beatrice goes to the supermarket to buy food for the guests, soon to arrive. As she gets back and puts things inside the refrigerator, her other niece comes in the house. She just landed from Miami. She falls on the floor and howls like a wounded animal. Beatrice is an intruder, she wants to disappear. There is too much pain. Before she leaves to give them their privacy, she hugs her niece and says: *According to Tibetan Buddhism, he is suspended in the bardo now, like in a dream. You can cry all you want for the next two days. He will wake up from his dream and understand he died. That's when you have to stop, to let him rest in peace. He might come to you in a dream, and you'll talk to him. He will hear you and you'll find the closure you need.*

As soon as their friends arrive, she leaves to pick up her children. In the afternoon, she parks three blocks away. There are too many cars. She cannot come in the house and stands outside singing *La Guadalupana* with the crowd. She witnesses when they bring the statue of the *Virgin de Guadalupe* and pass it above their heads and set it up next to the painting.

The next days are madness. Beatrice's parents come. Her three siblings stay in her house. On Thursday, they all gather. On Friday the body is ready, and they have the wake. He was strong and healthy. His body was emptied out for organ donations. He was her only godchild. When she sees him, it is not Chito, it is just a body. He was handsome, athletic and charismatic. There is a crowd, young and old, many ex-girlfriends, little widows who wish they were that special woman he would have grown old with. There are rosaries all afternoon. It is Beatrice's first time on the receiving line. She can see why it's impossible to find the right words. *It's unnatural to bury a son. This is a horrible tragedy. What a terrible loss. Why wasn't he wearing a helmet?* She just nods. The guests are divided into two: those attending a social event and those who have seen death in the face. Their hugs give them away.

This nephew was different from everybody else. He got the name. He was the seventh Octavio Theriot, the third Octavio to have a tragic death. Beatrice's great-grandfather committed suicide. Her father's brother was dropped by the nanny and died at three months, and now with this childless nephew, the lineage ends.

In the middle of all the commotion, something strange happens at home. David watches a DVD obsessively. He chooses to see the last scene from *All that Jazz*. After a last concert, Roy Sheider, still wearing his black sequined shirt, is moved on a conveyor belt through a tunnel. At the end of the passage, Jessica Lange awaits him, dressed all in white as the angel of death. In the last scene, his cadaver is inside a plastic bag and the zipper is being closed. David plays, rewinds and repeats, plays, rewinds and repeats. Does he have a special perception of things?

Saturday is a beautiful spring day and they head to the church to say goodbye to his lifeless body. More words, more tears, more hugs. They disperse. The whole thing is exhausting. Beatrice hosts the last gathering Saturday evening. She wants everything to be perfect. He was her godchild, she was there when he was baptized, and the church received him as a child of God. This is the farewell. The dining room is full of trays with finger food, classical music in the background and no alcohol. Nobody wants an unexpected outburst. They want to believe he is in heaven. They have no idea what is happening. They do not want to part. They eat some more, talk, laugh, and fill the silence. Nobody wants to go. They want to stay together. They are afraid to lie in bed and talk to death face to face. They need the noise, the company, the trivial daily tasks to fill time and numb the spirit to this crazy design of life.

In the next week, there is a mass in Mexico City from the mother's side of the family and a mass in Monterrey from the father's side of the family. It is all awkward. His ashes are put in a catholic cemetery in San Antonio. He is the first and only one to be there. No previous arrangements were made. Nobody expected this to happen.

When seven weeks have passed, the surviving brother calls Beatrice. *What happens on the seventh week?* She had explained: *Buddhists believe the transition takes seven weeks.* He then tells her he had a dream on Monday night, seven weeks to the day of his brother's death. *I walk towards the beach and see him. He tells me to look up, and there's an explosion like a supernova. When I look back down he's gone.*

The next months it sinks in. Beatrice's brother lost his job during the recession. He was in debt, lost his house, declared bankruptcy and his family took a downward spiral. Her nephew's death is the lowest point, and it affects everyone. The person it affects most is her father. He feels his legacy is finished. Beatrice tells her mom about the dozen girlfriends he left behind and speculates if one of them might be pregnant. *That would be wonderful, it would get your father out of his depression.*

When Beatrice visits her parents in Monterrey, Blondie organizes a gathering with their friends. Some of them called or emailed. When they get together, everybody has something to share. At this point, everyone has had a fair share of tragedies. Beatrice is an outsider. Her life is different. The changes were subtle.

In the summer, Blondie invites Beatrice to her apartment at the beach for a week. They will supervise her daughter and some friends. Blondie sets an alarm at noon to make sure she is up by the time Beatrice gets there. The next day Beatrice, who has been sleep deprived for a decade, wakes up at noon herself. The electrical hurricane shutters turn the room into a black cave. There are three maids to serve them, two locals, the third was flown in. Blondie and Beatrice chat while the teenagers watch movies and play cards. Blondie tries to update her with local gossip, but she cannot remember all those people from her past. Beatrice picks up after herself and takes things to the kitchen. *Please don't, you'll ruin my help.*

One evening before they go out to dinner, Beatrice knocks on Blondie's door to see if she is ready. She enters and sees Blondie sitting, watching her iPad while her maid fixes her hair, like she was Marie Antoinette. This image shocks her. At that moment, Beatrice realizes how different their two lives are.

Beatrice is still an outsider in San Antonio but has lost her place in Monterrey. Her previous life does not exist anymore. When she moved to Nuevo Laredo, she burned some ships, then some more when she moved to Laredo, Texas. Blondie was her last ship. Beatrice will blow magic powders and have it as a miniature golden souvenir on her desk for those lonely days when she feels she does not belong.

This same summer, Beatrice's brother-in-law is traveling with his new girlfriend to Europe. The in-laws are traveling with the girl's parents, supporting the union. She is a blonde blue-eyed Heights queen, handpicked by her mother-in-law. She is twenty-two years younger than Beatrice. The relationship is getting serious. Beatrice prepares for the possible wedding by making an appointment with a plastic surgeon.

At night, when she looks at herself in the mirror, she pulls her face up to see what it would look like if she got a facelift. When her mother was about her age, she got her eyes done. Blondie says the sooner the better the job and the less noticeable it is. Her sister Alexandra, just got her eyes done and is happy. She said: *I looked tired and I did not feel tired. I wanted my face to match my attitude.*

Beatrice's first appointment is in middle of September. The doctor looks like a normal plastic surgeon. That means he looks like a doll. *I am here because I want to rejuvenate myself. What is the difference if I do it now?* He says all his patients are different and some wait until they are older. Beatrice talks to his assistant, goes over numbers, and makes an appointment to get the job done during Thanksgiving week. Elliott does not support her decision, so she uses her savings to pay for the whole thing.

The weekend before the operation, Beatrice dyes her hair, she will not be able to do this for a while. She takes David for respite care. She fills the refrigerator with food. The Christmas tree is up, and her meds are numbered next to her bed. She has a list of movies to watch and books to read. On Monday morning, she does not eat or drink anything. Elliott drives her there, she registers, gets her plastic bracelet on and signs a waiver. In the questionnaire, they ask her about her will. She understands then, she is about to lose consciousness, and there is a risk of dying. She thinks of her nephew. They take her in and Elliott leaves. A nice nurse, with a soft sweet voice takes her vitals. The doctor comes in to greet her. Beatrice says a little prayer.

May all the people here be alert and present, may they use the talent to its full potential. Thank God for letting me have the resources to pay for their services. Amen. She wants them to do their best. Next, she is introduced to the anesthesiologist, and then she is gone. When she wakes up, she tries to talk but her words come out wrong. They do not understand. She says it as loud and as clear as possible.

They will not be able to take care of me! I need to hire someone!

Yes, they will, sweetheart. Don't worry. Just relax.

Beatrice is not in control anymore. She cannot undo this. She is at the mercy of others. She feels like a train ran over her. She cannot see or hear well. Her head feels three times its size, and she moves slowly. Before she leaves, she puts sunglasses and a scarf around her mummy head. Her sister-in-law drives her home. Beatrice lies in her bed. She cannot take her meds on an empty stomach and drinks liquid yogurt, like the doctor suggested. She feels nauseous and throws up. A few minutes later, she wants to throw up again. Both she and her sister-in-law reach for the trashcan at the same time, hitting her front tooth. Fortunately, she does not lose it.

Elliott brings her gelatin and saltines. The vomiting stops. Beatrice sits there paralyzed, fearful of moving. She takes her meds and gets ready to sleep. Elliott sleeps on the sofa. The next day, he takes her to see the doctor. The vomiting did not affect the sutures. She goes back home and sits in bed. Because of the ointments she cannot see, watch television or read. Her son was diagnosed with autism ten years ago, and she is not used to asking for help. Her children were always first. The secret reason she had surgery is she is afraid her husband will leave her. They have been together for eighteen years, but one of the first things she learned about autism were the high divorce rates.

On Wednesday, Elliott takes her to the doctor to get the wrap removed and her hair washed. She holds a towel over her deformed face. When she goes home, she sees the scars. The deformity of her cheeks makes her look like the Joker, and the stitched worms frame her eyes. She cries. Her head feels like a basketball. The swelling is an internal sensation. Her smile is gone.

Beatrice sits on her bed and looks out the window. She can see now life's perfect design. Humans are born to their designated caregiver. Babies are cute, so someone will want to take care of them. They improve, walk and talk. They learn what their designated parents teach them, so they are liked even more. If they like music or sports, the children love music or sports. Then they become independent, build their lives. Maybe they change the world, maybe they do not. As humans become too worldly bodies fail. When it is time to go, bodies do not serve fun purposes like eating with gusto, drinking with enjoyment and fornicating lustfully. In old age, hearing and seeing are compromised. When it is time to go, people detach from their useless bodies gladly.

On Friday Beatrice's teenage son says:
Mom are you sure about this? You look deformed.
She asks Elliott: *Do you think it was worth it?*
Ask me in two weeks.

He does not cheer her up, but puts the ointment on her sutures. Now he realizes how much she does and how necessary it is that she continues doing it.

Beatrice never imagined that such a shallow action would bring her such deep thoughts. To acquire beauty, she must let it go. As a vain woman, she is an expert at hiding behind makeup, but she cannot wear any. She must see her deformed face for three weeks. No costumes. No show.

Beatrice dresses up to go see the doctor. For the first time in a week, she is not wearing sweatpants. When the doctor opens the door, she starts crying.

I look ugly.

Looks like you had surgery. He makes her laugh.

After two weeks, she can recognize herself in the mirror. It was an intense journey to live without movies and books, steak and wine, Facebook and Internet, just in silence, being present and aware. None of this would have happened if she would have refilled the Vicodin and Xanax prescriptions.

With time, her face looks normal. She recovers her expressions and is relieved to look like herself again. She thought her outside would match her inside, but the rejection scars autism has lacerated into her soul are still there.

Chapter 10.1   **1995**

The Fantastic Four correspondents receive the New Year in a cheap restaurant in Venice, California. As the night progresses, we walk on the fishing pier. All these places are a cliché in my mind. I have seen them many times. Just standing here is surreal. I feel the humid breeze, hear the ocean and see the dark horizon ahead. I decide it is time to resign and find myself at an impasse. I do not want to go back home, but I cannot stay in Los Angeles, my work permit will soon expire. One of my colleagues knows someone in Univision and she gets me a job interview.

I fly to Miami and stay at her friend's house. He just landed a job as the host of a live contest show. As we drive to the studio, I can see that this is the capital of Latin America. If it were possible, it is even more *nouveau riche* than LA. The tropical ambience and pastel-colored buildings give it a retro feel. The traffic is bad, water everywhere and few highways to choose from. I spend the day waiting for an interview with Mr. Peimbert, head of news in Univision Miami.

My host works with an audience in a competition. The set is colorful. The studio is lit with artificial light only. The crowd is plain. The world of television is fake and shallow, no real fame or fortune. In front of the camera, it is all about sprayed flat hair and matte makeup. Any evidence of grey matter is behind the lens. This could be Dante's Hell vestibule and there could be a plaque with the inscription *Abandon all hope, those who enter here.* A toxic fog of vanity fills the air. Every human here wants the camera to capture them and give them the love they did not get as children. We are trapped in a room hard to describe, a sterilized space station. It is a desirable manmade plastic world with perfect people.

I get my interview. My lack of enthusiasm is evident. After experiencing television from the inside out, I want to bounce back to the world of news and journalism. This is an island of make-believe pulled by black strings coming from the ego. My visit is brief, efficient and a failure. I came to Miami because a Tarot reader told me that I was going to find *the one* in the United States. Underneath my choices, the drive is always to find love. The more I progress professionally, the deeper the romantic yearning. When I land back in LA, I understand that the end is near. The correspondent is the lion in the news kingdom. The only higher level is the war correspondent, and those people are addicted to action like it was meth.

After resigning, morning time freezes. I had been on a high for so long, I barely had time to think. I play solitaire on my computer and wonder about the cards I have been dealt. All those press conferences and interviews, what difference does it make? The carrousel of news will never stop. When we leave, others will come. We are faceless, nameless and replaceable. It is a clear container that gets filled and emptied every day. While I ran like a rat in a running wheel, my friends had real human babies. The correspondent from *El Universal* just had a baby girl. The correspondent from *Excelsior* is moving to Europe with his wife, and the radio correspondent is trying to find a job in LA to stay. I want to go back home, have a family and kids. I want to live a normal life.

The sofa bed I just bought at IKEA is returned, my friends get my plants. I buy two extra suitcases and a one-way ticket to return home. I go for my last walk on the trails, close to the Griffith Observatory. It is a cool day. You can see the city; downtown is close. The ocean is in the distance. This is farewell. Goodbye Mexican immigrants and Pete Wilson! Goodbye press conferences and the Fantastic Four! Goodbye Hollywood and the perfect people!

I am back in Monterrey, in my parents' house, turning twenty-eight, without a boyfriend, jobless, in the midst of the worst Mexican peso devaluation ever. From one day to the next, everything is worth half. Late at night, I call my friend in LA and talk to her. She is two hours behind. She is kind enough to hear my complaints.

After six months of being in LA, I am not used to socializing the Latin way. I attend a social gathering during which my mother's friend asks me all kinds of questions, while holding my hand. Who is this woman? Why is she grabbing my hand? When will she let go? Do I have to answer all her questions? Doesn't she realize how rude it is to intrude? I am not normal anymore. I miss my news tribe, my senseless purpose of creating information. I want to jump back on that carrousel after all.

I get together with my friends from middle school for lunch. We meet at a local restaurant. They sit divided by their children's schools. To my right are the conservative Catholics, who enrolled their offspring in the same low academic level dead end where we grew up, hoping to turn them into soldiers of the Legion of Christ. To my left, are the *avant guarde* mothers who chose the non-denominational American School, with the high-quality, secular, international teachers. I sit and listen to them talk about their maids, diapers, breast feeding, strollers, recipes and cleaning supplies. There is nothing for me to contribute to the conversation.

How was Los Angeles?

It was great. Thank you.

They do not want to know, they do not care. It is small talk. They feel comfortable putting me in the same box. No disruptions, no dissonance, no contradictions. I am envious, but do not want to be one of them or have my future children trapped in this itty-bitty world from birth to death. Reentering gets harder every time. Coming back from New York was hard, but others went to boarding schools as well. Coming back from Paris was harder, but now coming back from Los Angeles is something out of the Twilight Zone. I look around the table and none of them has a career. I am on my own. Their carrousel is run by Sunday family lunches, baptisms, birthday parties, beauty salons, Diet Coke and gossip in the afternoons.

There is a new television network in town, *Television Azteca*. I have an interview and get offered a social program called *Hola Monterrey,* which I refuse, arguing that I am a serious journalist. Somebody else gets it and tries to turn it into an aristocratic circus, interviewing the rich in their homes. I get to participate in the news segment with a commentary, but the new channel is not well organized. The economic crisis is hitting them hard. I never get paid and leave. There are few job opportunities, and I do something I have always wanted to do, participate in group therapy. My mother finds me a group. I need to understand why I go out with "works-in-progress," men who are emotionally unavailable, leading to relationships with no future.

The therapist is a psychologist and psychiatrist. He has groups in the afternoons. He just created one where I can fit in. The therapy is cheaper, paid by eight people. There are more participants, and we meet for an extended time. Everyone gets an opportunity to speak. In the past, I felt I could make the therapist be on my side and get away with a lot. That is not an option in group therapy. It is not easy to manipulate eight people.

There is a bit of everything: a pampered wife in a bad marriage, a fifty-year-old spinster living with her brother, a gay man inside the closet, a divorcée studying psychology, a man going through a midlife crisis, and a high functioning woman with Cerebral Palsy. We try to learn to live with an issue or resolve it. It feels like a board of directors. I get the opinion of more people on one problem. As I progress, I find a person I clash with. It is the middle-aged man. He has a dominant mother and wife. It bothers me how he does not stand up for himself. He is a new beast to me. My father is the king in my house, and his authority is never questioned. This man has glasses and a double chin, that reinforce his weak image.

I have to ask. Do you sit at the head of the table?
Sometimes, it depends.
Do you have a space you call your own, an office, a desk?
I don't. I am at work most of the time.
You need to have a place in your house that belongs to you only.
I am the dominant woman, the punching bag for his training.
When you go out to bars, who do you go with?
I have a group of guys I've been dating for years.
That's not the way it works. When you go out to meet a guy you can't be with a guy. The men in the bar don't know you don't like the man you are with. When you are sitting with a man, even if he is gay, you are not available. To meet guys, you have to go out with girls. The best number is two, it's easier to pick up in pairs.
I like going out with guys. They drive, pick up the check and have interesting conversations. I don't like going out with girls. It takes forever to agree on a place, and it's uncomfortable if she meets somebody and I don't or vice versa.
I'm telling you, if you want to meet men, you go out with women. That's the way it is. You need to stop going out with people you don't like. You're wasting your time. For example, that guy who takes you to art galleries, how long have you two dated?
We don't date. We might see each other once a month.
Answer the question. How long have you dated him?
His brother is married to my best friend, the four of us hang out.
How long?
Ten years.
And you don't like him?
Not romantically.
Every time you go out with this man, you are wasting your time. If you want to meet someone get rid of these guys. Make yourself available.

I commit to my group therapy. I promise to stop seeing the guys who are headed nowhere. Of the singletons, the one who is hardest to let go is Frank. He is handsome, a great catch in my fantasy land. In real life, he has built himself a moat, with crocodiles around his fortification and is trapped inside his tower like *Rapunzel.*

My support group continues searching for an endless list of blind dates. Every unhappily married woman I know is a matchmaker at heart who feeds on other women's romantic life. My sister-in-law gives me a book called *How to find a man in twenty-five days and keep him twenty-five years.* It gives meticulous advice on how to put yourself out on the market for Mr. Right. There are two useful advices: the first, if I am going out, I need to dress up, go to the right place, sit at a well-lit table, and smile; the second, I need to make a list of the things I am looking for. I write down twenty qualities I want, then put the list to the test and find the five non-negotiable I need. To get this exercise done, my anthem is *Vision of Love.* Before I put pen to paper, I hear this song to remember that destiny is treating me kind and will carry me through to the man who is waiting for me. I recreate my vision of love because it is not too late.

I want a man who is single, masculine, has a beautiful smile, a nice family, strong hands, speaks good English, is healthy, Catholic, well mannered, and most important wants to be with me, court me. I have no idea where I am going to find him, but have to trust that there is someone out there just for me. Someone who has a sense of identity beyond Monterrey. I leave the list inside a drawer, a quiet prayer said with divine intention and sent into the universe. Something shifts in me. We go to the beach and I buy a Brides magazine. My father asks:

What are you doing with that magazine?
I am getting married, Dad.
Really? Who are you marrying?
That doesn't matter. It will come.

Even I surprise myself with the answer, more so because I believe in what I am saying for the first time in a long time. *Matrimonio y mortaja del cielo baja* (Matrimony and death descend from heaven) What is under my control is my discipline and dedication.

After taming my pride, I call the director of The Daily, newspaper number two. This is betrayal to the team at The Compass, but there is no going back. The director of The Daily is a fallen angel who used to be the star at The Compass. He knows I was a ghost writer for the editorial. We agree to meet, and I drive to see him. The offices are smaller. The computers are old, and the director's office is modest. He believes he can make a difference. We cheer each other for leaving The Compass and convince ourselves of the potential this newspaper has. I am welcome, with no hesitation, I get a space in the editorial page twice a week. It is the end of the summer. By the time I publish an editorial it is Independence Day in Mexico, and my column is a reflection on independence. How symbolic!

The man who was meant to be president of Mexico was shot last year. The new president came to be through an unprecedented birth. The political landscape is being recreated, threatening the stability of an old system. We have NAFTA now. Through an open economy, more than legal merchandise comes in. The country changes and so do I. Having my own column is a big step forward, living with my parents is a big step back. The timing was perfect. My three brothers are married. Alexandra is still in Mexico City, and Isabelle is off to a boarding school in Boston. I move into the boys' three hundred and fifty square foot room, far away from my parents. When Isabelle comes back, she will move into my old bedroom and be next to them. I get my own telephone line, buy office furniture and a fax machine. My income is limited, but my savings from Los Angeles are significant, and my salary was in dollars. This is my opportunity to finish my book of short stories. I review the details and get ready to publish it next year.

An old film professor from college is teaching a script workshop, and I sign up along with twenty other students. Many come in with Oscar-winning ideas. After a few weeks, there are only two students left. I am one of them. The three of us, including the teacher, have weekly meetings to discuss our scripts. This writing project trains me to describe places and acquire an ear for dialogue. I do not know what I am going to do with this, but I work on it fearlessly. The subject is a woman turning thirty who cancels her wedding at the last minute. My eagerness to have a voice is strong after having been a ghost writer. It feels like "coming out" of the writing closet.

The news anchor, I went out with a few years back, offered me a segment in his morning show, reading my commentary. Working in television will be an opportunity to market myself and let my voice be heard. They do not pay much, but it is a new experience. I drive to the studio early in the morning and spend twice as much time in makeup as I do in front of the lens. I am forced to spice up my wardrobe. For television, they require bright colors; white burns the image.

What do I write about? My bag of tricks is not as full as I thought. Not having my previous boss's information and network leaves me to my own devices. The two subjects that distinguish me are immigration and women. I witnessed something painful and complex in Los Angeles. It had a deep meaning and struck a chord leaving a vibration in my soul. The new eureka that occurs to me is that my father is an American by birth. My insight into the differences between Mexico and the United States come from within. My American background is what makes me different from other women. The reason why I will never match a Mexican man is because my father is not a Mexican. When he is alone with his two sisters, they speak English. When you pinch him, he does not say *Aaee* he says *Ouch*! He likes pancakes not *chilaquiles*, hamburgers better than *tacos*. My mother has traveled alone dozens of times. My friends' mothers travel with their husbands. I am too opinionated, too independent and too ambitious. I recently met an American with a Texan father and a Spanish mother. There is no chemistry, but it feels easy.

Christmas holidays approach. Having good savings and a flexible job, I make plans with a friend, another single professional. We go to South America. I have always wanted to go. That is where my parents went for their honeymoon. Nobody knows, but I cling to the idea that I will meet someone by chance. Something is coming.

Chapter 10.2   **2005**

You organize your life in boxes. The house in Laredo, Texas is not ready yet. The first two weeks you do what hundreds of families do every morning, cross the border to drop off your kids in school. If you cross the International Bridge before eight, you miss the lines, after eight you never know. You are not complaining, at least both sides of the border abide by the same time zone. Elliott recalls when he was a child, Nuevo Laredo was on Mexican time and Laredo, Texas was on American time. He had to wake up at five-thirty. Daylight savings time is used on both sides now.

As you pack your life, it materializes into objects that you review one by one. Now that David is two years old, you can dispose of things that were necessary until recently. As Elliott's secretary is pregnant, you give her the beautiful crib, changer and rocking chair. You sell the custom-made brown sofas. You do not have a place for them. There is no library in the new house. You will use the leather sofas for the living room. The animal trophies will be donated to a museum in Monterrey. There is nowhere to hang them. You give your beautiful koi fish to your mother-in-law so she can put them in her fountain. The lucky bamboos cannot come; plants cannot cross the border. No need to pack the VHS, you do not use it anymore. Your new closet is smaller, you give away gently worn clothes. You pack the wedding gifts, some are re-gifted. You are not having the kind of help you had in Mexico.

You sit and wrap beautiful objects in newspaper: silverware, china, trays, serving plates, linen napkins, tablecloths, flower vases, and candlesticks. These exquisite gifts were for a life that is not viable anymore. You pause for a moment and close your eyes. You did not want to think about your vacation and the debut in New York, but now the memories pour into you like water.

You are sixteen and dread the social events prior to the International Debutante's Ball. The social gathering is a brunch in Manhattan on Thanksgiving week. You are staying with a friend in a small town in Connecticut. You take the train into the city. As you stand at the station freezing, you wear a nice off-white wool suit your mother bought you at Saks. The cab drops you off at some club, where you are supposed to mingle with eligible young bachelors. One of the attendees is a real Rockefeller. A snobby guy asks you to dance. He introduces himself, and after saying his name he says *the fourth* with pride. You are miserable, dancing with this snob. He sees your bulldog face. He lifts your chin with his index finger and says: *Smile, darling.* You give him a fake smile.

Your mother's escort was chosen by her mother. He was the son of a top executive at NBC. Your mother did not like him. She chooses your escort while having dinner at the 21 Club. He was having dinner with his parents. They started a conversation. She mentioned the ball. He accepted. He had just moved to New York. Mr. Broda is a handsome, working, college graduate, six years older than you. In one of the rehearsals, a group of students from West Point join you, line up and you approach them. You choose the soldier that will carry your Mexican flag. In the rehearsals, you practice bowing.

Your mother orders you to go to Manhattan and get a head start on the search for a dress. You force yourself to go to Saks and Bergdorf. It is intimidating to deal with the boutique ladies. You find a dress you love, but it is expensive. Later, at one of the events, a Cuban designer hypnotizes your mother, and she spends twice as much for a dress you do not even like. You are eager to wear her long leather gloves, that you would try on as a girl.

The day of the event, you are busy. Your father has a sore throat, and your mother is tired. You take a nap. You wake up late and only have half an hour to get ready. Your hair looks horrible, and you have to wear your fat size-six dress. The limousine picks you up at the hotel. You drive straight through Park Avenue. Your mother insists you look out the window.

Look, look at the PanAm Building. Never forget this.
She gets a teenager's reply. *Yeees, mooother.*

You get off and run to the salon where pictures are taken. After the photographs, you line up, and greet all seven hundred guests one by one. Your shoes are killing you. You are lined up in alphabetical order. The girl from Alabama gets authentic conversations with the guests. You get reruns further down the alphabet. There are two of you from Mexico, and you go second, you hear *Meeexico? I was in Tihhuanna, twenty-two-years ago,* twice.

Finally, the moment comes, and you stand in line, waiting to go out into the Grand Ballroom of the Waldorf Astoria. To your left, the soldier has the Mexican flag; to your right Mr. Broda waits in tails, white tie and white gloves. When they say your name, you walk to the center and bow. Then you walk to the end of the room, turn and make a full bow. You do not do the Texas dip. Only girls from Texas go all the way down to the floor. After all the debutantes are presented, including a real German princess, you dance to Lester Lanin's live band music. It is the first time you dance with your father. You do not know how to follow his lead.

You open your eyes, get up, out of the closet, and walk to your room to call your mother. She is busy and you insist on talking.

You told me to look out the window and I did. You told me to remember and I do remember. I remember everything! I am sorry I was a rude teenager.

I am glad. I still remember my debut like it was yesterday.

An international move is a nightmare. It requires a detailed inventory. If the officers at the checkpoint open one box and do not find what is supposed to be there, the move is cancelled. It is not a one-time move. You have boxes brought to your house every other day. Once the construction workers leave, mattresses are set up and beds are made. You sleep there for the first time the second week of January. Every day you unwrap and organize items. It does not matter where you put them, everything feels wrong. David is not sleeping well. He wakes up in the middle of the night and stays awake for a couple of hours. you stay with him in his room to make sure he does not wake up Tomas or Elliott. The next morning, you have to take them both to school. When you come back, you talk to the cable man, the curtain installer, explain things to the new maid, and try to make some sense of this new life. One morning, feeling exhausted, while sitting in the box room, you cry.

This will not last forever. You only have to talk to the cable man once. He tries to calm you down, treating this move as if it was a normal move, but it is not. You did not choose to move. You had to move because people were being killed. You did not move from one house to another, but from one country to another. You are not crying for curtains or carpets, you are crying for the promise of a Mexican life lived in Mexico. Your tears are from the animal pain of losing your herd, for being yanked from your place in the world. It is not the ashtrays that are misplaced, it is you, your family, and your future.

One week after the move, you have David's appointment in San Antonio. You drive to a place called Village of Hope, which offers services for children who are having developmental delays. There was nothing wrong with David as an infant, except for digestive issues. The concern is that he started walking late and his speech is limited. You go into the meeting with him. There are a lot of professionals there. The team includes: a developmental pediatrician, speech pathologist, occupational therapist, behavior therapist, social worker, and parent-clinic coordinator. They play with him, ask him questions, observe him and take notes. When he does not do what he is supposed to, you excuse him.

He is tired. He doesn't know you. Let me try.

When you leave, he is officially diagnosed with Pervasive Developmental Disorder. That is an elegant way of saying they do not know what is wrong with him. They give you a lot of information to read. Most of it has to do with developmental delays, learning problems, attention deficit hyperactive disorder, autism and Asperger syndrome. They express their inclination towards autism. After the meeting, the drive back home feels long. You talk about your options. Elliott suggests you move to San Antonio, but you have only been in Laredo, Texas one week. The decision needs to be made for four people, not just one.

You do not agree with the diagnosis. Over and over the image that comes to your mind is Dustin Huffman in *Rainman*. David likes being held. He is not autistic. There are services from the state called Early Childhood Intervention. They come to check on David's wellbeing. You get another appointment with a pediatric neurologist. He educates you and explains that every child with autism is unique.

Choose one therapy and stick with it. If you try too many things at once, you will not know what works. Take care of your family and take care of your marriage. One of the best things you can do for this child is make sure he has a family.

Of the possible symptoms there are, two you cannot deny. David does not point at things, and he does not pretend play. You learn there is something called the Autism spectrum: mild, moderate and severe. The diagnosis eclipses the relocation.

You still have to finish hanging the paintings and unpacking the boxes, but it does not matter anymore. The housewife treadmill has been turned off. It is winter, the days are cloudy, rainy and cold. This house is dark. Every member of the family goes to their corner. The original plan had an open space in the center for a patio, but it is a room with no windows. It becomes Elliott's man cave where he hides. You get a studio that you turn into your office and a small television room. The boys have their television room closer to the kitchen, overlooking the back patio. The dog likes this garden. You now have somebody else's grown trees to enjoy.

Tomas is not used to a big school. The first day that he has lunch in the cafeteria he tells you *Mom, today we went to eat at a restaurant.* He had been to small schools only. He is struggling because his English is limited. He has to learn it overnight. He wants to make friends and talk to them during recess. While Tomas is adapting, David's behavior issues become undeniable. They cannot handle him well.

You visit a lawyer to go over the paperwork required to apply for your residency. Before you deliver your visa, you accompany Elliott on a last trip. Once you return, you submit your papers and cannot leave the United States for four months. You have been married for five years to your American husband, a requirement to prevent people from having pretend marriages to get a green card. When you show up at Immigration Services, you bring your photo albums to prove you have a real marriage.

One late spring afternoon, you take your boys swimming to the Country Club. There is a sign that says *No lifeguard on duty.* You ignore it because you have your swimming suit on and will swim with your boys. After only fifteen minutes, someone comes and asks you to leave. *I don't need a lifeguard, I am taking care of my children.* They insist, and you wrap them up in towels and leave. When you get home, you are upset and tell Elliott what happened. *They have to do it for liability. If someone drowns, they are responsible.* This makes you even more angry. This is your first learning experience as an American resident.

David is now in a Montessori school. This system camouflages his differences, because everybody works at their own pace. He does things so obsessively that it is noticeable. When he pours water from one container to another, he does it for twenty minutes non-stop. The lack of sleep is getting to you. He wakes up at one and stays awake until four.

You have a meeting with the school district to plan for his education in the system. When the meeting is about to start they ask if you want the meeting in English or Spanish. Elliott insists the meeting be in English. That is your second learning experience as a resident in Texas. You always choose English. At the border, speaking Spanish is not an asset.

In one of those lunches at the Country Club you converse with an American woman. At some point in the conversation, you say you are all American. She gets furious. *I am the only American.* You explain to her Mexico is part of North America. *Mexico is part of South America.* You remind her that Canada, the US and Mexico signed the North American Free Trade Agreement. Later you explain to her that she is Christian and you are Catholic. *We are all Christian.* For Catholics, everybody else is Christian.

Your brain shifts not only to using English, but also absorbing a new perspective. You watch American shows on television. You assume Immigration Services have psychological studies leading them to come up with the four months. It is a change from one season to another. The day you get your papers back, you cross over to the Mexican side to buy hot sauce and chili candy. When you go to your previous house, you hear your footsteps echo in the empty space. You get flashbacks of your babies. The past cuts like a knife, slicing sharply into then and now.

One year prior, your sister Alexandra brought her son to see a developmental doctor called Dr. Unruh. She insists David should see him. After a long wait, you get an appointment. This man comes to see his Mexican clientele every four months. When you enter his spacious office, he stands up. He is dressed in a suit and is six feet six inches tall. He shows David some textured books, funny toys, and makes him follow a light with his eyes. He is cold, blunt and strict. He wants to make sure you are committed. He explains the importance of diet and gives you a handout that says cow's milk is like rat poison. *I need to make sure you are going to follow my instructions. If you refuse, there are other mothers waiting to sit in that chair.* Intimidated, you reply *I will follow the program, sir.* You go back to the waiting room and then talk to his wife, who explains the routine. You have to do the occupational therapy every day for half an hour. The exercises are simple and stimulate his brain from the outside in. By tapping on his head and extremities, you reactivate the brain network. For his sensory issues, you brush his arms and legs, use a vibrator to stimulate his muscles, roll him on the floor and turn him in a chair for balance. The hardest part is following the gluten-free, dairy-free diet and giving him the supplements.

When you try to do the routine, it is almost impossible to count the thirty seconds right arm, thirty seconds left arm and so on. You buy a tape recorder to record the whole routine. Once the recording is done, you train the help to do the routine. This way, while they work with David, you can drive Tomas to his Tae Kwan Do classes and sit in the car reading a book. Reading literature in the car is like time travel.

As you settle into your new American life, Elliott starts a low-residency graduate program in North Carolina. He attends classes one long weekend every month. Besides being busy with his job and traveling for hunting, now he will do homework and commute to school.

The further you go from Monterrey, the less you know what is going on there. You get a call from the editorial director. After ten years of writing for the newspaper, he questions your essays. Some are too general and some are too specific. Before they let you go, you resign to let the blow hit you softly. You feel like a dated housewife with nothing important to say. The newspaper in Nuevo Laredo will still have you, and you continue writing locally.

This has been a tough year: you lost your country, your house, your job, and the dream of neuro-typical Mexican children.

Chapter 10.3   2015

Beatrice is meeting with her writing group every other week. Her writing is becoming personal. Her 5W 1H shotgun has been put away. No more what, who, where, when, why and how. Her exploration is not outward but inward.

On a Saturday morning in late February, she prints the last three essays she wrote to put them in a binder. One of them is written in a letter format to an ex-boyfriend. She leaves them on a table while she goes for a late morning walk. When she comes back Elliott says he is going to visit a friend and will come back later in the afternoon. It takes him two weeks to tell her that he read the essay. Unknown ideas simmer in his mind for fourteen days and the distance between them grows even more. Beatrice thought the piece was a review ribbon that tied the past neatly into a bow of closure, but it has taken a life of its own. It ties some things and unties others. Her writing interferes with reality.

Beatrice is participating in a Dream Workshop to learn to interpret the hidden clues of her unconscious. She has a dream where she is in Disneyland carrying a bag of stuffed animals. When she gets to her room, the bag turns into a book. Like in *Jumanji*, real animals come out. She sees a thick long snake slide down and slither out of her room over the balcony. The previous day, she read in the Bible about the bronze serpent that was put on a pole to protect the Israelites. The snake in her dream, coming out of a magical book, has healing powers.

For spring break, they leave David at the respite care facility and take Tomas on a hunting trip to Argentina. Things are still tense with Elliott, and Beatrice gets the silent treatment. They spend a few days in

Buenos Aires, and she walks to the *Recoleta*. As she sits quietly thinking about her life, she remembers being in this exact same spot twenty years ago, wondering about her future. She followed Ester Vilar's guideline on finding a younger man, but Vilar did not include instructions on what that would look like after twenty years. Her brother-in-law is formalizing his relationship with a young, tall, American girl. Suddenly, Beatrice appears older, shorter and more Mexican. This girl is a local queen. Beatrice was a debutante in another place, another time, another life. False promises were made. The illusion of importance was created, a well-built path led her to her golden cage. How did she think she was going to survive? If Romeo and Juliet had married, they would have divorced. The clan call is engrained in the reptilian brain. It is the truest alliance. She can see how Elliott is longing for his siblings. Beatrice is now out of context, appraised differently, devaluated like the peso. She is too loud, too emotional, too warm. She is now a has-been of a has been. Twenty years ago, she had a profession, friends, family. Now, she is a shadow of her former self. Skins were shed, identities lost, lives tossed.

Beatrice gets back and takes a writing workshop with a Texan historian and hires her to read her essays. The historian suggests she get rid of the personal stuff and focus on the history. Beatrice decides to continue with the interviews. She feels the need to understand who the Wicked Witch of the West was. Now that she in San Antonio she interviews her acquaintances.

Beatrice has a friend whose grandmother has known the Wicked Witch of the West for sixty years. She gets an interview with her. Beatrice visits her beautiful apartment. This woman is in her late eighties. She is small and has short white hair. They sit in the dining room and start talking.

Our husbands went to high school together. When she left Maurice, we grew apart. It was a huge scandal. She left her children when the youngest was only nine years old. Do you mind if I smoke a cigarette? She was not glamorous back then. Maurice wasn't generous with her. She dressed like everybody else and had no jewelry. As she speaks she blows smoke. Her shaky hands hold the cigarette. *She would sleep until noon. It was her butler Philip, an African-American man, who took care of Maurice and the children. It was Philip who took the kids to school and fed them. When Maurice fell off a horse, it was Philip who settled him in the basement and nursed him back to health.*

The second interview is with her ex-sister-in-law, a sweet woman who was born and raised in Brazil. The connection is through a friend. Beatrice interviews her in the friend's house.

She was kind to me. I was married to her younger brother. She was an interesting woman, loved attention, active, full of energy. She had a television program where she would interview dignitaries, cover cultural and social events. When she was helping your grandfather build the Church of the Holy Spirit across the border, she got us to make donations of religious artifacts for the side chapel.

The information they provide is limited. Beatrice remembers she published a book titled *Aphrodite and Me* and orders it. When the book arrives, she observes the cover. It shows the Wicked Witch of the West dressed like a mermaid, coming out of the ocean, with her characteristic massive long blonde hair, her collagen injected full red lips. She got this picture taken in her late seventies. In the book, she discusses the subject of *discovering sensuality and romance at any age.*

She was born in 1928. Her father left her mother, who gave piano lessons to earn a living. Her mother accompanied her on the piano when she sang at the Officers Club and at base hospitals. Maurice was a pilot in World War II. They married when she was nineteen. They borrowed two hundred dollars to get married and had a short honeymoon in Dallas. They settled in a small apartment and had their first child within the first year. Five more followed. They were not strict with school attendance. None of their children went to college. Maurice gave up flying and tried his luck in real estate and became a successful contractor. When she was twenty-six-years-old, they moved into their twenty-four thousand square foot house in Alameda Circle.

Their relationship started with the church project. Your grandmother was still alive, one of the cousins remembers. *The help knows everything. The rumor is after a few drinks they would sneak down to the basement.* When Octavio's wife died in 1963, he became a regular guest in her house. They even fixed the attic for him. In 1964, Octavio invited Maurice and his wife to Africa, but only she went with a girlfriend. Three years later, he invited the whole family on a trip around the world, starting in London and ending in Hawaii. While in Rome, the couple fought, and Maurice returned to the United States. She continued the trip. When she and the children landed in San Antonio, Maurice wanted a divorce.

She got a one day divorce in Mexico on July of 1967. It was not a proper divorce, Maurice had shady businesses impossible to trace. On March of 1968, seven days before she turned forty, they married. The family didn't support the marriage. She had her seventh child with Octavio when she was forty-two-years-old.

She chose a lot at Bosques de las Lomas and drew up plans for a house in Mexico City. When Octavio refused to build it, she insisted that if it was not built the way she wanted it, it would not be built at all. *Casa Arabesque*, a thirty-three thousand square foot house was finished in 1973. It could seat six hundred guests, host charity functions and fashion shows including Givenchy, Yves Saint Laurent, and Oscar de la Renta. She had dinners for Ronald Reagan, Cary Grant and Ricardo Montalban.

An event planner who worked for her for years tells the story of a famous diamond ring Octavio bought her. She complained about the size of the stone. He had given big diamonds to his first wife. She had him exchange it. He gave her a thirty-carat diamond ring: *Is this big enough?* He said.

When Octavio's mother died, fighting over ownership of the businesses began. The brothers sued him in Mexico and the United States. They froze his assets. The feast lasted only five years. She was vulnerable. She was a United States citizen, and her husband was seventy-three years old. With what he got in the settlement, he tried to remake his fortune by buying Texas ranches and digging for oil. In 1982, Mexican banks were nationalized, and the Mexican peso was devaluated from 22 to 150 pesos per dollar. She sued Maurice for what he owed her from the divorce. She got her Alameda house back and some assets. They continued a high life style and hosted grand parties for celebrities like Mikhail Baryshnikov.

While Octavio was trying to rebuild his business in Nuevo Laredo, he suffered an accident and fell in a ditch at a construction site. From then on, his health deteriorated. Having to pay outrageous medical expenses, they went back to Mexico City. Some believe he had ALS. He ended up in a wheelchair for a year, fully present without being able to move. The only time his son visited, Octavio looked at him and cried. It was a powerful moment. The nurse waited in the next room. On December of 1986, he died at the age of eighty-two, distanced from his siblings, children, nephews and nieces. Before Octavio's mother died, she made her family promise they would bury him next to her. His widow agreed. The funeral was quiet, not too crowded. After all the lawyers, after all the fights, the family showed up. The widow had no allies. People remember she was alone in the receiving room.

When Beatrice was growing up, she saw that her mother did what her father said, her father did what Octavio said, and Octavio did what the Wicked Witch of the West said. This woman was at the top of the food chain and single handedly destroyed the clan. With time, it became obvious that the couple was selfish. They did not think of anybody but themselves. *After desire has conceived, it gives birth to sin; and sin, when it is fully-grown, gives birth to death. James 1:15*

There is an upcoming wedding. Elliott's brother is getting married and this means a new family dynamic. A business consultant specialized on Family Business works with them. They participate in family therapy sessions. The more Elliott reconnects with them, the more distant he is from Beatrice. They start arguing because the new fiancé is not going to sign a prenuptial agreement. Beatrice was told not to take it personally, that when the time came, the others would sign as well. Turns out it was personal. Their grandfathers' quarrel has been hanging above them like Damocles' sword, a constant threat to their weak alliance.

In June, Beatrice goes on a birthday trip with two of her writer friends. The pair is thick as thieves, and she feels like the third wheel. While they are eager to do everything, Beatrice wants to rest. She was recently diagnosed with chronic fatigue by a wellness doctor. For her birthday, they have a nice lunch overlooking the city. Her birthday resolution is to write that book that she has been talking about for years. She cannot seem to find the right angle, there are so many things to explore. One of her birthday gifts is a book titled *Liar's Club*, written by Mary Karr, a memoirist who changed the genre forever. Memoirs were reserved for famous people, but Karr, who had a less than perfect childhood, believed her life mattered and wrote about it. Karr shares painful family secrets, finding healing for herself and the reader.

In July, Beatrice goes with Elliott and Tomas to Spain. While Elliott hunts, she takes Tomas on tours of Madrid and Barcelona. They watch movies, walk the streets and visit museums. When Elliot joins them, he does not leave the room. There is a hunting emergency. A famous male lion living in a game reserve in Zimbabwe, called Cecil, was lured and killed by an illegal party of big game hunters. Elliott knows the killer and is doing damage control.

Tomas is still asleep. Beatrice walks alone in the *Parque del Retiro*, enjoying the beautiful day and looking at the families. There are boats on the lake and couples rowing. She sits on a bench to feel the breeze and look at the tall trees. When she was young, being raised by a city lover, she thought every city was unique and nature was all the same. Now, she can see it is the other way around. It is nature that is unique, and cities are all the same. It is these parks that give cities their true flavor.

Close to the lake, there are all kinds of vendors. Beatrice sees an old lady with her tarot cards and walks up to her. *How much for a reading?* She has little cash, but it is enough. She says to divide the cards in three groups, and ask three questions. Beatrice decides to ask about her three men: Elliott, Tomas and David. The reader does not know the order. Tomas is first. *This one had a hard time, but is about to start a new stage in his life, it will be a good one.* David follows. *This one is a hard worker, he will accomplish more than you think he can.* It is Elliott's turn. *There is turmoil. Big changes are coming.* Beatrice stops her and says thank you.

The intuitive psychologist, who leads the Dream Workshop, organizes a trip with a group of hippie women, Beatrice signs up. In August, they spend a few days in Sedona, Arizona, known for having four energy vortexes. They go on hikes, do journey dancing, read the runes daily, have Reiki sessions and do breathing work. At the end of the day, Beatrice retires to her solitude. The energy at these locations resonates and strengthens her inner being.

Beatrice comes home energized to start the school year. David had a good summer attending a camp in the mornings. Tomas is starting high school in an all-boys Catholic school. She applies for a writing mentorship for the second time but does not get it. The mentor is kind enough to read her material on the side and give her some feedback. Over coffee he says: *Get rid of all the historic stuff, the value is in the personal stories.*

At the beginning of October, on a Thursday evening, Elliott and Beatrice are invited to the club for her brother-in-law's engagement party. After he gets down on one knee and gives his girlfriend a ring, there are pictures. They all sit in a private salon to have dinner and toast the soon to be bride and groom. As dinner progresses, Beatrice realizes that she never got a real proposal. Elliott just made her pick a hand and she got an earring. His brother did not want to use the other earring. He wanted a bigger stone for his fiancée. Beatrice can see both families chatting and smiling. This is a true family alliance. She did not get that either.

Two weeks later, she is walking out of her Bible study, wearing cheap shoes made with elastic bands, and as she walks over some rocks to get to her car, her left foot bends and she falls. She gets in the car, surprised with how much it hurts. She gets home and starts limping. Elliott does not believe her pain. She drives herself to the emergency room, and she is told that her fifth metatarsal is splintered. She leaves on crutches and gets an appointment with a foot doctor. The next appointment she needs foot surgery. During her convalescence, her home is turbulent. Elliott fixed the cellar and has people over for wine every other night. Tomas is caught in an alley drinking with a friend and gets a ticket for an MIP, minor in possession.

Elliott starts hanging out with his brother's bachelor friends. Tomas is miserable in his new school, and Beatrice is homebound. After one of the charity galas that she attends with her orthopedic boot, she has a nightmare. Elliott and Beatrice are in a marble hallway, dressed formally. There are beautiful fine wood doors to this corridor. Out of one comes somebody and pulls him in. Beatrice hears a werewolf grunting. When Elliott comes out of that room, he has been bitten and turned into a vampire. His eyes are different.

Everything changes that day. She demands that he drink somewhere else, her house is not a bar. They have used the D word in conversation, but now he is determined. He wants a divorce and asks her to find a lawyer. She thinks he is confused, but follows his instructions to dance along the rhythm of this crazy midlife crisis.

She calls a lawyer friend to ask for options. Elliott wants her to file by the first day of the new year. He is in a hurry. She makes an appointment on December 24th in the morning, even the secretary suggests she reschedule, but she explains that they need to get this done. After a short visit with the family Christmas dinner, once the pictures are taken, she comes home with David.

On Christmas morning, Beatrice sees Mary Karr, the writer, announces a writing workshop in Patmos, Greece next summer. Beatrice pays her deposit, determined to celebrate her fiftieth birthday in Greece and write that memoir once and for all.

After thirty years of the break down, she knows her mind is strong and reliable.

Writing always makes things better. Her pen is the scalpel that opens hidden stitches. The ink is a healing antiseptic. As she enters the forest of her mind and catches fireflies, her pen is the light beam that illuminates dark corners, the laser that reaches infinity and opens her immortality.

Made in the USA
Middletown, DE
07 January 2019